THE PAIN RELIEF SECRET

How to Retrain Your Nervous System, Heal Your Body, and Overcome Chronic Pain

SARAH WARREN

TCK PUBLISHING.COM

ISBN: 978-1-63161-072-1

Sign up for Sarah Warren's newsletter at
somaticmovementcenter.com/signup

Published by TCK Publishing
www.TCKpublishing.com

Get discounts and special deals on our best selling books at
www.TCKpublishing.com/bookdeals

Check out additional discounts for bulk orders at
www.TCKpublishing.com/bulk-book-orders

Contents

Medical
Disclaimer

This book is not intended to be a substitute for the medical advice of physicians. The reader should regularly consult a physician in all health matters, particularly with respect to symptoms that may require diagnosis or medical attention.

As we grow older, our bodies—and our lives—should continue to improve, right up until the very end. I believe that all of us, in our hearts, feel that this is how life really should be lived.

—Dr. Thomas Hanna
Founder, Clinical Somatic Education

Why You're in Pain

We live in a time of incredible advancement in medical technology. Doctors give people new hips when their old ones wear out, new arteries to replace clogged ones, and drugs to manage almost any condition. Scientists can grow new body parts in labs, and doctors routinely use robots to perform surgeries on patients who may be thousands of miles away. It sounds like the stuff of science fiction.

These feats would have been impossible and practically unimaginable just a few centuries ago. Back then, people were more concerned with eliminating the viral and bacterial infections that ran rampant through populations, killing thousands of people in a single outbreak. The practice of vaccination, widely considered to be the greatest accomplishment of modern medicine thus far, has turned these epidemics into distant memories for much of the world.

The near elimination of external threats to human health has extended life expectancies in many countries, but it's also opened the door for new threats to quality of life. In the Western world, our successful dominance over our environment has brought with it a sedentary lifestyle, man-made toxins, nutritionally deficient and chemically enhanced food, and new kinds of stress that we are ill-equipped to handle.

As a result, most of us live relatively long lives during which we encounter a myriad of internal threats. Heart disease, high blood pressure, mental illness, ulcers, cancer, autoimmune disorders, obesity, diabetes, chronic pain, and physical degeneration have become the norm. We accept and even assume that we'll experience one—if not several—of these conditions by the time we reach middle age.

Until very recently, the approach of treating an ailment from the outside in—with antibiotics, vaccination, or surgery—was entirely appropriate, given that most threats to people's health came from outside their bodies. But while Western medicine works miracles on a daily basis, it hasn't successfully addressed some of the internal threats people face today. Far too many people suffer from chronic pain, loss of mobility, and musculoskeletal degeneration. Science has shown that these debilitating problems can be prevented and even reversed, but very few people get the proper help and treatment they need.

To make things worse, pharmaceutical companies create drugs that keep chronic lifestyle-related conditions and chronic pain effectively under control. These drugs give you the illusion that your conditions are being cured, when in reality they do nothing to address the underlying causes.

Like so many people today, your reliance on doctors to treat you with medicine and surgery keeps you from realizing that you have a tremendous amount of control over your own health. This mental block is exceedingly evident when it comes to muscle and joint pain and degeneration.

The myth that your body will inevitably break down and that you must experience pain as you age is so ingrained that you've probably never stopped to wonder why this breakdown occurs and if it might be avoidable. As a result, the scientific research around pain is devoted to to developing new drugs that simply manage pain conditions and new surgical techniques that fix worn-out joints instead of investigating the underlying causes of physical decline.

While there are many causes of chronic pain, including cancer, autoimmune conditions, and neuropathy, most musculoskeletal pain and degeneration occurs because of the way that you habitually use your body. The way you sit, stand, and move makes your muscles chronically tight and sore, compresses your joints and nerves, and puts stress on your bones, often to the point of causing significant pain and damage to the structure of your body.

Throughout your life, you develop unique ways of standing and moving. Most animals come out of the womb already knowing how to move—picture the fawn who awkwardly stands up less than an hour after being born and is soon trotting around—but humans require at least a year of motor learning to reach the same degree of proficiency. And while most animals complete their motor learning process by the time they're a few years old, you continue to learn new motor skills and habits throughout your life.

You develop muscular patterns based on a vast array of factors. Your physical and emotional environment, your reactions to stress, your personality, the injuries you sustain, the sports you play, and any physical training you engage in all contribute to your habitual posture and movement. Like all humans, your incredible capacity to learn sets you apart from other animals and makes it inevitable that you will acquire a pattern of muscular habits that is entirely unique. No other human being on the planet moves quite like you.

You're probably familiar with this learning process: It's the way you develop muscle memory. When you repeat a movement like swinging a golf club, the neurons involved in controlling that movement develop increasingly stronger connections. Existing synapses begin to fire more efficiently, and new synapses are formed. As a result, your golf swing becomes more automatic, reliable, and forceful the more often you practice.

Despite what the term implies, muscles have no memory of their own. They're controlled by your nervous system, which likes to be as efficient as possible because making fast decisions helps you survive. When your nervous system notices that you keep repeating the same movement or posture, it begins to make that movement or posture automatic. As the muscular pattern becomes more deeply learned, the control and memory of the pattern shifts to different areas of your brain. This process allows the parts of your brain responsible for making voluntary decisions to focus on new things that require conscious attention.

The process of acquiring muscle memory is not limited to athletes, nor is it limited to learning complex movement patterns like swinging a golf club. The same learning process goes on all the time within your nervous system every day of your entire life, even if you sit at a desk all day and then sit on a couch watching TV at night.

Some people choose to work with their muscle memory, actively training and retraining certain muscular patterns in pursuit of a goal like winning an Olympic medal, performing heart surgery, or typing faster. But that's not the norm: Like most people, you're probably unaware that that you're engaged in a constant process of subconsciously reinforcing old movement patterns and learning new ones.

This innate, automatic learning process serves an important evolutionary purpose. You can imagine how critical muscle memory was to survival hundreds of thousands of years ago. Back then, only the fastest and fittest of our ancestors survived, and the ability to move quickly and automatically under stress often meant the difference between life and death.

Your survival today, however, does not depend on being able to move quickly. The process of learning and automating muscular patterns is hardwired into your nervous system, however, so it occurs whether you want it to or not. And for the most part, acquiring muscle memory is enormously beneficial. Without muscle memory, you'd spend all day figuring out how to brush your teeth and get dressed for work. The number of conscious decisions and voluntary movements needed to complete the most basic of tasks would overwhelm you.

However, this automatic learning process also makes it very easy to develop damaging muscular habits. Since your nervous system wants to help you be as efficient as possible, it will remember any movement or posture that you choose to repeat—even if the movement or posture could potentially cause pain and damage over time. Once learned, these habits feel so natural that they seem to be innate and unchangeable. They are, in fact, so deeply learned that they're nearly impossible to change unless you learn how to retrain your nervous system.

This automatic learning process has been part of humans' neural functioning for as long as we have been a species, yet only recently have chronic muscle and joint pain and degeneration become such widespread problems. One reason for this is increasing life spans. The longer you live, the more time you have to develop muscular habits, and the greater the chance that some of the habits you develop will damage your body. And the older you get, the more deeply learned your habits become, and the more impact they have on your health and functioning.

However, a 2016 review by researchers at Children's Hospitals and Clinics of Minnesota showed that 20–35% of children and teenagers worldwide experience chronic pain, and a 2017 study of 2,732 Polish children and teenagers showed that at least 67% have at least one postural defect. Certainly, it can't be aging that causes a young person to have chronic pain or poor posture. This brings us to the second reason for the increase in pain: our repetitive and all-too-sedentary lifestyles. Repetitive activities, whether they be playing video games for hours on end or competing in sports, quickly create habitual patterns. Being sedentary is just as detrimental; when your body isn't moving, your muscles become tight, connective tissue loses elasticity, and pressure is put on joints and nerves. You need to keep moving throughout the day to stay healthy, but you also need to move in a variety of patterns to avoid muscle and joint damage and chronic pain.

The third reason you experience so much pain and physical breakdown is the type of stress you likely deal with in your daily life. Current lifestyles are drastically different than they have been for most of human existence. The human nervous system evolved to cope with short-term, life-threatening stressors, like being chased by a tiger or being unable to find food. But in all likelihood, your life today is rarely physically threatened and you perceive minor events, like traffic or an impending work deadline, to be major crises. Many of these psychological stressors never go away, so your stress response is constantly activated. As you'll learn in this book, stress causes and exacerbates many pain conditions by increasing muscle tension, triggering postural reflexes, and increasing how much pain your nervous system perceives and creates.

If you're like most of my clients, who come to see me after trying everything under the sun to relieve their chronic pain, you know that most of the solutions available for pain relief don't work very well. They aren't effective because they don't address the underlying cause of your problem: the way that you habitually use your body.

Therapies that passively manipulate the structure of your body, like massage and chiropractic adjustments, attempt to fix your pain from the outside in. These therapies incorrectly assume that your body's structure is the problem. The real issue is how your neuromuscular system is functioning, and this can only be changed through an active learning process. To keep yourself out of pain, you must change your learned muscular patterns by "rewiring" your nervous system.

The fact that your function—the way you habitually stand and move—leads to muscle and joint pain and degeneration is not news. Many health professionals recognize this, yet they continue to try to fix musculoskeletal issues by manipulating the structure of your body. When their techniques have limited success, your pain and degeneration seem mysterious. Maybe you chalk it up to overuse or old age and assume that nothing can be done to improve your condition. But that assumption couldn't be more wrong.

The life-changing news here is the fact that you have the ability to eliminate most muscle and joint pain and prevent degeneration by retraining your muscle memory. Over the past hundred years or so, an increased understanding of how the nervous system works combined with a great deal of exploration of movement techniques have allowed somatic educators to figure out exactly how to change deeply learned muscular patterns and release subconsciously held muscle tension. The results in many cases seem miraculous, but it's really just science. The techniques of sensorimotor education that have been developed will change the way the medical community and society as a whole think about musculoskeletal pain and degeneration.

There will come a time—maybe in 5 years, maybe in 50—when taking care of your neuromuscular functioning will be akin to eating a healthy diet and exercising. It will be widely accepted that you have just as much of an ability to prevent muscle and joint pain and degeneration as you do to prevent heart disease, obesity, and diabetes. Getting to this point will require a significant shift in thinking, but it is only a matter of time.

Why I Wrote This Book

I learned about a groundbreaking method of sensorimotor education called Clinical Somatics while I was exploring various approaches to movement, yoga, and physical therapy. As I read Thomas Hanna's classic book *Somatics*, I knew immediately that I had found something big. I began to practice his movement techniques, and felt my injuries and chronic tightness left over from years of intensive ballet training slowly melt away. I gradually became looser, more relaxed, and free from pain and physical discomfort. Looking back on the past 11 years since I started retraining my nervous system with Clinical Somatics exercises, it feels as though my body has been aging backward. I never dreamed that I would feel better in my body at 40 than I did at 20!

My goal with this book is to explain what causes most muscle and joint pain and degeneration, and to show you that you have the ability to prevent, alleviate, and eliminate many pain conditions by retraining your nervous system. I have seen people who suffered from back, neck, and hip pain; sciatica; scoliosis; and other debilitating musculoskeletal conditions for years become pain free in a matter of weeks. So despite what many people believe, you don't have to fall apart as you age. You can prevent and relieve most muscle and joint pain, stay active, and feel great in your body—and you can do it yourself.

What You're About to Learn

In this book, we'll start by talking about how and why your nervous system creates the sensation of pain, and how stress makes your pain worse. Then we'll discuss motor learning and how learned muscular habits can put you in pain and cause damage to your body. Understanding the science of pain sensation and motor learning is an important part of your healing process. Knowing the inner workings of your brain and your body is incredibly empowering. Armed with this knowledge, you'll no longer feel hopeless about your pain, and you'll be better able to figure out exactly what is causing your pain so you can fix the problem for good.

Throughout the book, we'll talk about how specific conditions like sciatica, scoliosis, carpal tunnel, and many others can result from habitual posture and movement patterns. You'll learn how your repetitive daily activities, athletic training, stress, and even your personality contribute to muscular habits and pain.

You'll read the stories of pioneering educators who helped develop methods of neuromuscular education that will change your life and the way you feel on a daily basis. You'll learn how to get out of pain and keep yourself pain free by practicing Clinical Somatics exercises. You'll become aware of things you're doing in your daily life that could be causing or worsening your pain. You'll get the tools and knowledge you need to free yourself from pain and move forward with your life.

This book is for you, no matter who you are, how old you are, or whether or not you have chronic pain. You are human, and this makes you susceptible to the cumulative, negative effects of learned muscular habits. I hope to educate and inspire you to take control of your musculoskeletal health. It's a process that requires some time and dedication, and it can only be done by you, from the inside. I promise that the payoff—the ability to relieve your own pain, release chronically held muscle tension, and improve your posture and movement throughout your life—will be well worth the effort you put in.

This information and the exercises you'll learn in this book will forever change the way you feel, the way you move, and the quality of your life.

Let's get started.

CHAPTER 1

How Pain Affects Your Life

If you're reading this book, you're likely suffering from chronic pain or know someone who is. At least 100 million Americans, or one in three, live with chronic pain. It's a debilitating condition that affects your ability to work, exercise, focus, relax, do basic household tasks, get a good night's sleep, and fully enjoy life. The amount of pain people have learned to live with is shocking: More than a third of the world's population is in some type of pain, most or all of the time. In the United States, the number of people who live with chronic musculoskeletal pain is almost double the number of people who suffer from heart disease, stroke, cancer, and diabetes combined.

The Staggering Cost of Pain

In the United States, pain disables five times more people than heart disease. When the medical expenditures for pain care are combined with the decreased productivity and missed work that result, the cost to the US economy is around $600 billion each year. To put this in perspective, heart disease costs the country $317 billion annually, and cancer costs $125 billion, so chronic pain costs more than heart disease and cancer combined. Yet since chronic pain isn't a life-threatening condition, there is little urgency around finding a real solution to the problem. Because they aren't offered a way to get out of pain, most people believe they have to live with the pain and simply manage it with medication.

The cost of pain comes out to around $2,000 per person per year in the United States—not just for people in pain, but for every single man, woman, and child. A nationwide survey by Research!America found that 57% of Americans think pain research should be one of the medical community's highest priorities, and that they would be willing to pay a dollar more per week in taxes to increase federal funding of pain research and treatment.

Instead of spending money on developing new pain medications, researchers should proactively try to understand the underlying cause of pain and explore real solutions. If they don't, the number of people suffering from pain, as well as health care costs, will continue to rise.

Got Pain? There's a Drug for That

The first stop for many pain sufferers is the drugstore, just as the first step for most doctors is to write a prescription for medication. From the 1990s through 2012, prescription rates for narcotic pain medications skyrocketed. The increase was partly due to a few studies published during the 1990s suggesting that opioids, the powerful group of painkillers that includes morphine, codeine, oxycodone, and hydrocodone, might not be as addictive as previously thought. Future studies showed that opioids were in fact highly addictive, but the damage had been done, and doctors began to prescribe the drugs more freely.

At the same time, pain sufferers were speaking up about being undertreated. The pharmaceutical industry took advantage of the situation. When Purdue Pharma introduced OxyContin in 1996, it launched an aggressive marketing campaign. The company led pain-management conferences, targeted doctors who were the highest prescribers of pain medication, increased bonuses paid to their sales representatives, and offered free prescriptions for the drug. It worked: sales of OxyContin grew from $48 million to almost $1.1 billion in just four years, and by 2004 OxyContin was one of the most abused drugs in the United States.

In 2011, a whopping 238 million prescriptions for narcotic pain medications were filled in the United States. And while the prescription rate has been gradually declining since 2013, there were still 57 opioid prescriptions written for every 100 Americans in 2017. In an effort to control the situation, in 2016 the Centers for Disease Control drafted protocols designed to limit the length and frequency of opioid prescriptions.

Prescription opioids bind to specialized nerve endings in the same way that heroin, an illegal opioid, does. The resulting pain relief and sense of euphoria make these drugs not only highly effective, but also highly addictive. Just a week or so of regular opioid use can lead to dependency, in which the brain begins to depend on the drug for normal functioning. Repeated exposure to opioids leads to tolerance, a state in which the brain needs increasingly higher dosages to achieve the same effects. Too often, opioid use outlasts the pain condition, leading to lifelong addiction and even death.

The accessibility of prescription opioids, the speed at which they lead to dependency, and the desirable feelings they produce has led to a high rate of abuse. There are now twice as many people dependent on or abusing prescription pain medication as are addicted to cocaine. Three out of four of the people who are addicted to prescription opioids are using medication that was prescribed to someone else, and the vast majority of the drugs are obtained for free from family or friends.

Having a doctor's prescription for narcotic pain medication often gives people a false sense of security; they think it's okay to give the drugs to a friend or leave them easily accessible in a medicine cabinet. But as availability increased during the 1990s, opioid addiction tripled within just 10 years. These drugs quickly became more commonly abused by addicts than tranquilizers and sedatives. And the results have been nothing short of tragic.

The number of emergency room visits due to overdose of prescription painkillers increased by 34% in just one year between 2016 and 2017. Larger doses of painkillers, often sought by those whose addiction has increased their tolerance for the drug, can cause breathing to slow so much that respiration stops altogether, resulting in a fatal overdose. There are now more overdose deaths involving prescription opioids than there are deaths involving cocaine and heroin combined.

Now that the dangers of abuse, addiction, and overdose are being recognized, the drug manufacturers are in a race to develop abuse-resistant drugs. Some of these new drugs are manufactured in such a way as to ensure a slow release of the drug, and others have safeguards such as an outer shell that is difficult to crack. The US Food and Drug Administration is beginning to strongly favor drugs that have abuse-resistant properties, and is taking some products that are more easily abused off the market.

These safety measures are a step in the right direction, but the ease with which prescription painkillers can be abused is only part of the problem. The larger issues are that the drugs are being overprescribed in the first place, and that many patients are not being screened and treated for addiction. Frighteningly, most doctors receive only a few hours of training in medical school on how to prescribe controlled drugs and identify addiction; some receive no training at all.

There's a growing movement to educate doctors about safe prescription practices and limit the conditions for which opioids are prescribed as well as the amount dispensed. While many people favor these trends because they increase awareness about the risk of addiction, others see potential negative consequences. Older patients and people living in rural areas often have difficulty making the trip to see their doctor, which can make getting a refill quite challenging. And there's a fear that more stringent prescription drug laws could encourage those suffering from chronic pain to turn to illegal drugs. Many people who become addicted to prescription opioids turn to heroin because of its availability and relatively low cost.

With all of the problems created by overprescribing, you would hope that at least the people suffering from chronic pain were getting some relief. But it turns out that prescription pain medications manage pain effectively only about half the time—not a great success rate for a treatment that poses so many serious risks.

Under the Knife

When drugs don't work, many Americans turn to surgery to find some relief from their pain.

Blue Cross Blue Shield reported that rates of elective orthopedic surgeries increased by 44% between 2010 and 2017. Many of these surgeries are being performed on younger patients; the National Center for Health Statistics found that between 2000 and 2010, the number of hip replacement surgeries in people ages 45–54 more than tripled.

The efficacy of hip and knee replacements in particular continues to improve, fueling a new mentality: Your body will inevitably break down, but that's no problem—you can just get your joints replaced! This attitude makes people feel justified in pushing their bodies until they break instead of taking the time to pursue nonsurgical solutions to their pain, such as physical therapy. As a result, more elective surgeries are performed each year, driving health insurance costs higher.

A prime example of this problem is the surgeries that are performed for back pain. Back pain is the type of pain most frequently experienced by Americans, and it's the leading cause of disability for those under the age of 45. So it's no surprise that back surgery is the most common type of orthopedic surgery, being performed 1.2 million times each year in the United States. An analysis published in the *Spine Journal* in 2018 found that between 2004 and 2015, there was a 62% increase in the number of elective back surgeries performed in the United States. Unfortunately, unlike joint replacements, back surgeries are not nearly as consistent in their effectiveness.

An analysis of Medicare recipients with lumbar stenosis published in *The Journal of the American Medical Association* examined the rates and outcomes of complex spinal fusion surgery compared to simple decompression surgery. It showed that the number of complex fusion surgeries performed each year increased by 1,500% in just a 5-year span, and rates of rehospitalization and life-threatening complications were higher among the patients who had more complex surgeries. The average cost of a complex surgery was $80,088, more than three times the cost of a simple decompression surgery at $23,724.

Naturally, both doctors and patients are genuinely attracted to new technology and more aggressive procedures in hopes that they'll provide better outcomes. Patients also want fast, effective solutions for their pain. But many patients mistakenly assume that surgery will correct the problem simply because it's presented as an option. After all, why would there be surgery for back pain if it didn't work?

In addition to being the most expensive option for pain relief, surgery has inconsistent and often harmful outcomes. In a large cohort study published in 2011, researchers reviewed the records of 1,450 workers' compensation subjects in Ohio who had diagnoses of disc degeneration, disc herniation, or radiculopathy (nerve compression) and were candidates for spinal fusion. Of the patients who had the surgery, only 26% had returned to work two years later. Of the patients who didn't have surgery, 67% had returned to work. Spinal fusion was unsuccessful at relieving pain and reducing disability 74% of the time, and patients would have been 2.5 times more likely to get better if they had avoided surgery. The study also found a 41% increase in the daily use of opioid pain medications among the patients who had surgery, indicating that surgery may have introduced further pain and led to opioid dependence.

One reason for the high rate of failure in back surgeries is that many people are misdiagnosed as good candidates for surgery. Often, back pain patients can avoid surgery if they and their doctor take the time to pursue physical rehabilitation. At an annual meeting of the American Academy of Pain Medicine, a panel of doctors led a session entitled "Failed Back Syndrome" in which they discussed the overuse of and lack of success from surgery in back pain patients. The doctors reported no difference in outcome between surgically and nonsurgically treated back pain patients, and they argued in favor of physical rehabilitation and more stringent preoperative evaluation.

When the structure of the body is damaged beyond the point that rest and improved movement can allow it to repair itself, surgery is typically the best course of treatment. But when function is the issue— as is the case with most people who have chronic musculoskeletal pain—studies consistently indicate that physical rehabilitation is the better choice. It has a higher rate of success, is less expensive, and has far fewer risks than surgery or medication.

To shift out of the surgery-focused trend, some big changes are necessary. Doctors must be educated about the effectiveness of preventive care compared to surgery, and communicate this to their patients. Insurance companies must start covering more types of preventive care. And as a patient, you need to do your part by educating yourself about your condition and getting opinions from multiple doctors. You should also recognize that in many cases there are no magic pills or surgeries that will cure your pain forever. You must put in the work required to take care of yourself on a daily basis so that you can get out of and stay out of pain.

Living in Pain

If you've been in pain for an extended period of time, you understand the profound effect it has on your emotional state, ability to focus, and desire to go about regular daily activities. Maybe you've even been forced to adapt to your condition by making major life changes such as taking disability leave from work, changing jobs, or moving to a home that's easier to manage.

Family members and friends who haven't experienced chronic pain can find it hard to sympathize. Like so many things in life, you don't know what it's like to live in chronic pain until you've gone through it yourself. Pain is a very real condition with serious health implications, including an impaired ability to make decisions, increased risk of psychological disorders, and even structural changes to the brain. If you or a loved one in chronic pain is depressed, anxious, or has trouble handling normal daily activities, it's most likely the effect of the pain.

Research shows that chronic pain can affect both the structure and functioning of the brain, and these changes might help explain some of the cognitive, emotional, and behavioral impairments that often accompany pain. Compared to control subjects, chronic pain patients are shown to have between 5% and 11% less volume in the neocortex, the part of the brain responsible for higher functions such as rational thought, language, spatial reasoning, motor control, and sensory perception. This decrease is equivalent to the effect that 10–20 years of normal aging has on the brain. The effect of chronic pain on brain volume is directly related to the duration of pain; each year living in pain decreases the size of the neocortex.

The regions of the brain that tend to be most affected are the prefrontal cortex and the right thalamus, both of which are involved in pain perception. The stress that often accompanies chronic pain is a likely contributor to this neurodegeneration, as the stress hormone cortisol has been shown to cause brain cells to wither away and die. Lifestyle changes resulting from chronic pain, such as avoiding physical activity and mentally challenging tasks, may also contribute to the reduction in brain matter.

Imaging studies show that regions of the brain involved in making emotional decisions are also involved in chronic pain. To explore this connection, researchers at Northwestern University Medical School and SUNY Upstate Medical University paired chronic back pain patients with healthy control subjects on the Iowa Gambling Task, a card game that measures emotional decision-making abilities. The chronic pain patients performed poorly compared to the control subjects, showing the negative impact chronic pain has on your ability to make decisions.

Another study at Northwestern University used functional magnetic resonance imaging to monitor brain activity while subjects executed a simple visual attention task. Chronic pain patients displayed reduced activity in several areas of the brain that are part of the "default-mode network" or DMN. Altered DMN activity has been linked to decision-making difficulties as well as depression, anxiety, and sleep disturbances—all of which affect chronic pain sufferers.

A whopping 86% of pain sufferers are unable to get a good night's sleep. This lack of sleep contributes to a state often referred to as the "terrible triad" of suffering, sleeplessness, and sadness. Inadequate rest alone is enough to make someone not in pain become irritable. For people with chronic pain, the combination of fatigue, irritability, depression, and unrelenting pain becomes a vicious downward cycle that can lead some to desperately resort to overuse of painkillers, unnecessary elective surgeries, and even suicide.

Another major challenge is that people suffering from chronic pain tend to feel like they have no understanding or control over their pain. Despite all that modern medicine knows about the human body, the medical community still understands relatively little about pain—so much so that 85% of lower back pain sufferers receive no definitive diagnosis.

The lack of a diagnosis often leads patients to develop anxiety and depression around their condition. Imagine feeling like you're crazy because your doctor says there's nothing wrong with you, even though you're in constant pain and nothing seems to help. That's the experience of far too many patients who suffer from pain. Studies show a higher rate of depression among patients who have undiagnosed pain than those with diagnosed pain conditions.

People who suffer from pain for at least six months are more than four times more likely than nonsufferers to be diagnosed with depression. And as pain becomes more severe or complex, symptoms of depression worsen. People with two or more areas of pain are six times more likely to be depressed, and people with three or more areas of pain are eight times more likely to be depressed.

Compounding the issue is the fact that depression is vastly underdiagnosed, especially in pain patients. A 2003 review published in the Archives of Internal Medicine found that at least 50% of patients with major depression are not diagnosed accurately, and those who present with pain symptoms are even less likely to be diagnosed correctly. Depression alone is the fourth leading cause of disability worldwide, and is projected to be the second leading cause by 2020. Pain and depression share biological pathways and neurotransmitters in the brain, so they often coexist, exacerbate one another, and respond to similar treatment.

Doctors need to be educated about the connection between pain and depression, and be vigilant about screening for depression when chronic pain is an issue. If you suffer from chronic pain, understanding why you're suffering from depression could also help you feel more in control of your condition. Knowing that lessening your pain could simultaneously improve your depression, and vice versa, might motivate you to make the necessary lifestyle changes to get well.

The Effects of Chronic Pain

If you're in chronic pain, do you notice the effects that it has on your mood and ability to live a normal life? If you have a loved one who suffers from chronic pain, have you noticed changes in them since their pain began?

Chronic pain has become a large-scale public health issue that dramatically worsens quality of life for many people and creates a sizable and growing financial drain on our health care system. The core of the issue is that the medical community does not know how to address the underlying cause of most chronic musculoskeletal pain. Why are drugs and surgery, which are effective roughly 50% of the time, their go-to treatments? The answer that "these are the best solutions we have" is simply not good enough anymore.

It's time to take back control of your body and your life. As you'll learn in this book, it's possible to prevent, alleviate, and even eliminate most musculoskeletal pain simply by improving the way that you habitually use your body. Creating these changes in your muscular patterns cannot be achieved with a prescription from a doctor or a surgical procedure. You must actively retrain your nervous system to release subconsciously held muscle tension and change painful posture and movement patterns. Your musculoskeletal health is in your hands, and the sooner you accept this, the better off you'll be.

CHAPTER 2

How and Why You Feel Pain

In 1950, psychologist Gordon McMurray was examining one of his most unusual cases yet. He was administering strong electric shocks to a young woman and she was not reacting. Scalding hot water and a freezing ice bath elicited no reaction either. He went so far as to subject her to acts of torture: inserting a stick up her nostrils, pinching her tendons, and injecting histamine under her skin. Still nothing.

McMurray was amazed to see that the woman's heart rate, blood pressure, and respiration remained unchanged during what should have been painful experiences. Certain reflexes were absent as well; she didn't blink when her corneas were touched, and she couldn't recall ever having sneezed or coughed. She could recognize the pressure of a pin prick, but didn't withdraw or wince in pain.

The young woman's medical history provided more clues about her mysterious condition. Once, as a child, she had bitten off the tip of her tongue while chewing food. Another time, she'd accidentally knelt down on a radiator when looking out a window; she didn't even notice the heat and suffered third-degree burns.

The young woman revealed that after a day at the beach she would have to carefully inspect her feet to make sure there were no cuts. She'd been hospitalized many times due to small skin wounds that had gone unnoticed until they became infected. She was embarrassed about her condition and was curious about the reactions to pain that she observed in others.

As she grew older, the woman had begun to experience a great deal of joint damage, and had several orthopedic operations. Her knees, hips, and spine were quite inflamed, and the connective tissues and surfaces of her joints were damaged. It's not surprising to find someone in their eighties in this condition, but this woman was only in her twenties.

Despite multiple surgeries, her joints continued to be worn away because of the way she was standing and moving. You instinctively shift your weight, roll over in bed, and adjust your posture when you feel discomfort in your joints. But this young woman could not feel these protective sensations, so her body, particularly her joints, deteriorated rapidly.

The dying tissue surrounding her eroded joints was highly susceptible to infection, and lack of blood flow to the joints made it difficult for her immune system to do its job. At the age of 29, the young woman suffered severe infections that could not be brought under control. The bacterial infections began in her joints and spread into her bones and marrow, resulting in osteomyelitis. During the last month of her life, she reported feeling discomfort, tenderness, and even pain in her left hip. Incredibly, an examination of her nervous system after her death showed no abnormalities.

This young woman, known simply as Miss C., is the best-documented case of a condition known as congenital insensitivity to pain with anhidrosis, or CIPA. There are fewer than 60 documented cases in medical literature. CIPA is an autosomal recessive disorder, meaning that a person must get two copies of a specific mutated gene, one from each parent. This mutation prevents pain-detecting cells from developing normally, and as a result the person is born without the ability to feel pain or sense temperature.

CIPA patients hurt themselves without realizing it. Self-mutilation is common, not because the patients wish to do damage to themselves for any psychological reason, but simply because they can't feel the pain that their actions should produce. CIPA patients often bite their fingers, lips, tongues, and the insides of their cheeks. There are stories of people who suffer from appendicitis and feel only slight pressure in their stomachs, but are saved by a family member or doctor who understands their condition. And one case study tells the story of a man who walked on his fractured leg until it was completely broken.

Most CIPA patients do not live past the age of three, and there are extremely few who live past 25. About half of all CIPA deaths are related to the inability to feel pain and the other half are due to overheating. The A in CIPA stands for "anhidrosis," which means that the body is not able to produce sweat. Without this natural cooling mechanism, CIPA patients experience extremely elevated body temperature known as hyperthermia, which can lead to death.

A life without pain might sound very appealing, especially to someone who suffers from chronic pain. But feeling pain is essential to our survival. Most of us learn quickly through experience to avoid harmful or dangerous stimuli because we know they will elicit the unpleasant sensation of pain. Children with CIPA must be taught things that are obvious to the rest of us, like that they shouldn't bite their fingers, touch hot stoves, or jump from trees.

As you grow up, pain modifies your behavior without you even realizing it. Yet as an adult, you likely hear messages that contradict your instinct to avoid pain. Coaches tell you to be tough and play through the pain. Doctors tell you that pain is a part of getting older, and you think you just have to live with it. So your behavior can be modified in the opposite way as well; you can learn to ignore the sensation of pain to the point that you do structural damage to your body—much as a CIPA patient would do.

How the Nervous System Works

Pain is your nervous system's way of telling you that something is wrong. It often means that actual damage to the structure of your body is likely to occur soon. This type of pain is called nociceptive pain.

Feeling pain can also mean that something is abnormal in the way that your nervous system is processing the sensation of pain. You experience neuroplastic pain when your nervous system becomes oversensitive as a result of being in chronic pain.

You can also experience pain when structural damage is done to your nervous system. This type of pain, called neuropathic pain, can result from an injury, autoimmune disorder, genetic condition, degenerative disease, stroke, vitamin deficiency, infection, toxins, diabetes, or alcoholism.

Before we dive into the mechanics of how you feel pain, let's talk about how your nervous system works as a whole. Your nervous system controls or helps to regulate every function of your body, from breathing and digestion to voluntary movement, consciousness, and thought.

The structure of your nervous system is divided into the central nervous system (CNS) and the peripheral nervous system (PNS). The CNS is made up of the brain, brain stem, and spinal cord. The PNS consists mainly of peripheral nerves, which extend from the spinal cord to the extremities (Illustration 1).

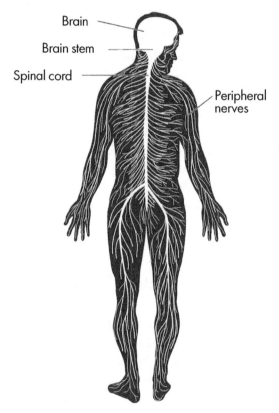

Brain

Brain stem

Spinal cord

Peripheral nerves

Illustration 1: The structure of the nervous system
(Peter Lamb © 123rf.com)

Your brain makes all your voluntary decisions, like where to go for dinner and which shoes to wear. Your brain stem controls functions that are essential to life, like breathing and heart rate. Even if you experience brain damage, you can continue to live as long as your brain stem is intact and functioning correctly.

Your spinal cord carries signals from the brain and brain stem down to your peripheral nerves, and sends sensory information back up to your brain. Your spinal cord also coordinates certain reflexes and movement patterns independent of your brain and brain stem.

Your peripheral nerves are the final piece of the puzzle, delivering messages to and receiving sensory information from skeletal muscles and organs. Your PNS is divided into the somatic and the autonomic nervous systems. The somatic nervous system receives sensory information from skeletal muscles and skin, relays it to the CNS, and controls voluntary movement by telling skeletal muscles to contract.

The autonomic nervous system automatically regulates bodily functions like heart rate, breathing, and digestion; reflexes like sneezing and coughing; and sexual arousal. It is further divided into the sympathetic and parasympathetic nervous systems. The main purpose of the sympathetic nervous system is to stimulate your automatic response to stress, which we'll talk about in chapter 3. The parasympathetic nervous system automatically helps your body return to normal functioning after a stressful event.

Your nervous system carries out all of its actions through neurons, or nerve cells. The approximately 100 billion neurons in your nervous system receive information, make sense of it, communicate with each other, and send commands to your skeletal muscles and organs.

Each neuron is made up of a cell body (soma), dendrites, and an axon. The soma contains the cell nucleus and controls the function of the neuron. Dendrites are branchlike structures that extend from the cell body. They receive information in the form of electrochemical messages from other neurons and transmit them to the cell body. The axon then sends these messages from the cell body to other neurons (Illustration 2). Neurons have many dendrites, but they can only have one axon.

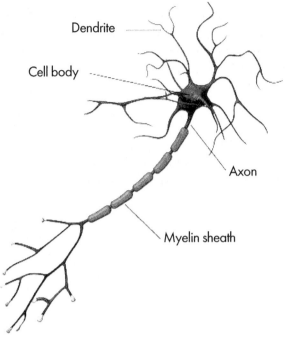

Illustration 2: The structure of a neuron
(adapted from 3drenderings © 123rf.com)

Nerves are bundles of axons that travel from your spinal cord to your extremities (or directly from your brain and brain stem to your extremities, in the case of cranial nerves). Axons that carry messages from your spine to your hands and feet have to be quite long. The sciatic nerve, which runs from the lumbar vertebrae to the big toe of each foot, is made up of the longest axons in the body—approximately three feet long. To put this in perspective, if cell bodies in the sciatic nerve were the size of tennis balls, the dendrites would be about 33 feet long and the axons would be half a mile long.

Neurons communicate with each other through synapses, where the terminal at the end of an axon transmits information to receptors at the end of a dendrite. Substances called neurotransmitters facilitate the transmission of the neurons' messages (Illustration 3). Over time, as certain neurons communicate with others repeatedly in the same way, neural pathways are created, modified, and strengthened. These pathways create your behaviors, habits, and perceptions of the world.

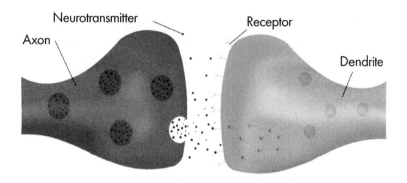

Illustration 3: The synapse
(adapted from Joshua Abbas © 123rf.com)

Now that we've covered the basics of how your nervous system works, let's talk about how and why it creates the sensation of pain.

Nociceptive Pain

Recall that there are three types of pain: nociceptive, neuroplastic, and neuropathic. We'll start by talking about nociceptive pain, the type that occurs when your physical body is being damaged or at risk of being damaged.

When you feel nociceptive pain, two things take place. First is nociception, which occurs when damaging stimuli are detected by the peripheral nerves, and the nerves send a message to the brain saying, "Hey! Your body is being hurt or might possibly be hurt soon! Do something now so it doesn't get worse!"

Second, when that message reaches your brain, a perceptual process creates the actual sensation of pain. That sensation is a not-so-gentle reminder to your consciousness that something is wrong with your physical body.

Now let's take a more detailed look at how nociception works. Your peripheral nerves form a vast network throughout your body. There are more than 1,000 nerve endings in just one square inch of skin. And while you're most often aware of nerve sensations on your skin, nerve endings are present throughout your muscles, joints, blood vessels, and most organs as well.

Some of these nerve endings are specialized receptors called nociceptors, a term derived from the Latin word *nocere* which means "to hurt." Most nociceptors respond to all potentially damaging stimuli, but some respond selectively to mechanical stimulation such as strong pressure, thermal changes such as extreme heat or cold, and chemicals such as histamines.

When you encounter a potential physical threat, whether it be external like stepping on a thumbtack or internal like twisting an ankle, your nociceptors sense that their membranes are being bent or stretched. They spring into action, sending an electrochemical message to your brain.

If cells actually become damaged, they release substances such as proteases, potassium, and adenosine triphosphate (ATP). These activate nociceptors, which in turn send the message to the brain that physical damage has occurred.

Nociceptors don't just passively receive and transmit information; they also actively change the environment surrounding the injury and facilitate the healing process. Nociceptors release substances called neuropeptides that help transmit messages to your brain, widen blood vessels to increase blood flow to the injured area, and even stimulate cell growth. That means that as soon as you feel pain, your body is already responding to try to heal the damage.

The message that cells are being damaged is carried to the brain by two different types of nerve fibers. The first, A-delta fibers, carry messages relaying acute pain. They transmit the messages that cause the immediate sensation of pain you feel when you step on a thumbtack or twist your ankle. A-delta fibers are able to carry the pain signal quickly because they are surrounded by a layer of myelin, a substance made up of lipids, protein, and water. This is called the myelin sheath (Illustration 2) and it acts as insulation around nerve fibers. The more heavily myelinated a nerve is, the faster it's able to transmit messages.

The second type of nerve fibers that transmit pain signals are C fibers. Between 60% and 70% of all sensory nerves fall into this category. C fibers are unmyelinated, so they transmit signals relatively slowly—1 to 2.5 meters per second, unlike the speedy myelinated fibers, which transmit messages at rates between 6 and 100 meters per second. C fibers transmit the signals that result in dull, aching, throbbing, long-lasting pain. While acute pain demands that you react quickly, chronic pain is less often life-threatening, so the nervous system isn't in as big of a rush to communicate the message.

Nerve fibers carrying pain signals travel along multiple pathways as they travel to your brain. Some of them synapse with other neurons in your brain stem, which projects information to the rest of the brain for interpretation. Other nerve fibers pass through the brain stem and synapse in the thalamus, a part of the brain that acts as a switchboard, relaying sensory signals to the rest of the brain (Illustration 4).

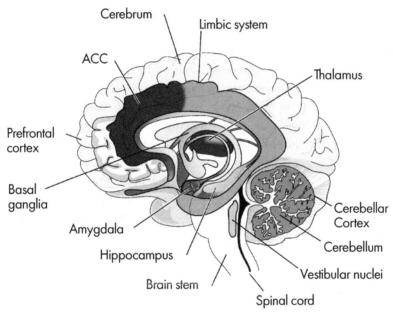

Illustration 4: Brain areas involved in chronic pain and motor learning
(adapted from Peter Lamb ©123rf.com)

Pain is perceived, processed, and created by an interaction of virtually all areas of your brain, including areas that might seem unrelated. And new research shows that the parts of the brain involved in creating the experiences of acute versus chronic pain are somewhat different. Chronic pain patients show unique activity in the limbic system and prefrontal cortex, parts of the brain involved in emotions, mood, memory, behavior, and decision-making. This activity may represent evidence of the neural changes that cause the transition from acute to chronic pain as well as the emotional and cognitive changes that result from being in chronic pain.

Nociception and Muscle Pain

The idea that stepping on a thumbtack would cause pain makes sense from an evolutionary point of view; this external threat might damage your physical body, so your nervous system wants to warn you immediately when it occurs. But sometimes pain arises from internal sources like chronically tight muscles. Tight muscles can feel achy, sore, and sometimes extremely painful, especially if a muscle is in spasm. It might not seem like tight muscles would put your life in danger, but they do, and your nervous system knows it.

To understand why tight muscles are so dangerous to your survival, let's start by examining what's happening inside your muscles when they're working. The brain sends a message to your muscles saying, "I'm going running—time to get moving!" In response, your muscles begin to contract and release in a coordinated pattern of movement.

In order to contract, your muscles use ATP as a source of energy. ATP is used in numerous other physiological functions as well, including synthesizing DNA and perceiving taste. It also participates in nociception because damaged cells release ATP, which activates nociceptors. Because of its important role in so many processes, ATP is constantly being synthesized and consumed by your body in large quantities.

Muscle fibers store only a few seconds' worth of ATP, so when you start running your body must produce more of this energy source almost immediately. And as long as your brain continues to send the signal to keep running, your body will try its hardest to keep up. When muscles require more energy, your liver changes stored glycogen into glucose and sends it into your bloodstream. The glucose combines with oxygen to create ATP, with water, carbon dioxide, and heat released as waste products. This process, called aerobic metabolism or aerobic respiration, is one of the reasons why you breathe heavily when doing aerobic exercise; your body needs extra oxygen to produce energy for your muscles. It's also why you get hot when you exercise.

Sometimes, no matter how hard you breathe, you simply can't take in enough oxygen to keep up with your muscles' energy demands. When cells don't get enough oxygen, they're forced to create energy through a far less efficient process called anaerobic metabolism. In this process, glucose is synthesized into ATP without the help of oxygen, and lactic acid is produced as waste.

As lactic acid is produced, your body quickly breaks it down into lactate and hydrogen ions. The lactate is carried by the blood back to your liver, where it's converted into glucose and either consumed as energy or stored as glycogen for future use. Likewise, your body efficiently takes care of the hydrogen ions with the bicarbonate buffering system. Bicarbonate combines with the hydrogen ions, forming carbonic acid, which is then converted into water and carbon dioxide. The carbon dioxide is exhaled through your lungs, contributing to your increased rate of breathing.

You feel the negative effects of anaerobic metabolism when you're exercising so hard that this recycling process can't keep up. The dull ache and burning sensation you feel in your muscles during strenuous exercise is a result of a buildup of hydrogen ions that activate nociceptors. In addition, a variety of waste products increase the acidity in your muscles, making it difficult and sometimes impossible for muscle fibers to function properly. Acidity and energy depletion lead to muscle fatigue—the state at which you feel like you simply can't go on. If you stop to rest and give your systems a chance to catch up, your muscle pain slowly fades and your muscle function is restored.

The way your body produces energy for your muscles provides a natural defense mechanism against overexertion. Muscle pain and fatigue force you to slow down, preventing you from doing permanent damage to yourself. So the next time you have to take a break due to exhaustion or a burning sensation in your muscles, say a little "thank you" to your body for keeping you in check and preventing you from hurting yourself.

As a side note, there's a difference between the muscle pain felt in an active muscle and the delayed onset muscle soreness (DOMS) that tends to peak around 48 hours after a challenging workout. Most research suggests that DOMS is a result of structural cell damage that occurs during strenuous exercise. The damaged cells release substances that repair and create muscle cells; some of these substances also activate nociceptors. Consider this soreness a reminder from your body to take it easy because you pushed it a little too hard a couple of days ago. As your muscle cells are repaired, the irritating substances are flushed out of your system, and the soreness goes away. Muscle growth occurs during rest, so if you're trying to build strength, you should wait until your soreness goes away to do another strenuous workout.

Now, back to why tight muscles hurt: In normal movement, your muscles contract and release, contract and release, over and over again. When muscles release and get a chance to rest, metabolic wastes are flushed out of your muscles, making the pain go away and restoring full function. However, when your muscles are in a constant state of contraction, as often results from stress and repetitive activities, this recycling process can't happen efficiently.

Muscles that are constantly contracted are working very hard even if you're standing still. As you can imagine, they require a great deal of energy in the form of ATP. But unfortunately, contracted muscles squeeze the blood vessels in the area, restricting blood flow and reducing the amount of oxygen and glucose that can be carried to the working muscle. This compression does not create long-term problems when muscles are given a chance to relax. But when muscles are held in a state of contraction for too long, constant compression of the blood vessels leads to ischemia, a condition in which lack of oxygen and nutrients can lead to pain, loss of function, cell damage, and even cell death.

Lack of oxygen flow means that cells must use anaerobic metabolism to create energy. When a muscle is held tight, this process happens constantly, even during sleep. Lactic acid is continuously produced and broken down into lactate and hydrogen ions. The constant contraction has the same effect as a strenuous workout; the waste recycling process can't keep up and hydrogen ions build up in the muscle, activating nociceptors and causing chronic muscle soreness and pain. So if muscle pain resulting from constant contraction is what you're feeling—which it most likely is, since this is the cause of most chronic muscle pain—then your pain should go away when your muscles release and oxygen flow is restored.

Now you understand the mechanical reasons why tight muscles hurt. As for the evolutionary purpose of this type of pain, consider the consequences of chronically tight muscles. First, lack of blood flow can lead to cell death. Second, tight muscles restrict movement, meaning you'll have a harder time moving quickly and defending yourself if attacked. Lastly, tight muscles and the dysfunctional movement patterns that go along with them often cause structural damage to muscles, connective tissues, joints, and bones.

Considering all the potential damage that tight muscles can cause, it's no wonder that your nervous system wants you to pay attention to it, and do so through the sensation of pain.

Nociception and Inflammation

If it seems like you hear a lot about inflammation, you're right. It's become the latest buzzword in the health world due to research showing the link between inflammation and many chronic conditions including cancer, heart disease, type 2 diabetes, depression, and dementia. Ever since these "diseases of civilization" began to take the place of infectious diseases, researchers have been searching for an equivalent to germ theory—the nineteenth century discovery that led to groundbreaking advances such as antibiotics, immunization, and pasteurization. During the 1990s and early 2000s, research that demonstrated the role of inflammation in diseases such as cancer and diabetes began to accumulate. As the body of evidence continues to grow, the medical community may now be converging on a unified theory of chronic disease based on the concept that low-grade systemic inflammation is an underlying and maintaining factor in many chronic lifestyle-related and toxin-induced conditions.

When musculoskeletal pain is the problem, however, the type of inflammation that's typically involved is localized inflammation, which occurs at the site of an injury or infection. When cells of your body are being damaged or attacked, whether by bacteria, a thumbtack, or repetitive strain, your immune system is activated. Your immune system does not discriminate between physical trauma and infectious invaders. Proteins called pattern recognition receptors detect both microbial pathogens and physical cell damage, and your immune system responds in the same way to both types of attacks.

When these threats are perceived, your immune system goes into high gear in its effort to remove harmful stimuli and begin the healing process. Within moments, blood vessels dilate and increased blood flow makes the area of injury or infection feel warm and appear red. Capillaries become permeable, allowing white blood cells to move from the bloodstream to the injured area. This causes swelling, which helps to isolate the invaders or damaged cells from the rest of your body.

Both immune system cells and damaged cells release substances known as inflammatory mediators, which facilitate the inflammatory process. Some of these mediators activate nociceptors, causing the pain that you feel with inflammation, like when you have a sprained ankle and it gets swollen and sore. Immune system cells can spread inflammatory mediators indiscriminately, so unaffected areas near the injury or infection sometimes feel painful as well.

Inflammation that occurs immediately after an injury or infection, called acute inflammation, isolates and disposes of pathogens, allows damaged cells to be removed from the area, and initiates the healing process. Despite these well-known beneficial effects of inflammation, and the fact that excess use of anti-inflammatory medication is known to slow wound healing, anti-inflammatory drugs continue to be widely overprescribed because they temporarily relieve pain.

A study published in 2011 by researchers at the Cleveland Clinic in Ohio brought some evidence to light that should affect the way that anti-inflammatory drugs are used. The study examined inflammation in muscle injuries, and found that inflammatory cells produce a large amount of insulin-like growth factor, a substance that greatly increases the rate at which muscle cells regenerate. When you try to reduce acute inflammation with anti-inflammatory drugs, you actually slow down your body's natural healing process.

Acute inflammation continues only as long as the damaging stimulus is present. Once the pathogens or damaged cells have been isolated and disposed of, the inflammation response winds down. Remaining cells are repaired, inflammatory mediators degrade, and blood vessels return to normal. All in all, acute inflammation is a good thing. It's chronic inflammation, which occurs when a harmful stimulus remains present for an extended period of time, that has negative effects.

Chronic, localized inflammation occurs most often as a result of poor body mechanics. If you constantly put unnatural or excessive strain on your knees, for example, you can easily damage cartilage, tendons, and ligaments. In its constant effort to protect you, your immune system will wage war against the damaged cells. The resulting inflammation is a common cause of joint pain. It will continue as long as the source of the problem—the habitual movement pattern that damages your soft tissues—is present.

If the movement pattern and resulting inflammation persist, permanent structural damage can occur. Joint tissues are slowly destroyed by both physical wear and tear and the immune system attack. Without these protective tissues, bones rub against each other, causing pain as well as damage to the bones themselves. Remaining healthy joint tissue is replaced by scar tissue, resulting in loss of function and even deformity of the joint.

You suffer through much of this inflammation, pain, and structural damage simply because of the way you habitually stand and move.

Neuroplastic Pain

If you're past a certain age, a friend or family member has probably encouraged you to do crossword or Sudoku puzzles to keep your mind active. Brain training and brain fitness programs are all the rage thanks to research that came out in the 1990s demonstrating that, contrary to popular belief, humans are capable of generating new brain cells throughout their lives.

The term neuroplasticity describes the ability of your brain to change and grow. Moreover, a great deal of research has shown that the entire nervous system, from the brain to the spinal cord to the peripheral nerves, can change depending on the input it receives. Your nervous system is plastic, and that's a good thing.

Until recently, the nervous system was thought to be hardwired to sense and perceive pain in a predictable, unchanging way. We now know that changes within your nervous system affect the way you experience pain. Pain you feel as a result of these adaptations is called neuroplastic pain.

If inflammatory pain continues for even a day or so, the nervous system begins to adapt to the continued nociceptive input. Inflammatory mediators released in response to cell damage not only activate nociceptors, but also increase their sensitivity. So the longer the inflammation continues, or the more often an injury is repeated, the more sensitive your nociceptors become. The resulting state of hypersensitivity, called peripheral sensitization, describes adaptive changes that occur in the PNS that increase the amount of pain you feel.

Peripheral sensitization contributes to the conditions of hyperalgesia and allodynia. If you experience hyperalgesia, your nociceptors respond more strongly than usual to potentially damaging stimuli. Your nociceptors correctly sense a threat, but they sense it to be much greater than it actually is, prompting you to scream in response to stubbing your toe instead of letting out a more appropriate "ouch!"

People with allodynia perceive normally nonpainful stimuli as painful. Brushing a hand against the skin or picking up a warm plate might elicit pain, when under normal circumstances those stimuli wouldn't evoke pain or might even feel pleasurable.

As with peripheral sensitization, pain can become heightened if your CNS becomes sensitized. Central sensitization occurs when repeated or sustained activation of nociceptors leads to adaptations in your spinal cord and brain that increase your perception of pain. During inflammation, neurotransmitters and neuropeptides are released and send pain signals to your brain. Over time, these substances alter the function and activity of the pathways that the pain signals take to the brain. Neurons in the spinal cord become increasingly responsive to pain signals, and more spinal neurons are recruited to receive input from peripheral nerves.

Similar adaptations take place in your brain. Injury and inflammation make neurons more responsive, and lasting pain leads to an increase in the number of neurons that respond to pain signals. Studies of amputees show a positive correlation between the magnitude of pain experienced and the degree of reorganization in the brain. It can be a vicious cycle: The more pain you feel, the more your nervous system adapts, and the more pain you feel as a result of the adaptations. This means that getting an injury that keeps you in pain for weeks or months could set you up to feel even more pain in the future.

Central nervous system sensitization doesn't just make injured areas feel more painful. When your brain and spinal cord become hypersensitive, they can react strongly to stimuli in areas of your body that are far from the original injury. One study showed that people with chronic neck pain were hypersensitive to electrical stimulation and heat in their legs. In another study, chronic tension headache sufferers were found to be hypersensitive to applied pressure on their fingers. A third study found that people with osteoarthritis were hypersensitive to muscle pain, and experienced increased pain in parts of their body not directly affected by their osteoarthritis.

The process of sensitization plays a role in the transition from acute to chronic pain. Adaptations in your brain, spinal cord, and peripheral nerves can outlast the original injury and lead to structural changes, which include the sprouting of new nerve endings and the formation of new synapses between neurons. For example, in long-lasting muscle inflammation resulting from damage to muscle fibers, not only do nerves become sensitized, but new nerve endings grow and nerve density increases. And the more nociceptors that exist in an area and can be activated, the more pain you feel. Once structural changes have occurred in your nervous system, pain can persist even if little or no damage is being done to the tissues of your body. In this way, painful injuries that linger can cause you to feel more pain in the future, even after the injury heals.

Recognizing the role that sensitization plays in developing chronic pain, researchers are looking for ways to prevent patients from becoming hypersensitive. Their approach involves preventing or reducing pain as soon as possible in order to limit sensitization. One strategy used in surgery is called preemptive analgesia. It entails administering an analgesic, such as morphine or epidural anesthesia, before an operation to reduce postoperative pain. While more research is needed, some studies of preemptive analgesia are quite promising, showing decreased rates of chronic pain six months after thoracic surgery, breast cancer surgery, and lumbar spine surgery.

While acute pain serves a crucial evolutionary purpose, chronic pain seems to have no value. It does not protect against tissue damage, nor does it promote healing. Even worse, chronic pain can spiral out of control when your nervous system adapts to increased nociception by becoming hypersensitive, increasing the amount of pain you feel and leading to further changes in the nervous system. Thankfully, research has shown that in many cases, the changes are reversible and normal functioning can be restored. This shouldn't come as a surprise—your nervous system is plastic, after all.

While you can't change the fact that your nervous system maladaptively responds to pain, you can use this knowledge to reduce your chances of developing chronic pain, and to reverse chronic pain if you have it. When you become injured, have surgery, or develop chronic pain, you should be cautious about doing things that make the pain worse.

This doesn't mean that you should lie immobile on the couch or overmedicate yourself to avoid feeling the pain. In most cases, movement is necessary for optimal healing, and overuse of pain medications can bring about a host of other problems that can be far worse. But it's important to understand that the more often your nociceptors are stimulated, the more sensitization is likely to occur. So, running on an already injured and painful knee will not only damage the joint further, but may also increase the amount of pain you feel in the future.

Neuropathic Pain

Sometimes during the course of an injury or illness, nerves can become damaged. Neuropathic pain is caused by damaged nerves sending incorrect signals to other parts of the nervous system. Symptoms include tingling, numbness, and shooting or burning pain.

There are more than 100 potential causes of nerve damage, including physical trauma, autoimmune disorders, genetic conditions, degenerative diseases, stroke, vitamin deficiencies, infections, toxins, and alcoholism. About 30% of peripheral neuropathy cases are linked to diabetes. The reasons for this are not completely clear; some theories point to high glucose levels, while others believe decreased blood flow or depletion of metabolites are the cause.

Peripheral nerves are very good at regenerating after injury, growing on average between one and two millimeters per day. This process, called neuroregeneration, can allow nerve sensation to be restored and pain from nerve damage to go away. When injuries are extensive, doctors may perform surgery to graft portions of healthy sensory nerves onto damaged nerves. Occasionally, an injured nerve can form a neuroma, which is an abnormal growth of nerve tissue. While neuromas themselves are generally benign, they can cause significant nerve pain.

Unlike peripheral nerves, damaged nerves in the spinal cord face many challenges. The environment surrounding spinal nerve cells is hostile to regeneration, because it contains proteins that cause nerves to grow in the wrong direction and others that prevent nerve growth. On top of that, spinal nerves must grow in two directions (both toward the brain and toward the periphery), and this added challenge decreases their chances of successful regrowth.

Scientists have developed a technique that combines stem cells—which produce substances that promote nerve growth—with biomaterials. This method forms guidance channels within the spinal cord, creating a hospitable environment for neural regeneration and allowing spinal nerves to grow in the right directions. Another promising approach involves using polyethylene glycol–based biomaterials to fuse cell membranes at the site of the injury. This method repairs physical damage, reduces scar formation, and promotes nerve cell regeneration. These techniques offer a great deal of hope for people with pain and/or limited mobility resulting from spinal nerve damage.

Why Chronic Pain is So Complex

It's important to understand that in many cases of pain, especially chronic pain, multiple mechanisms are involved. Activation of nociceptors, changes in the nervous system, and actual nerve damage can work together to produce the unbearable aching, throbbing, and burning sensations that keep you awake at night and miserable during the day. As a result, many pain conditions continue to confuse and frustrate the people who suffer from them as well as the medical professionals who do their best to help.

One such example is cancer pain. Chemotherapy drugs can be one cause of neuropathic pain associated with cancer, but radiation, surgery, infections, a tumor pressing on nerves, and chemicals released by a tumor can all contribute to nerve damage and pain. A tumor large enough to damage nerves will likely damage surrounding tissue as well, thereby activating nociceptors; inflammation resulting from the damage will create more pain. And if these causes of pain persist, they'll likely to lead to adaptive changes in the nervous system that will increase and prolong the pain.

The severely painful, debilitating condition known as complex regional pain syndrome (CRPS) is another example of all three pain mechanisms working together. With a score of 42 out of 50, CRPS is the most painful condition on the classic McGill Pain Index, ranking above amputation and natural childbirth. Few studies have been done to determine how many people suffer from CRPS, but best estimates suggest that somewhere between 60,000 and 400,000 Americans have the condition at any given time.

CRPS typically develops after an injury, trauma, surgery, or infection. It often begins as pain in an arm or leg and then spreads, sometimes affecting the entire body. The most recent research suggests that CRPS is due to dysfunction of the nervous system on many levels. Nerve damage is a major factor, caused both by the trauma that may have initiated the condition and nerve degeneration, which can occur over time. Compression or entrapment that puts pressure on a single nerve has been reported to cause CRPS symptoms as well. Maladaptive neuroplasticity also contributes, causing nerve sensitization and dysregulation of circulation. Along with burning pain, tingling sensations, and hypersensitivity, nervous system dysfunction in CRPS patients causes swelling, changes in skin color and temperature, joint stiffness, loss of motor control, tremors, abnormal sweating, and changes in hair and nail growth.

Currently, the most promising drug treatment for CRPS is ketamine, a common general anesthetic. Ketamine works by blocking a glutamate receptor called NMDA (N-methyl-D-aspartate). Glutamate, an amino acid, is released in large quantities in response to a prolonged or intense painful stimulus. Overstimulation of NMDA receptors by glutamate can cause central sensitization, so blocking NMDA receptors can allow the nervous system to return to normal functioning.

It's interesting to note that ketamine can also be used as a treatment for depression. By blocking NMDA receptors, glutamate builds up in the nervous system and stimulates other types of glutamate receptors. This helps the brain to form new synapses and repair the neural damage resulting from stress that is so often present in depression.

Medication, physical therapy, and counseling are all recommended for CRPS; often a combination of these treatments over a period of months or years will yield gradual positive results culminating in near or full recovery. But just as the cause of CRPS is not well understood, patients often recover from the condition mysteriously and miraculously. A population-based study in Olmstead County, Minnesota, followed 74 people with CRPS from 1989 to 1999. The study found that 74% of the CRPS cases resolved over the ten-year period, and often the patients recovered spontaneously.

Why Emotions Make Pain Worse

Pain can be a confusing experience for anyone, and it becomes even more so when you consider how the sensation is created. While it feels like a bodily experience, that experience is actually created by your brain. The emotional parts of your brain, including the anterior cingulate cortex, the insular cortex, and the amygdala, are responsible for the unpleasantness that comes with pain. The more those areas are activated, the worse your experience of pain becomes.

Brain-imaging studies have demonstrated this quite clearly. In one study, researchers at the University of Montreal hypnotized a group of test subjects and told them that they would feel no pain. By doing this, the researchers essentially "turned off" the emotional parts of the test subjects' brains. When the test subjects and the control subjects dipped their hands into hot water, the sensation-processing part of the brain was activated to the same degree for both groups, showing that nociceptive stimulation was the same. However, the emotional brain areas of the subjects who had been hypnotized did not light up, while those of the control subjects did. The pain stimulation and pain signals sent to the brain were the same for both groups, but the emotional reaction and experience of the pain was quite different as a result of the expectation set by the researchers.

On the flip side, anticipating pain before it occurs can worsen your experience of pain. Have you ever exclaimed "ouch!" immediately after stubbing your toe, before actually feeling the pain? You've seen your toe hit the corner of the coffee table, felt the pressure of the corner against your toe, reflexively yanked your foot away, and possibly uttered a four-letter word—all before feeling the sensation of pain. The anticipation, often intensified by the memory of past toe stubs, is enough to make you react as if you're actually feeling pain.

When your emotions get involved, your experience of pain is heightened. In chapter 3, we'll explore how the anticipation of pain, along with stress, anxiety, and depression, work together to prolong your pain and make it much worse.

Endogenous Opioids: Natural Pain Relief

People have been using drugs for thousands of years, seeking out substances that will relieve what ails them or give them an unnatural high. One of the oldest drugs known to man is opium, a highly addictive substance obtained from the dried sap of the opium poppy. Evidence of opium poppies has been found in archaeological sites in Switzerland, France, and Spain dating to 5500 B.C. and earlier, and Sumerians living in lower Mesopotamia cultivated the plant as early as 3400 B.C. The Sumerians referred to the opium poppy as the "joy plant," so they were quite aware of its euphoric effects and likely used it for both medicine and recreation.

Opium made its way west, and by the sixteenth century it was being prescribed as a painkiller. In the early 1800s, chemists isolated two of the active ingredients in opium: the alkaloids known as morphine and codeine. In 1827, E. Merck & Company, the German chemical and pharmaceutical company now known as Merck & Co., Inc., began commercial manufacture of morphine. Opium and its derivatives were heralded as gifts from God because they came from nature and were powerful at relieving pain, reducing anxiety, and inducing a sense of euphoria.

In 1874, English researcher Charles Wright first synthesized heroin by boiling morphine. People quickly embraced this potent, fast-acting drug. Opioid use wasn't regulated, and by the end of the century hypodermic syringe sets for personal use were sold in the Sears, Roebuck and Co. catalog. The Harrison Narcotics Tax Act of 1914 was the first move by the US government to regulate the sale and distribution of opioids, which were becoming a widespread problem. By 1924, the Heroin Act banned the sale of heroin entirely.

The group of drugs once thought to be harmless had been criminalized. Physicians were hesitant to prescribe them, and some patients were undertreated due to the tight controls. Not surprisingly, the black market for opioids flourished. The problem of addiction reached epidemic levels during the decades following World War II.

During the 1970s, several groups of scientists identified specific nerve endings that are receptors for opium and its derivatives. These opioid receptors are located throughout the CNS and PNS, but are most concentrated in areas of the brain that process pain information. This groundbreaking discovery answered the question of how opioids work: By binding to opioid receptors, they block the nociceptive information traveling from the spinal cord into the areas of the brain that process pain information.

This discovery immediately raised another question: Why would the brain contain receptors for substances derived from the opium poppy? The obvious answer was that the body must naturally produce substances with a chemical structure similar to opioids.

The race was on to find these substances, and within two years researchers had isolated endogenous opioids, the most famous of which were named endorphins (a contraction of "endogenous," meaning naturally occurring, and "morphine"). Endogenous opioids function both as hormones and neuromodulators, modifying the behavior of other neurotransmitters. In addition to blocking pain sensations, endogenous opioids have since been found to play roles in appetite, mood control, immune response, and regulation of sex hormones.

The existence of endogenous opioids also explained a phenomenon known as stress-induced analgesia. In contrast to hyperalgesia, the increased sensitivity to pain that you learned about earlier in this chapter, analgesia is the inability or reduced ability to feel pain. That's why substances that reduce pain are called analgesics.

In the 1950s, anesthesiologist Henry Beecher published a study in which he compared pain intensity in wounded World War II soldiers to the civilian population. He found that only 32% of wounded soldiers, compared to 83% of civilians with similar injuries, requested narcotics for their pain.

In 1977, French neurobiologist Roger Guillemin demonstrated that the pituitary gland releases a certain type of endorphin in response to acute stress. Further research showed the release of other endogenous opioids, particularly enkephalins, in response to acute stress. This research explained what Beecher had observed—that when someone experiencing acute stress, such as being in combat, they actually feel less pain due to the release of natural opioids.

Unfortunately, these analgesic effects of stress don't last forever. They tend to be short-lived, possibly because your opioids are temporarily depleted. Another important aspect of this phenomenon is that stress-induced analgesia typically occurs when there's an external stressor that takes attention away from the pain—like someone threatening your life, or the need to escape a burning building.

Your natural analgesics serve an evolutionary purpose: They allow you to run fast or lift heavy objects even if you're injured. But what about acute stress that isn't life-threatening? It turns out that exercise elicits the same stress response, triggering the release of endogenous opioids that act in numerous areas of the brain, spinal cord, and peripheral nerves to dull pain and produce a sense of euphoria. While this well-known "runner's high" is a great incentive to exercise, it can numb the pain that should signal an injured athlete to stop and rest. Stories abound of athletes like Kerri Strug and Manteo Mitchell who kept going in spite of an injury that would normally cause crippling pain.

Looking for a way to get a runner's high without exerting any effort? Try acupuncture. The ancient Chinese technique of inserting needles into specific points on the body stimulates the release of natural opioids, providing relief from pain. Acupuncture also helps improve a variety of other conditions that use opioids as neurotransmitters, such as depression, immune system disorders, and sexual dysfunction. Since 360 out of 361 acupuncture points in humans are located near major nerves, it's hypothesized that acupuncture works by stimulating the pain pathways and neuroimmune pathways through which the nervous system and immune system communicate with each other. And while scientists don't yet agree on exactly why inserting needles causes the release of opioids, studies have proven the effect by using a drug called naloxone that blocks opioid receptors. When naloxone has been administered, opioids are unable to connect with opioid receptors, and the effects of acupuncture are negated.

Endogenous opioids help demystify another phenomenon as well: the placebo effect. Placebos, traditionally sugar pills, bread pills, or colored water, were often given instead of pharmaceuticals to patients during the nineteenth century as a way to calm and comfort them. The benefits of placebos were widely accepted, but the effects were thought to be psychological in nature. Researchers used to believe that placebos had a stronger effect on patients who were less intelligent and more neurotic, but we know today that this isn't true.

The placebo effect was linked to the release of opioids in 1978, when a study examined the placebo effect in dental postoperative pain. When patients were given naloxone to block their opioid receptors, the placebos stopped relieving their pain. More recently, brain-imaging studies have shown that opioid release and placebo administration activate the same areas of the brain. Statistically, the placebo effect accounts for about 50% of a medication's effectiveness. So for reasons that are not yet fully understood, simply believing that your pain will go away is enough to stimulate your natural pain-relieving mechanisms.

How Have You Experienced Pain?

Now that you're familiar with how and why you feel pain, and how your body can naturally relieve pain, take a moment to reflect on the pain you've experienced in your life.

- Can you think of times when you've had a chronically tight, painful muscle?

- Have you ever had pain continue long past the original injury?

- Have you had nerve damage resulting from an injury or illness?

- Have you ever felt pain relief or improved mood after exercising?

- Have you ever suspected that your relief from a health condition was due in part to the placebo effect?

CHAPTER 3

Why Stress Makes Pain Worse

Modern Homo sapiens have been evolving for at least 300 thousand years. For most of this time, humans lived a nomadic, hunter-gatherer lifestyle, moving with the seasons and following their sources of food. Daily life was focused on physical survival: finding food, preventing and healing from injuries, and defending against attack. People evolved to expertly deal with these acute stressors, automatically speeding up certain body systems to help fight the stressor, and automatically returning to normal functioning when the source of stress was gone.

The Purpose of Stress

When you perceive a threat to your survival, your sympathetic nervous system initiates the "fight-or-flight" response, temporarily creating a super-powered human capable of lifting heavy objects and sprinting very fast to outrun an attacker.

The stress response increases your blood flow, breathing rate, and production of energy for muscles. Your blood thickens, beginning the clotting process so that you don't bleed to death if injured. Muscles tense as they ready for action, and postural reflexes prepare you to either stand up and defend yourself or curl up into a ball. Your body releases endorphins so that pain or injury won't slow you down. Functions of your body that are not essential for fighting or fleeing, like digestion, immune response, and sexual arousal are inhibited to allow your body to devote itself fully to surviving the stressful event.

Then just as swiftly, as soon as you believe that the source of stress is gone, your parasympathetic nervous system automatically cues the functions of your body to return to normal. Heart rate and breathing slow down, muscles relax, and the digestive, immune, and reproductive systems resume their work.

Evolution prepared humans extremely well for chasing down dinner and defending against attack. But over the past 10 thousand years or so, since the development of agriculture provided reliable sources of food and allowed people to settle down in one place, sources of stress have changed. Once your basic needs are met, your stressors shift from the physical—those that directly affect your survival—to the psychological.

Unfortunately, emotional, social, and financial events can trigger your stress response in the same way that physical stressors do. It all comes down to perception; if you perceive something to be a threat, your stress response is activated. But unlike acute physical stress, from which you are quite adept at recovering, psychological stress stays in your mind and constantly activates your stress response.

Short-term physical stress generally has positive effects on the body by stimulating cellular repair and regrowth. It's the long-term activation of the stress response that gets you into trouble. When you constantly worry about work, deadlines, debt, relationships, and ironically, your health, your recovery response never kicks in.

Blood pressure remains elevated and your blood stays thick, increasing your chances of clots, strokes, and heart attacks. You may take shallow breaths, inflating your chest instead of your lower belly, and you find yourself short of breath. Your muscles stay tight all the time, ready for action. These chronically contracted muscles use a great deal of energy, causing you to feel fatigued. Stress hormones keep your immune system suppressed and blood sugar levels high, leading to brain-cell death. In the end, your response to psychological stress usually causes more damage than any of the sources of stress could have caused in the first place.

When it comes to chronic pain, there are two particularly relevant aspects of the stress response. The first, which is the focus of this chapter, is how chronic stress worsens your experience of pain. The second, which we'll discuss in chapter 9, is the way your neuromuscular system responds to stress: by tensing muscles and bringing you into reflexive postures, preparing you to fight or protect your body.

In chapter 2, we talked about how being in chronic pain leads to adaptive changes in the nervous system that increase pain sensation. We focused on mechanical changes in the structures that transmit pain signals to the brain and those that perceive pain in the brain. But mechanics are only part of the story. The way you react to pain is actually responsible for most of the unpleasantness that comes with painful stimuli. Stress makes you react more strongly, worsening your experience.

When you perceive stress, a series of hormones released in the brain triggers the adrenal gland to secrete hormones called glucocorticoids. These bind to glucocorticoid receptors, which are present in almost every cell in the body. They suppress the immune response so that all of the body's energy can be used to fight the stressor. They also increase and regulate the amount of glucose in the bloodstream, ensuring a constant supply of energy. They even improve your memory of events in which you feel strong emotions.

So far, glucocorticoids are sounding pretty good. In fact, synthetic glucocorticoids called corticosteroids have been used since the 1950s as medications for a variety of conditions in which the immune system is overactive, such as allergic reactions, asthma, dermatitis, hepatitis, inflammatory bowel disease, joint inflammation, lupus, multiple sclerosis, and rheumatoid arthritis.

But as the saying goes, moderation in all things. Prolonged activation of the stress response causes levels of glucocorticoids in the bloodstream to be constantly elevated. Just a few weeks of stress causes neurons, particularly neurons in the hippocampus (Illustration 4), a part of the brain involved in memory and learning, to begin to wither and die. So over time, high glucocorticoid levels can lead to diminished memory and attention.

Ironically, the hippocampus plays a role in inhibiting glucocorticoid secretion. So the more stress you experience and the more damage is done to your hippocampus, the less effective it is at regulating glucocorticoid levels, and the more glucocorticoids build up in your system. This is a vicious cycle that can make it difficult to reduce your level of stress.

Glucocorticoids have the opposite effect on the part of the brain called the amygdala (Illustration 4), which is where your perception of pain comes into play directly. The amygdala, along with the hippocampus and the rest of the limbic system, helps process emotional reactions and memories. Prolonged high levels of glucocorticoids actually enhance amygdala function, stimulating neuron growth and making synapses more active and sensitive. Some pain pathways pass through the amygdala, which helps create your emotional reaction to pain. When the amygdala is overactive, your reactions to pain are intensified, making your pain feel worse than it actually is.

How to Reduce Your Stress Level

If you want to reduce your stress, the first step is to identify the specific situation, event, or person that is causing the problem. Often, a single problem can make you feel stressed about everything in your life by affecting your mood and altering your perception. To counter this, take out a pen and piece of paper and make a list of everything that causes you stress.

Now, look at your list. Consider each item, and figure out how to take control of it. This may mean making changes to your work schedule or job expectations, addressing issues in a relationship, or dealing with difficult financial problems. If you find yourself making excuses for why you can't make the necessary changes, just remember:

1. There's a solution to every problem.

2. Your stress will get worse if you don't take action.

3. You are the only one who can make these changes. No one else will do it for you.

4. You're smart enough and strong enough to handle it if you work hard at it.

In addition to taking control over the sources of stress in your life, you'll also need to think about how you might be creating stress for yourself. If you're like many people, the underlying cause of your stress is habitual thought patterns. Do you perceive situations to be stressful when in reality they aren't that big of a deal? Do you spend a great deal of time worrying and creating unnecessary stress in your mind?

It's not the experiences themselves but the way you perceive and process them that determines the effects they have on your stress level, muscular patterns, and pain. In a study of over 48 thousand Swedish military recruits between the ages of 18 and 24, over five thousand of them had back problems—and the strongest predictor of their back pain was their ability to manage stress. Another study showed that among migraine sufferers, headaches could be predicted not just by stressful occurrences but also by the subjects' interpretations of events and their ability to cope with them.

Two people in identical situations can perceive and react completely differently—one person can become stressed and suffer health problems, while the other can just smile and shake it off. Can you think of people you know who always seem to be stressed out? Catastrophes occur for them on a daily basis, and they're always worrying or freaking out about something. More than likely, they don't encounter more stressful situations than the average person. But do they have more stress in their lives? Absolutely, because they create it.

Your thoughts are simply electrochemical reactions, consisting of messages sent between neurons. Repeat the same thought over and over, and the neural pathways involved in that thought get stronger. Your thoughts can trigger the release of neuropeptides that travel through your body, creating physiological responses, changing the structure of cells, and even altering your DNA, leading to accelerated aging and increased rates of cancer and heart disease.

If you perceive a situation to be stressful, your stress response is triggered. You also influence how you'll react in the future by worrying about potentially stressful situations ahead of time. Just as worrying about pain can make the pain worse, worrying about a potentially stressful situation can make it feel much more stressful. If you find yourself worrying and stressing before anything bad happens, you must learn to break that pattern or you'll continue to suffer the ill effects of unnecessary stress.

You may not feel like you can choose how you react because your responses and thought patterns have become habitual. But remember that your nervous system is plastic—you can retrain your thought patterns, and you can change how you react to potentially stressful situations.

As you go through your daily life, notice what happens when you experience stress:

- Does your pulse race?

- Do your thoughts become fixated on the stressful situation?

- Does stress affect the way you react to nonstressful things?

- Do you take the stress out on your family, friends, or coworkers?

- Does your posture change?

- Do your muscles get tense?

- If you're in pain, does your pain get worse?

- How does your body feel when you're stressed?

- Where in your body do you feel stress?

Once you've begun to notice your habitual reactions to stress, you can begin to change them. When you feel stress, take a deep breath into your lower belly, hold it for a few seconds, and exhale as slowly as you can. Breathing slowly and deeply like this (known as diaphragmatic breathing) stops your body's stress response and triggers your parasympathetic nervous system. Activating this part of your nervous system is the antidote to stress on a physiological level.

Next, analyze your situation and look at it objectively. Can you find a way to remain relaxed and deal with the situation? If you can, you'll find that not only is your stress reduced, but the stress of other people involved is reduced as well. The unnecessary stress that you and the people around you experience creates unpleasant living and working environments, negative expectations, impatience, poor communication, and a decrease in productivity. Stress and emotions are literally contagious, because the mirror neurons in your brain make you feel the emotions of the people around you (we'll talk about this more in chapter 12). You have the ability to turn a potentially stressful situation into a neutral or even positive experience for everyone just by modifying your reaction.

It takes time and conscious effort to retrain your habitual thought patterns and reactions, but it's worth it. Try it today: Notice one potentially stressful situation that you encounter, take a deep breath, and try to relax and turn it into a positive experience. Practice this every day and soon you'll find that your new pattern of reacting to events has become habitual, and you'll feel much less stress overall.

Anxiety and Pain

Repeated activation of your stress response can lead to generalized anxiety disorder, a mood disorder characterized by excessive worry, nervous behavior, irritability, restlessness, fatigue, difficulty concentrating, muscle tension, and problems sleeping. In laboratory experiments, artificial stimulation mimicking the effect of glucocorticoids on the amygdala caused rats to develop a condition similar to anxiety.

People who suffer from chronic anxiety are in a state of heightened stress that never goes away. They are always on edge, worrying about things that will most likely never happen. Their heightened anticipation of negative events causes them to overreact to a variety of stimuli, including pain. In laboratory studies, anxious patients reacted more strongly to hot and cold stimuli than did control subjects, withdrawing their fingers more quickly and rating their pain higher. Similar results were found when pain-related anxiety was induced in healthy subjects, showing that someone without generalized anxiety disorder can develop anxiety around a specific type of pain.

Anxiety sufferers also remember their pain as being worse than it actually was. In studies of people undergoing dental procedures, those who had the highest levels of anxiety before the procedures not only reported higher levels of pain than control subjects, but were also the most likely to overestimate their pain three months later. Sadly, their unrealistic memories of the pain only serve to increase negative anticipation, making their next dental procedure even more painful.

Studies like these led to research that tested the efficacy of antianxiety medications such as diazepam and chlordiazepoxide for pain relief; these drugs are now regularly prescribed for people with chronic pain. Antianxiety drugs work with the reactive component of pain perception; by slowing down the nervous system and making it less reactive, they dampen the experience of pain.

Stress, memory, and pain come together in an anxiety condition called post-traumatic stress disorder (PTSD). People most often develop PTSD after an experience that is, or that they perceive to be, threatening to their own or someone else's well-being. The condition may arise from a single experience, such as a car accident, attack, or natural disaster, or as a result of repeated exposure to a highly stressful situation, like combat or long-term abuse.

People with PTSD tend to suffer from recurring thoughts and nightmares, forcing them to relive the traumatic event and experience the stress that came with it over and over. PTSD patients experience higher rates of chronic pain and more intense chronic pain than both control subjects and anxiety patients. Various studies report that up to 80% of people with PTSD experience chronic pain, and that the severity of PTSD symptoms correlates directly with the severity of their pain.

Not only do anxiety disorders worsen the experience of pain, but simply being in pain can cause you to develop anxiety. Being in pain is stressful. The pain makes you agitated and reduces your ability to focus and concentrate. You might worry about not being able to keep up with normal work and activities, and you worry that the pain won't go away. The pain keeps you up at night, and the lack of adequate rest increases your stress levels. You may feel isolated because others don't understand what you're going through.

Worst of all, people in pain often feel like they have no control over their pain. Research shows that 45% of chronic pain patients develop one or more diagnosable anxiety disorders. And up to 50% of people with chronic musculoskeletal pain, serious burn injuries, and other painful pathologies such as fibromyalgia, cancer, and AIDS exhibit symptoms of PTSD. In fact, people who experience chronic pain are four times more likely to develop PTSD than those without pain. Chronic pain and anxiety disorders are often mutually maintaining conditions in which each exacerbates the other, creating a downward spiral that makes getting out of pain all the more difficult.

Depression and Pain

Imagine one person with anxiety and another with depression. The anxiety sufferer has elevated energy in the form of agitation and nervousness. In contrast, the depression sufferer has lower-than-average energy, is unable to get excited about anything, and finds it difficult just to get out of bed. Yet it turns out that stress is instrumental in developing depression, and glucocorticoids are again to blame. Research shows the correlation of stressful life events and chronic stress with an increased risk of depression. So despite seeming low energy, depressives with elevated glucocorticoid levels experience a great deal of stress and turmoil. While anxiety sufferers express their stress outwardly, depressives internalize their stress, which causes them to withdraw socially and feel lethargic.

People suffering from depression are often unable to take pleasure in activities they once enjoyed, and stress is part of the reason. Stress and the resulting release of glucocorticoids affect pleasure pathways in the brain, raising the threshold needed to perceive pleasure. A stressed lab rat temporarily becomes depressed, requiring stronger than normal stimulation of its pleasure pathways to elicit a sense of pleasure. Based on this research, you might guess that people taking synthetic glucocorticoids as medical treatment would experience an increased risk of depression, and you'd be right.

What about serotonin, dopamine, and norepinephrine, the famous neurotransmitters that have been implicated in depression? It turns out that glucocorticoids can affect how much of these substances the body produces, how they are broken down, and even the quantity and function of their receptors. Abnormalities in the levels of these neurotransmitters and how their receptors work play key roles in depression; for some people, elevated levels of stress hormones are the causative factor. For these people, drugs that lower glucocorticoid secretion and inhibit glucocorticoid receptors have been shown to be effective antidepressants.

So now that you have some understanding of the relationship between stress and depression, let's examine how depression affects your experience of pain. While anxiety worsens your experience of pain by increasing worry and reactivity, depression worsens pain by intensifying negative emotions like sadness.

The effects of negative emotions on pain perception can be induced even in healthy control subjects with no chronic pain and no depressive symptoms. One study asked three groups of volunteers to read statements describing positive, neutral, or negative moods. The volunteers were then asked to try to experience their assigned mood.

When subjected to a painful cold stimulus, the subjects in the negative mood group reported more intense pain than the control group, while the subjects in the positive mood group reported less pain than controls.

Certain parts of the brain are responsible for creating these negative emotions, and these same parts of the brain play a role in creating the unpleasant sensation of pain. One part of the brain that is particularly important in both depression and pain is called the anterior cingulate cortex or ACC (Illustration 4), an area of the brain located just in front of the limbic system.

When people are shown photos of their loved ones who have passed away, brain scans show their ACC lighting up. Electronically stimulating the ACC also causes people to experience abstract negative emotions. Depression sufferers tend to have elevated levels of activity in their ACC all the time compared to control subjects. In cases of debilitating depression, an experimental surgical treatment called bilateral anterior cingulotomy, which severs the connections between the ACC and the rest of the brain, may be able to decrease depressive symptoms.

When sensory pain information is sent from the periphery of the body to the brain, the ACC helps create the unpleasantness of pain by creating a negative emotional state. Brain-imaging studies show that the ACC can be essentially "turned off" by hypnosis, allowing people to be subjected to painful stimuli and feel no pain.

The good news is that the pathway connecting sensory pain information and the ACC seems to be highly plastic, like most of the nervous system. The degree to which the ACC is activated depends largely on your emotional state and your behavior when you react to pain. So can you improve your emotional state, learn to modify your reactions, and reduce your experiences of pain? Absolutely.

Recall from earlier in this chapter the role that the amygdala plays in anxiety, and how glucocorticoids elevate amygdala function. Activity in the amygdala is elevated in people with depression as well. In anxiety sufferers, the amygdala helps create the emotional states of fear and worry. In depression sufferers, the amygdala tends to be overactive all the time, responding to everything with a feeling of sadness and worsening the experience of physical pain.

As with pain and anxiety, the pain-depression relationship goes both ways; depression worsens pain and chronic pain can cause depression. The two conditions often maintain and exacerbate each other. Suffering from pain that never goes away is enough to make even the most cheerful person begin to have a negative outlook on life. Combine being in pain with the stress of missing work, the inability to do everyday activities, and feeling socially isolated, and a mood disorder seems almost inevitable.

To top it off, people in chronic pain rarely get a full, restful night of sleep. Research shows that sleep deprivation reduces your ability to control your emotions and makes you overreact to normally neutral situations. A healthy person feels grumpy when they don't sleep well for a night or two, so just imagine what months or years of inadequate sleep can do to your emotional state.

Numerous studies report that well over half of chronic pain patients suffer episodes of major depression or symptoms of depression. Rates of depression increase predictably with pain symptoms; the longer someone has been in pain, the more intense their pain, and the more areas of pain in their body, the more likely they are to experience depression. Sadly, the symptoms of depression are often overlooked by medical professionals, so many chronic pain patients suffer with undiagnosed depression.

A newfound link between depression and pain is substance P, a neuro-transmitter that helps transmit nociceptive information from the PNS to the CNS. When levels of substance P are lowered or its receptors are blocked, pain is reduced. Research shows drugs that block substance P can also be effective antidepressant medications, and common antidepressant drugs can lower levels of substance P. Why? Because substance P is often released along with serotonin, dopamine, and norepinephrine.

If you're in pain and substance P is being secreted to help transmit pain signals, it's likely that serotonin, dopamine, and norepinephrine are being secreted too, leading to potentially abnormal levels of these substances. So simply having nociception occurring in your body can increase your risk of depression, even when other emotional and behavioral factors are taken out of the equation. Likewise, suffering from depression can elevate your levels of substance P, worsening your experience of pain.

How to Alleviate Anxiety and Depression Naturally

While medication can be part of a successful treatment approach, here are four things you can do to alleviate your anxiety or depression naturally:

- **Participate in talk therapy.** There's no substitute for talking out loud about what's bothering you. Fear often keeps anxiety and depression sufferers from seeking help from others. If you're scared to talk to someone, know that literally hundreds of millions of people out there are suffering just like you are, and they're all scared too. Conquering the fear will help you get past your condition and move forward. It's much easier to solve your problems when you're able to talk about them with an expert. If you're not comfortable talking to someone in person or going to a support group, there are other options like text, phone, and video chat therapy services.

- **Take control.** For anxiety and depression sufferers, regaining a sense of control over their lives is a huge part of recovery. If you have anxiety or depression, you should go through the process of listing your sources of stress. If you can't figure out how to take control of them, ask someone else to look at the list and give you an objective opinion. It can be difficult to see your problems objectively when you've been stuck in them for so long. While you can't control everything in life, it's important to gain a sense of control over the things you actually can change—like your behavior, choices, and situations you can improve.

- **Make exercise a habit.** Exercise stimulates the release of endorphins, which not only block pain sensation, but also help to regulate mood. Exercise also releases and helps regulate levels of serotonin, dopamine, and norepinephrine. Physical exercise—particularly aerobic exercise—is a crucial part of recovery from anxiety and depression.

- **Take time to relax.** Simple relaxing activities like soaking in a hot tub, getting a massage, or taking a walk in nature will trigger your parasympathetic nervous system, making you less reactive to potentially stressful situations. Plan some relaxing activities in your schedule every day, and don't think of them as being indulgent—recognize them as a critical part of your recovery.

Fibromyalgia

Now we come to the most mysterious pain condition of all: fibromyalgia. While many factors are likely involved in developing this condition, one of the most common causes is stress. Fibromyalgia sufferers have been shown to be more vulnerable to the negative effects of stress, have impaired and maladaptive coping mechanisms, be more likely to catastrophize, have higher levels of neuroticism, and have higher rates of anxiety, depression, and PTSD.

Fibromyalgia affects about 10 million Americans, and between 75% and 90% of fibromyalgia patients are women. Women are more likely to suffer from fibromyalgia than men at least in part due to hormones. Estrogen, the female sex hormone, is protective against pain. But women's estrogen levels fluctuate throughout the month, and fibromyalgia sufferers report more pain during times of the month when their estrogen levels are low. Testosterone, the male sex hormone, also protects against pain, but women have a small amount of testosterone compared to men, and men's testosterone levels don't fluctuate the way women's estrogen levels do.

Social stigmas may also contribute to the higher rates of reported cases of fibromyalgia in women than in men. Men are less likely to go to the doctor when they experience pain because they don't want to appear weak. Also, doctors often overlook fibromyalgia as a possible diagnosis in men because it's thought of as a female problem.

Muscle pain and fatigue are the two main symptoms of fibromyalgia. Traditionally, fibromyalgia has been diagnosed based on sensitivity to touch at 11 or more out of 18 specific tender points on the body. However, in 2010 a new diagnostic approach was adopted that will likely lead to an increase in the number of people diagnosed with the condition. The new criteria are based on how widespread the pain is combined with the severity and duration of the symptoms, which include fatigue, unrefreshing sleep, and cognitive issues. Many disorders such as Lyme disease, hypothyroidism, rheumatoid arthritis, sleep apnea, and lupus have similar symptoms, so when diagnosing fibromyalgia it's important to rule out all other possibilities.

Stressful or traumatic events such as car accidents, abuse, repetitive injuries, and acute illnesses have been linked to fibromyalgia. As mentioned earlier, chronic psychological stress is a common cause of the condition. Stress would certainly explain the fatigue that patients suffer, as well as the muscle pain, which could be the result of both chronic muscular contraction and sensitization of the nervous system.

Fibromyalgia can also begin with an illness. When your natural immune system response becomes overactive or prolonged due to stress, a host of issues arise such as fatigue, chronic inflammation, and autoimmune conditions that can cause pain as well as structural damage to joints, connective tissues, and organs.

As you might expect, depression is common among fibromyalgia sufferers. People with fibromyalgia have decreased activity in opioid receptors in the parts of the brain that affect mood and the emotional processing of pain. Researchers say that this reduced response might explain why fibromyalgia patients are likely to have depression and are less responsive to opioid painkillers.

For many people, it seems that fibromyalgia is the result of an ongoing cycle of chronic pain, psychological stress, overactive immune system response, lack of sleep, and sensitization of the nervous system. Researchers at the University of Oslo in Norway interviewed patients who had recovered completely from fibromyalgia, and found that they had not recovered as a result of a specific treatment, but rather by making changes to their lifestyle and reducing their stress levels.

If you or someone you know suffers from fibromyalgia, here are some lifestyle changes that can help:

- **Use talk therapy** to address sources of psychological stress such as abuse, accidents, or loss of a loved one.

- **Take control of lifestyle-related stress** by making necessary changes in your job, schedule, daily habits, and relationships.

- **Relieve functional physical pain** by improving body mechanics and releasing chronic muscular tension (we'll cover this in chapters 8, 14, and 15).

- **Commit to a regular sleep schedule** and take steps to improve sleep, such as limiting caffeine and alcohol, reducing stress, getting regular exercise, and creating a restful sleep environment. A weighted blanket, often recommended for anxiety sufferers, can promote better sleep by helping you relax and feel safe.

- **Boost the immune system** by reducing stress, engaging in regular moderate exercise, getting enough sleep, and eating a healthy, balanced diet.

The Immune System and Pain

When you think of your immune system, you probably think of winter colds that leave you curled up on the couch with cough drops, or allergies that make you break out in hives. You probably don't think of pain as being related to an increased immune system response, but the two often go hand in hand.

Sometimes your immune system gets confused and begins to attack healthy cells instead of foreign or damaged cells. The result can be one of more than 80 recognized autoimmune conditions. Stress tends to make inflammatory autoimmune reactions worse, increasing the pain that goes along with inflammation. For some people, a period of extreme stress triggers the onset of an autoimmune condition, such as rheumatoid arthritis, lupus, multiple sclerosis, Grave's disease, asthma, celiac disease, psoriasis, ulcerative colitis, or inflammatory bowel disease. Some studies show that up to 80% of autoimmune disease sufferers experience severe stress leading up to the onset of their disease.

One of the most common (and arguably the most painful) autoimmune diseases is rheumatoid arthritis (RA), which affects 2–3% of the world's population. In RA, immune system cells target the joints, attacking and slowly breaking down healthy cartilage. Then the synovium, the connective tissue that lines the joints, invades the cartilage and bone, causing permanent structural damage. Joints are often swollen, stiff, warm to the touch, and very painful.

Once an autoimmune disease has set in, stress often causes relapses or flare-ups. New research showing that psychological stress triggers an inflammatory response from the immune system indicates at least one reason why: Stress leads to inflammation, which leads to increased pain. Studies show that stressful events lead predictably to increased joint pain in people with RA. Sadly, doctors may dismiss stress as a factor in autoimmune diseases because these conditions typically respond well in the short term to high doses of corticosteroid medications.

This is a great example of the effects of acute versus chronic stress. In acute stress, the release of glucocorticoids temporarily suppresses the immune system so that all of the body's energy can be used to fight the stressor. Temporarily suppressing the immune system is a good thing for someone with an autoimmune disease because their immune system is attacking the wrong thing—their body's own cells. High doses of synthetic glucocorticoids simulate the natural response to an acute stressor, suppressing the immune response and giving the autoimmune disease sufferer some relief from their symptoms. In contrast, prolonged periods of stress and repeated stressful experiences cause the immune system to become perpetually overactive, triggering flare-ups and worsening pain. So as you might expect, corticosteroid medications are generally not recommended for long-term use.

How to Improve Immune System Function

Here are the best ways to balance your immune system function and improve your health naturally, whether you have an autoimmune disease or not:

- **Reduce psychological stress** (see "How to Reduce Your Stress Level" earlier in this chapter). Psychological stress triggers your fight-or-flight response, suppressing immune system function. Chronic stress increases your risk of viral infections and autoimmune disorders.

- **Commit to a regular sleep schedule.** Research shows that adequate sleep is instrumental for optimal immune system function. Like chronic stress, chronic lack of sleep weakens the immune system.

- **Eat a healthy, balanced diet.** Make sure your diet provides you with enough vitamins A, C, B6, E, and folic acid, as well as zinc, selenium, iron, and copper. If you suspect a significant vitamin or mineral deficiency, see your doctor for a definitive diagnosis.

- **Identify food intolerances.** Eating foods that you can't tolerate can increase inflammation and impair immune system function. If you think you might have any food intolerances, discuss your symptoms with a doctor.

- **Make time to exercise and relax every day.** Moderate exercise (in contrast to intense exercise and no exercise at all) improves immune system function. Exercise and relaxation also strengthen immunity by reducing your stress response and allowing your immune system to do its job.

Take a Holistic Approach

Humans are incredibly complex beings. Nearly all of your internal functions are interconnected, and most health problems exist on a spectrum. Grouping symptoms into conditions is useful, but the labels used to identify certain conditions can limit your understanding of what's happening in your body, thereby limiting the actions you take to heal. For most people, a holistic approach that treats the whole person by addressing psychological and physical symptoms and lifestyle-related factors will be the most successful.

Consider these questions as you begin to notice the connection between your own stress and well-being:

- Do you tend to come down with a cold or become ill when you've been stressed or haven't had enough sleep?

- Do you notice that stress and lack of sleep put you in a bad mood and increase your muscle tension and pain?

- Do exercise and a healthy diet improve your sleep and reduce your stress?

Take Control

It's safe to say that everyone will experience some negative effects of stress at some point in their lives. For most of us, the experience of stress is highly modifiable, and the triggers for stress are controllable. Stress has countless negative effects on all aspects of your health including pain, immune function, mental state, cardiovascular function, energy level, and ability to sleep. That's why reducing your stress is one of the best things you can do for yourself.

No matter how stressed you get, remember to focus on the things you can control. You can change your old stressful habits and help yourself heal.

CHAPTER 4

How You Develop Muscle Memory

When a baby is born, he is immediately overwhelmed by new sensations: the chill of the air, the warmth of his mother's touch, and the roughness of a blanket against his skin. This world is vastly different from his mother's womb. Now there is constant stimulation and seemingly no limit to the space around him.

Not yet able to crawl or walk, he explores with his eyes and ears. He recognizes faces and voices, and soon begins to interact by babbling and mimicking facial expressions. Around four months of age, his brain has developed some ability to gauge where objects are in space. With his developing depth perception, he begins to reach and grab for anything in his field of vision that seems interesting.

The infant's desire to move toward objects that he can now see, combined with an innate desire to be upright in gravity, motivates him to contract the muscles in the back of his neck so that he can lift his head and look around. Five or six months after birth, he learns how to contract the muscles in his lower back as well. Now he can move around on his own! Gaining control of these extensor muscles, which extend the spine and arch the back, allows him to crawl, sit, and eventually stand.

At this young age, the little boy is already developing learned motor patterns, sequences of movements that accomplish certain tasks. Each time he tries to climb the stairs, he makes conscious, deliberate choices about how to move his arms and legs. When something works, he repeats it. Soon he has developed a pattern that works every time: He puts his left hand up on the second step, then his right knee on the first step, then his right hand on the second step, and finally his left foot on the first step. He presses his left foot downward, pushing himself up toward the next step, and then starts the pattern again. The motor learning process is constantly at work in his nervous system every time he contracts a muscle or even thinks about moving.

With each repetition, the motor pattern becomes more deeply learned. Soon the boy can climb stairs quickly and easily, with little conscious effort. While the pattern that he created and taught himself has become so automatic that it seems to be innate, we know that it's learned through experience, practice, and repetition.

At birth, the size of the boy's brain was around 12 ounces, only a quarter of what it will weigh when he is fully grown. In contrast, most mammals are born with brains that are already at 90% of their adult weight. Within just a few hours after birth, many animals know how to walk and communicate with their species, and they rely largely on reflexes and instincts that are hardwired in their brains from birth. As somatic educator Moshe Feldenkrais said in his book *Body & Mature Behavior*, "Learning becomes the greatest and, indeed, the unique feature distinguishing man from the rest of the living universe."

As a general rule, the smaller the weight of an animal's brain at birth compared to its adult brain weight, the greater capacity the animal will have to learn and make conscious choices. Chimpanzees' brains are roughly half their adult size at birth; bottlenose dolphins are born with 42% of their adult brain weight. Elephants are born with just 35% of their adult brain weight, giving them an incredible capacity to learn. Like humans, elephants go through a learning period of about 10 years before they are considered fully mature.

But there's a downside: Your capacity to learn a seemingly infinite variety of motor patterns is one of the main reasons you're in so much pain. When your learned motor patterns make your body stand and move in unnatural ways, they can cause muscle and joint pain and degeneration. Before we dive into the details of how you develop learned motor patterns, let's talk about how your sensory perception affects the way you move.

The Connection between Sensing and Moving

Movement begins as sensation. When you sense that there's dust in your nostrils, you reflexively sneeze. You feel hunger and decide to get up and make a sandwich. Even voluntary movements unrelated to what you feel in your body, such as the decision to get out of bed and get ready for work, depend on sensation to determine the way that you move. You must be able to sense your body position and detect where objects in your environment are in relation to you.

There is constant feedback between your sensory and motor nerves. First, you sense what you feel in your body, where you are in space, and what's happening in your environment, and then you move your muscles accordingly.

In chapter 2 you learned about nociceptors, the nerve endings you sometimes wish you didn't have because they receive information that gets processed into the sensation of pain. There are many other types of nerve endings that receive different sensory information relating to what you see, hear, smell, taste, and touch in your external environment.

You also have nerve endings that sense your internal environment, providing information about body position, relationship to gravity, and temperature. Some sensory nerves send information to your brain, where it's translated into something meaningful to which you then respond. Other sensory nerves synapse in the spinal cord or brain stem, triggering automatic reflexes like sneezes and postural corrections. Three sensory systems in particular—visual, vestibular, and proprioceptive—play important roles in determining movement and posture.

Visual Sensory System

Your visual sensory system is incredibly complex. In the eye alone there are over 100 million photoreceptors, known as rods, cones, and ganglion cells, which take in light information. These make up the retina, a layer of tissue that lines the back wall of the eye. The retina processes light information and sends it to the brain via the optic nerve. Various parts of the brain then use this information to create your perceptions of depth, movement, shape, and color, as well as control your daily sleep and waking cycles.

Vestibular System

The vestibular system, responsible for maintaining your sense of balance, receives information about the movement of the head entirely from its internal environment. Within the inner ear is a structure called the vestibular labyrinth, which is made up of fluid-filled semicircular canals and the otolith organs.

When you move forward or backward, hair cells in the otolith organs give your vestibular receptors information about your acceleration and deceleration. When you turn your head, fluid moves hair cells within the canals; vestibular receptors connected to the hair cells relay information to the brain about how quickly and in what direction you're turning. If you spin around in circles a few times and then stop abruptly, you'll feel dizzy because the fluid in your semicircular canals keeps moving for a while after you've stopped spinning.

You usually process vestibular sensation at a subconscious level, automatically adjusting head and body position to remain balanced. You're typically unaware of your vestibular system unless it's not functioning normally. Vertigo is a symptom that indicates problems in the inner ear, causing dizziness, nausea, and other unpleasant sensations. Another common vestibular issue is motion sickness, which occurs when the brain is forced to deal with conflicting sources of visual and vestibular information.

Proprioceptive System

Your proprioceptive system works with the visual and vestibular systems to help you understand where your body is positioned in space relative to your surroundings. Proprioceptors are sensory receptors located in muscles and joints that sense muscle length, muscle tension, and changes in the angle and movement of your joints.

An accurate sense of proprioception is critical to maintaining healthy posture, relaxed muscles, and natural, efficient movement patterns. Your brain seamlessly blends information from the visual and vestibular systems with information from the proprioceptive system to give you a sense of balance, body position, and how you're moving through space. When your sense of proprioception is off, it becomes very easy to sit, stand, and move in ways that cause pain and physical damage to your body. (We'll talk more about this in chapter 5.)

Other Sensors

Along with proprioception, the sensations of pain, touch, and temperature are known as the somatic senses. Like proprioceptors and nociceptors, these nerve endings are spread throughout your body.

Mechanoreceptors, which can sense bending and stretching by stimuli as small as 0.006 mm high and 0.04 mm wide, detect touch and pressure in the skin, heart, blood vessels, bladder, digestive organs, and teeth. Specialized mechanoreceptors work with the brain to perceive variations in types of touch and pressure, allowing you to feel the differences between pressing, pricking, stroking, vibrating, tickling, and scratching. Your thermoreceptors are incredibly sensitive as well, able to detect a change of just 0.01 degrees Celsius. When pressure is strong enough or temperature is hot or cold enough to potentially cause damage, your nociceptors are stimulated, and you feel pain.

How You Move

All parts of your nervous system, from the brain to the spinal cord to the peripheral nerves, are involved in motor control. Let's start at the top, with the brain.

The cerebrum is the largest part of the brain, made up of the cerebral cortex and subcortical structures. The cerebral cortex is the outer layer of the cerebrum, responsible for the highest level of brain function, including thought, language, perception, memory, attention, awareness, and voluntary movement. All areas of the cerebrum located beneath the cortex can be referred to as subcortical.

Beneath the cerebrum lies the cerebellum, which is responsible for organizing your movement patterns (Illustration 4). The brain stem extends downward, relaying information between the brain and the spinal cord. The brain stem also controls processes that are most vital to survival, including breathing, heart rate, consciousness, and body temperature.

Each part of the brain plays a different role in controlling your movement. The cerebrum is responsible for strategy of movement; it's the "big picture" guy. The cerebellum is responsible for tactics; it figures out the sequence of muscle contractions necessary to carry out the movement and how to arrange the body in time and space. Finally, the brain stem and spinal cord execute the movement by sending signals that tell your muscles to contract.

Two parts of the cerebral cortex play important roles in how we move: The somatosensory cortex processes sensory information and the motor cortex controls movement (Illustration 5). Together, these areas span the brain across the head from ear to ear. Each cortex is made up of many smaller areas responsible for sensing and controlling different parts of the body; these areas of the brain can adapt to increased or decreased levels of input and use.

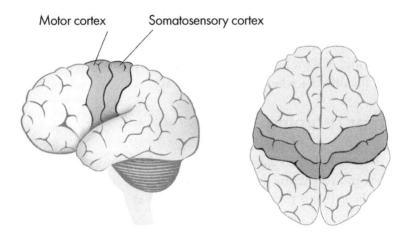

Illustration 5: The somatosensory and motor cortices
(adapted from Alila © 123rf.com)

For example, a person who had his right hand amputated would use his left hand a great deal more, and as a result, the areas of his brain that process the sensory information and control the movement of his left hand would increase in size. As your nervous system learns and updates motor skills throughout your life, this learning process causes structural changes in your brain. In other words, the ways you move your body will literally change the structure of your brain.

For the sake of simplicity, let's classify movements into two types: voluntary and reflexive. Voluntary movements are initiated by the cerebrum; they're movements that you deliberately decide to do and must learn how to execute, like tying your shoelaces or dancing the rumba.

Reflexive movements occur automatically and subconsciously. They are controlled by the spinal cord or brain stem, depending on what part of the body is involved. Sensory neurons carrying information from your extremities synapse with neurons in the spinal cord or brain stem; some will trigger an automatic motor response known as a reflex. As the reflex occurs, the sensory information continues to travel all the way to the brain, allowing for a voluntary response that may override the reflex.

Reflexes serve a critical evolutionary purpose. The nerves involved carry both the sensory and motor signals a much shorter distance—just to the spinal cord or brain stem and back to the extremities, instead of all the way to the brain and back. This saves a great deal of time and allows you to respond nearly instantaneously to potentially harmful stimuli. The difference in reaction time can mean the difference between life and death.

Motor Learning

Two significant changes occur in your nervous system as you learn a motor pattern: Neural pathways are created, modified, and strengthened, and the control and memory of the pattern shifts to different areas of the brain.

You may have heard the phrase "neurons that fire together wire together." This short phrase summarizes the synaptic plasticity theory of learning set forth by Canadian psychologist Donald Hebb in his 1949 book *The Organization of Behavior*. As we discussed in chapter 2, neuroplasticity is the brain's ability to forge new connections based on input and use. The concept of neuroplasticity had been previously proposed by others, most notably American psychologists William James and Karl Lashley, and Polish neuroscientist Jerzy Konorski, but it was largely ignored by the scientific community until Hebb brought the concept to the forefront in his groundbreaking book.

Hebb explained that "synaptic connectivity changes as a function of repetitive firing." In other words, when you repeat a movement like swinging a golf club over and over, the neural pathways involved in controlling that movement become stronger and faster. Not only do existing synapses begin to fire more efficiently, but new synapses are formed and other neurons are recruited to get in on the action. As a result, your golf swing becomes more automatic, reliable, and forceful the more often you practice.

Initially, both voluntary and reflexive movements occur and then cease completely. Once you decide to stop moving or the stimulus that triggers the reflex is removed, your muscles stop contracting and your body comes to rest. When you perform a voluntary movement many times, however, or if a reflex is stimulated repeatedly, your nervous system adapts.

Your nervous system likes to be as efficient as possible, because making fast decisions helps you survive. When you keep repeating the same movement or posture, it begins to make that movement or posture automatic, and you develop muscle memory. As the motor pattern becomes more deeply learned, the control of the pattern shifts to different areas of the brain. This allows those parts of the brain responsible for making voluntary decisions to focus on new things that require conscious attention.

To demonstrate how lower levels of the brain take over control of practiced movements, in 2010 researchers did brain scans of 10 people while they learned how to execute a simple finger movement. During the first two weeks of daily practice, the prefrontal cortex (Illustration 4)—the area of the cerebral cortex that plans complex behavior, makes decisions, and focuses attention—was highly interactive with other brain regions. After four weeks of practice, the prefrontal cortex was less active and its connections with other brain regions were weakened. The need for conscious attention was diminished as the subjects mastered their new skill.

Over the four-week test period, activity increased in the motor cortex (Illustration 5) and the basal ganglia (Illustration 4), a subcortical cluster of neurons that plays a role in learning, memory, voluntary motor control, and habit formation. Strengthened connections between the basal ganglia and the motor cortex are correlated with improved movement planning and control and decreased involvement from the prefrontal cortex.

The process of motor learning is gradual. The more times you repeat a movement, the more deeply it is learned, and the more automatic and less conscious it becomes. As movements become learned, not only does control of the movements shift to different areas of the brain, but storage of the motor memories moves as well.

For decades scientists have debated where long-term "muscle memories" are stored in the brain. Finally in 2006, they found their answer. By examining eye movements in mice, scientists in Japan found that short-term motor memories created in the cortex (outer layer) of the cerebellum become long-term memories when they are transferred to the vestibular nuclei (Illustration 4).

Research on the efficacy of visualization techniques has proven that you can practice motor skills and strengthen learned motor patterns without actually moving. By simply imagining yourself performing certain tasks, your brain functions in much the same way as when you physically carry out the actions. Brain scans show that you plan and prepare for both real and visualized movement in the same way, whether you perform the actions or stop before activating the primary motor cortex and carrying out the movements.

Visualization techniques allow athletes and performers to practice without sensory distractions, physical limitations, or risk of injury. In fact, an experiment carried out by Russian coaches leading up to the 1980 Olympics showed that not only does visualization work, but it can be more effective than physical training. The coaches separated their athletes into four groups: the first did 100% physical training, the second did 75% physical training and 25% visualization, the third did 50% physical training and 50% visualization, and the fourth did 25% physical training and 75% visualization. Remarkably, the athletes that showed the greatest improvement in performance were in the fourth group that spent most of their time visualizing their movements instead of physically training.

Learned motor patterns can remain with you for long periods of time even if they are not actively practiced. While synaptic connections will weaken, some vestiges of the neural pathways remain, and the memory of how to execute a movement can be stored. A study by L.B. Hill found that typing skills could be retained after two consecutive 25-year periods of not typing at all. Other research has shown that the abilities to juggle, drive, and solve mazes can be quickly remembered and reinstated after many years without practice. As the saying goes, it's just like riding a bike.

Despite the potential permanence of your learned motor skills, you do have the ability to learn new movement patterns well enough that they can override old ones. A wonderful example of this ability is golfer Tiger Woods, who has deconstructed and reconstructed his swing not once, not twice, but three times in less than two decades. Ever the perfectionist, Woods seems to take great pleasure in harnessing his analytical and kinesthetic skills in pursuit of the perfect swing.

You can learn an important lesson by observing what Woods went through the first time he changed his swing. Shortly after winning the 1997 Masters Tournament by a record 12 strokes, Woods approached his then-coach Butch Harmon about the possibility of improving his swing. Harmon agreed that it was possible, but cautioned Woods that it would be difficult to play competitively while making the changes. Woods refused to listen, insisting that he was capable of implementing the new swing while continuing to compete. He went on to have one of his worst seasons ever, entering a famous slump during the second half of 1997 and winning only one tournament in 1998.

Harmon knew what he was talking about. Weakening the grip, adjusting the takeaway, raising the left arm on the backswing, changing the clubhead angle, and coordinating the timing of the arms and hips were too many changes to make all at once while maintaining world-class performance. Harmon also understood that trying to learn how to swing a club in this new way would be virtually impossible while under the pressure of competition; this was why so many other golfers had failed in their attempts to change their swings.

Under stress, your nervous system relies on the fastest neural pathways for movement. The motor pattern that is most deeply learned requires the least amount of conscious thought, so the nervous system is able to carry it out most efficiently. Woods ran into trouble during the 1998 season because he was trying to use his new swing while it was still tentative and unreliable. The neural pathways controlling his new swing were not yet strong enough for the pressure of competition. The stress caused him to revert to his old swing, possibly creating some sort of hybrid of the two, as well as a great deal of frustration.

Harmon finally convinced Woods to take a year off from playing competitively so that he could learn his new swing from the ground up, one element at a time. Away from the stress of competition, Woods was able to practice his new swing slowly and consciously. As Woods experienced, by practicing in a nonstressful environment where old patterns were not triggered, he was able to develop and master a new movement pattern that became stronger and more efficient than the old one.

Just before the Byron Nelson Championship in May of 1999, Woods famously called Harmon and said, "I got it." Over the next two seasons, Woods won 17 PGA Tour events, including the 2000 US Open Championship, which he won by a record-setting 15 strokes. This was the first in a streak of four straight consecutive wins in the four major golf tournaments. From August 1999 to September 2004 Woods was ranked the number-one golfer in the world. The time and effort it took to change his swing had been well worth it, and Woods repeated the process again in 2004 and 2010.

Think About Your Movement Patterns

You learn and master new motor skills throughout your life. The next time you do the following activities, notice how ingrained your movement patterns are in your muscle memory. If you try to do these actions in a different way, you'll notice how difficult it is and how uncoordinated you feel!

- Brushing your teeth

- Brushing your hair

- Getting dressed

- Driving your car

- Walking at your normal pace

- Exercising

- Working at a computer

- Using your phone

- Preparing dinner

Although mastering these movement patterns allows you to get through your day efficiently, they can actually cause chronic pain and damage your body. As you're about to learn, the way you automatically, subconsciously use your body in daily life leads to most musculoskeletal conditions like back pain, scoliosis, disc problems, osteoarthritis, and many more. In the next chapter, we'll talk about the negative effects of muscle memory.

CHAPTER 5

Why You Lose Control, Sensation, and Awareness

Let's pretend you just started a new job, and it's your first-ever office job. All of a sudden you'll spend most of your waking hours sitting at a desk and working at a computer. Let's also pretend you're a bit nearsighted. Each time you sit down to work, you reach your head and neck forward a little in order to see the screen better. Then you lift up your hands, bringing your arms forward and rotating them inward so that you can type on the keyboard (Illustration 6).

I'd like you to really feel what it's like to be in this position. Wherever you are, please read the next few paragraphs and then put your book down so that you can try this exercise.

Sit up straight and tall with your feet on the ground right below or in front of your knees, head sitting easily on the top of your spine, eyes looking straight ahead, and arms hanging loosely by your sides.

Now, bring your head forward a bit as though you wanted to see a computer screen better, and as you do this, pay attention to what muscles you feel contracting. Did you feel where the contraction is happening? If not, do the movement again. You might have kept your torso stiff and just craned your neck forward using your neck muscles. Or you might have contracted your abdominal muscles, tucking your pelvis under and rounding your back. Most likely, you did some combination of these two actions.

Contracted neck muscles

Contracted pectorals

Contracted biceps

Contracted abdominals

Illustration 6: Muscle contraction in typical computer posture
(Marcin Balcerzak © 123rf.com)

Repeat the movement again, feeling your pattern of muscular contraction as you bring your head forward, and feeling the release of the muscles as you go back to your neutral starting posture.

Now bring your arms up in front of you and rotate your hands inward as if you're going to type on a keyboard, and as you do so, notice what muscles are working. If it's hard to feel this one, relax and start over, and try moving very slowly. You should feel your pectoral muscles as well as your biceps muscles contracting as you come into the typing position.

Each time you sit down to work at your new job, your neck muscles, pectorals, biceps, and abdominals all contract to bring you into your typing position. At first, this position is new to you and it will likely feel uncomfortable and tiring. You'll instinctively relax back in your chair every few minutes, and subconsciously find reasons to get up and walk around.

Day after day, you repeat this posture. Your nervous system says,

"Hey, she seems to like sitting this way. Let's help her out and just keep her in this posture all the time!" The control of this posture begins to shift away from your prefrontal cortex into lower brain regions where it's controlled automatically and subconsciously. You become accustomed to the feeling of being in this posture, and it feels more and more comfortable every day. Now you can stop wasting energy and conscious attention on your posture and focus on your work.

Muscle memory has the positive effect of making you more efficient, but it has the negative effects of reducing your motor control, sensation, and awareness. These can lead to posture and movement patterns that put you in pain and damage your body. Let's see what happens when these occur.

Why Your Muscles Stay Tight

When you want to move, the brain sends a message to begin the contraction phase of the muscles. This is the only type of signal your brain can send to your muscles; it cannot send a message to release. When the movement is complete and your brain stops sending the message to contract, your muscles automatically enter the relaxation phase and return to their normal resting length.

If your brain keeps sending a "contract" message to your muscles, the relaxation phase doesn't happen completely—or at all. The degree to which relaxation occurs depends on the frequency with which the brain sends a message to contract. The more often it sends that message, the less the relaxation phase can occur. When the message is sent at a very frequent rate, the relaxation phase doesn't happen at all and the muscles are in a tetanic contraction.

While this might sound like something you want to avoid, most skeletal muscle contractions are tetanic; you need sustained contraction to coordinate your movement and maintain balance and posture. In a voluntary movement like picking up and carrying a heavy box, however, the tetanic contraction occurs only for the few minutes that you're carrying the box. Once you set the box down, your brain stops telling your muscles to contract, and the relaxation phase occurs. That's because control of the movement happened in the conscious parts of your brain.

However, if you repeat the same posture or movement over and over, it gradually becomes automatic and you slowly cease to have conscious, voluntary control of it. When you repeat a posture or movement often enough, the muscles involved don't complete their relaxation phase. They continue to hold some residual tension, an unconscious partial contraction of resting muscles known as muscle tone or muscle tonus.

Like nearly everything else in your body, muscle tone exists on a spectrum. When muscles are abnormally loose, they're called hypotonic. When muscles are abnormally tight, as can occur with certain neurological diseases and conditions, they're called hypertonic. For most of us, the norm lies somewhere in between.

You need a certain amount of resting muscle tension to maintain your balance. A little bit of tension in your muscles helps you move more quickly, because your nervous system has to send fewer messages to carry out the movement. You develop varying levels of resting muscle tension in different muscles as a result of your habitual posture and movement patterns.

As you learned in the last chapter, motor patterns are created and stored in the brain. Your level of muscle tone is determined both by your learned motor patterns, which send the messages to your muscles to contract, and by a sensorimotor feedback loop that senses and maintains the length of your muscles.

This sensorimotor feedback loop is the gamma loop (Illustration 7). It's made up of alpha and gamma motor neurons, sensory neurons, proprioceptors called muscle spindles, and skeletal muscle. The loop operates between the spinal cord and the muscles, quickly and automatically maintaining appropriate muscle length.

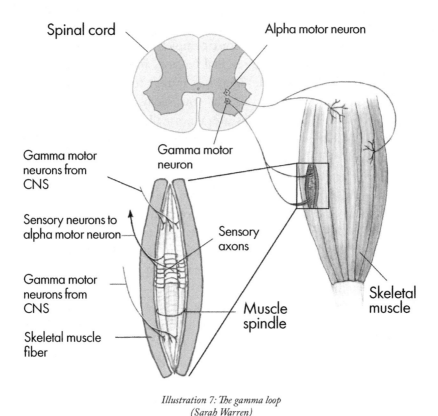

Spinal cord

Alpha motor neuron

Gamma motor neuron

Gamma motor neurons from CNS

Sensory neurons to alpha motor neuron

Gamma motor neurons from CNS

Skeletal muscle fiber

Sensory axons

Muscle spindle

Skeletal muscle

Illustration 7: The gamma loop
(Sarah Warren)

Alpha motor neurons innervate (supply with nerves) skeletal muscle, while gamma motor neurons innervate the muscle fibers within the muscle spindle. Alpha and gamma motor neurons relay messages from both the brain and the automatic feedback loop. Sensory neurons wrapped around the muscle spindle sense changes in muscle length and send this information to the alpha motor neuron, allowing it to regulate the length of the skeletal muscle.

Unfortunately, when repeated muscle contraction is signaled by the brain, the gamma loop can get out of whack. Overactive or imbalanced firing by motor neurons in the gamma loop can increase muscle tension and spasms and even cause severe spasticity or rigidity.

As you just learned, a certain amount of muscle tone is beneficial because it allows you to stand upright and move quickly. But when your muscles become so tight that you can't fully release them, bad things happen: The tight muscles feel sore and painful, they pull your skeleton out of alignment, compress your joints, increase your risk of muscle spasm and injury, and elevate your blood pressure.

Imagine that your leg muscles have become chronically tight because you're training for a marathon. As a result of overuse, your hamstrings, quadriceps, and calf muscles have developed a lot of residual muscle tension—maybe they're 20% contracted all the time. The tightness bothers you throughout the day, and you sometimes get cramps in your calves and hamstrings. But no matter how much you stretch, massage, or work on your muscles with a foam roller, they just won't stay loose.

External manipulation like passive stretching and massage has little to no effect on muscle tone because it doesn't change the messages that your brain is sending, and it doesn't have a lasting effect on gamma loop activity. To change the messages and return the gamma loop to normal baseline activity, you need to reprogram your nervous system with slow, conscious movement. You'll learn how to do this in chapters 9, 10, and 14. But this is only one piece of the puzzle. As you develop habitual muscular patterns, you also lose sensation and awareness, making it all the more difficult to change your patterns and get out of pain.

Sensory Adaptation

While your pain-processing system becomes more sensitive the more frequently your nociceptors are activated, your other sensory systems operate at their highest levels during and immediately after a new stimulus is presented. Within a short period of time, these receptors return to their normal resting state, even if the stimulus is still present. This is known as sensory adaptation.

Imagine going swimming in cool ocean water. When you first dip your toes into the water, it feels unbearably cold. If you stand there for a minute, letting the waves lap over your feet, you get used to the temperature and it begins to feel comfortable. Wading in deeper, you experience this phenomenon each time the water comes into contact with a new part of your body until you are fully submerged and the water feels much warmer than it did at first. Once this happens, your thermoreceptors—receptors that sense temperature—have returned to their resting state.

You adapt in a similar way to new sensations of touch, sound, smell, and taste. Wearing a new bracelet can be bothersome and distracting until you get used to the sensation of the metal touching your wrist. A repetitive sound like a car alarm is annoying at first, but quickly fades into the background. An unpleasant odor can be overwhelming as you enter a room, but within minutes you barely notice it. A sugary drink seems too sweet until you have taken several sips and become used to the taste.

When it comes to learned movement patterns and postures, your vestibular and proprioceptive systems adapt as well. Your vestibular system adapts when you're in motion at the same speed for longer than a few moments; so even when you're flying in an airplane at 600 miles per hour you feel like you're sitting still. Likewise, if you tip your head slightly forward or to the side, after a while the tilted position begins to feel normal. This adaptation is a function of both the vestibular and proprioceptive systems.

Remember, proprioceptors are sensory receptors located in your muscles and joints. Those in your joints quickly detect changes in joint angle, direction, and speed of movement. They're very good at sensing changes in joint positions as you move, but give you very little information about the resting position of your joints. This adaptability is helpful when you're in motion, but it allows you to get comfortable in harmful or awkward resting positions—like being slouched forward at a computer.

Muscle spindles, proprioceptors located within your muscles, are often referred to as stretch receptors because they sense and adapt to changes in muscle length. When a muscle is chronically contracted, your proprioception adjusts so that you feel like the muscle is not as tight as it actually is. In other words, as your muscle tone increases, the increased level of contraction in your muscles actually begins to feel normal. This can be a vicious cycle: As your proprioception adapts, your muscles stay tight, and your proprioception continues to adapt to higher and higher levels of muscle tension.

This loss of sensation is a key factor in developing habitual muscular patterns. As you sit at your computer day after day, your nervous system keeps you in slouched postures by contracting certain muscles. Your proprioceptive and vestibular systems allow you to get more and more comfortable in this position, even as you slowly damage your body. Slouching forward begins to feel normal and even good, and sitting up straight takes effort and feels uncomfortable. This makes improving posture very difficult; not only have you lost the ability to fully release your muscles, but sitting up straight actually feels wrong. If you're like most people, you probably remain blissfully unaware of this subconscious adaptation until, one day, it finally causes you pain.

Why Awareness Is so Important

The word "awareness" has acquired a vague New Age connotation, making it sound less important than it is. It's an essential and entirely real function of your brain: the state of being conscious of something. Awareness is critical if you are to avoid acquiring damaging motor patterns.

You can improve your awareness by focusing your attention: selectively concentrating on a specific thing and temporarily ignoring everything else. You can choose to focus your attention on any portion of the vast amount of sensory information coming into your brain. By focusing your eyes on one object, you can observe its tiniest details. By listening intently, you can hear a conversation happening at the next table in a noisy, crowded restaurant.

Likewise, you can focus your attention on your proprioceptive sensations. Let's use the simple example of tilting your head downward. This postural habit is becoming increasingly common among Americans due to constant use of smart phones and computers.

As you read these words, your head is likely tilted downward. Bring your eyes up and look straight ahead, so that your head sits straight up and down on top of your spine. Notice how this position feels different than tilting your head downward. Also notice how quickly you return to the downward tilted position. Which position is more comfortable? Can you feel certain muscles that are contracted or released in each position? Can you relax the muscles in your neck, shoulders, and chest so that looking straight ahead is comfortable? Take a few moments to really feel the differences in your muscles as you hold your head in each position.

Now that you've taken the time to notice the difference between what these two positions feel like, you will likely start to notice your head position more often. In fact, once you've noticed or learned something new it can be difficult to not notice it. This tendency of your brain to notice things you have just learned is referred to as the Baader-Meinhof phenomenon, also known as the frequency illusion or recency effect. When you focus your attention on something you haven't noticed before, like a new word or an internal sensation like the position of your head, you become more aware of it. Now each time you see that new word you'll consciously recognize it instead of subconsciously skimming over it.

Likewise, now when you hold your head tilted downward, your brain will recognize that proprioceptive sensation rather than ignoring it. Congratulations! You've just taken the first step toward retraining your muscular patterns—developing proprioceptive awareness of what your muscles have been doing when you weren't paying attention.

You can think of attention as being focused and active, and awareness as being broad and relaxed. If you begin to pay attention to your proprioceptive sensations, you'll become more aware of them. With practice, you won't need to work so hard at noticing your body position and movement. Awareness of your muscle tension, posture, and movement is a skill, and you've already begun to develop it simply by paying attention to the position of your head.

As you gradually learn a posture or movement pattern, you get used to the proprioceptive sensations that accompany it, and you begin to notice it less and less. This loss of awareness makes it very easy to fall deeper and deeper into your learned patterns, and also makes it very difficult to change them. To improve the way you use your body, you need to have an accurate sense of your starting point. And unfortunately, unnatural and damaging movement patterns feel natural and correct because you've adapted to them. You probably don't notice that you're developing a damaging muscular pattern until you feel pain or do actual harm to your body.

Your Ever-Changing Nervous System

I hope it's becoming clear how all of these processes work together. You are continuously sensing and moving, and that means you're continuously learning new motor patterns or strengthening existing ones. You are constantly becoming more and less aware of various sensations in your body as your sensory system adapts to the choices you make from moment to moment.

Most of us are born with the same innate ability and potential to sense, move, and learn. Yet throughout our lives we each develop such unique motor patterns that it's hard to believe we all started in the same place. Some people can bowl a perfect game, while others can flip around four times in the air on a snowboard. No one is born with those skills—they're developed through focused attention, practice, and repetition.

The good news is that you have the ability to focus your attention and improve your sensorimotor awareness, reduce your chronic muscle tension, and change your posture and movement patterns. The bad news is that most of the popular pain relief treatments and therapies won't help you do this, so any positive effects they have are only temporary. In the next chapter, we'll talk about the pros and cons of the most common pain relief options.

CHAPTER 6

The Pros and Cons of Common Pain Relief Treatments

By now you know that your learned motor patterns can lead to pain and damage the structure of your body. The problem comes from the way your nervous system tells your body to stand, sit, and move.

Conventional pain treatments, while they provide temporary relief, do not address the learned muscular patterns that cause your pain and damage your body.

In this chapter, we'll talk about how stretching, massage, chiropractic, physical therapy, medication, and surgery typically treat chronic pain, recurring injuries, and musculoskeletal degeneration. We'll discuss the benefits of each approach, and how they ultimately don't address the underlying cause of the problem.

Stretching

From a young age, you were likely taught that stretching is a necessary part of any workout routine. If you're involved in sports or physical training, you stretch to warm up, cool down, and during breaks to help you stay loose. Unfortunately, stretching usually doesn't accomplish much, mainly due to the myotatic reflex, more commonly referred to as the stretch reflex.

In the last chapter, you learned about the gamma loop (Illustration 7). The stretch reflex (Illustration 8) is a function of the gamma loop. When a skeletal muscle is stretched, its muscle spindle is stretched, too. The sensory axons wrapped around the spindle sense the increase in length and send this information to the alpha motor neuron in the spine. The alpha motor neuron then tells the skeletal muscle fibers to contract to protect the muscle from being torn. The neurons carrying these messages back and forth from the spine are among the most heavily myelinated in the body; this means that their messages travel faster and are more important to your survival than the sensations of pain, touch, and temperature.

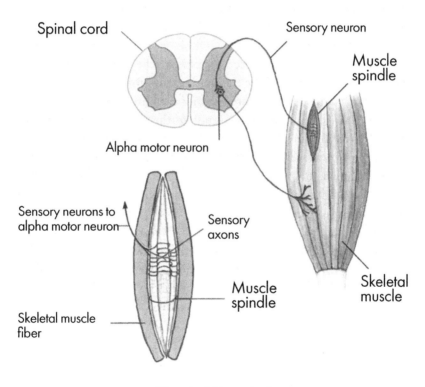

Illustration 8: The stretch reflex
(Sarah Warren)

One critical function of the stretch reflex is that it helps you stand upright. If you suddenly lean to the right side, the postural muscles on the left side of your vertebral column are stretched. When the muscle spindles in those muscles sense that they're being lengthened, they automatically send the message to contract to correct your posture. You're probably not consciously aware of how the stretch reflex automatically maintains your balance and keeps you from falling over—but you sure would notice if it weren't working properly.

The stretch reflex also prevents you from tearing your muscles, tendons, and ligaments. The knee-jerk reflex is a great example. When the doctor gently taps your patellar tendon just below your knee, it stretches the patellar tendon, the quadriceps tendon, and the quadriceps muscles. The muscle spindles in your quadriceps sense the sudden increase in length and automatically send the message to contract your quadriceps to prevent injury and overstretching. When your quadriceps contract, your foot kicks up. Absence of this reflex could indicate a possible neurological disorder, like receptor damage or peripheral nerve disease.

When you practice static stretching (the type of stretching traditionally taught in athletic training), the voluntary and involuntary parts of your nervous system are battling each other, trying to achieve opposite results. Your brain is sending the voluntary message to manually stretch your muscles by pulling on them. But despite all your efforts, your stretch reflex is automatically kicking in, contracting your muscles to prevent you from overstretching and tearing your muscles, tendons, and ligaments. It's like having one foot on the brake and the other on the gas.

So if the stretch reflex prevents you from manually lengthening your muscles, why does stretching sometimes make you more flexible? There are a few reasons. Prolonged static stretching pulls muscles and tendons past the point that they are able to lengthen. When this happens, you begin to stretch your ligaments. While this makes you more flexible, it can also loosen and destabilize joints. Once stretched, ligaments may never regain their original length and strength.

Second, prolonged static stretching can cause the stretch reflex to become much less active, leaving the muscles lengthened for a period of time. While you may feel looser after you stretch, the effects wear off fairly quickly. Often you'll feel your muscles begin to tighten up within just a few hours as your stretch reflex regains normal function.

For this reason, static stretching can decrease muscle performance by temporarily reducing the muscle's ability to contract, especially when it's stretched for a minute or more. This is not good if you're about to play an important game. An analysis of 104 studies conducted between 1966 and 2010 showed that static stretching before a workout reduces muscle performance, strength, and power. Many coaches and trainers have come to realize that the best way to warm up is to do a slow, gentle version of the movement you'll be doing in your workout. By consciously practicing the movement sequences and increasing blood flow to your muscles and connective tissues, you prepare both brain and body for optimal performance.

Finally, stretching can make you feel more flexible because when you stretch repeatedly you build up a tolerance to the sensation of pulling in your muscles. Even though it is by nature an uncomfortable sensation, with repetition it can become tolerable and even enjoyable. As a ballet dancer, I loved that feeling of pulling on my muscles and I craved it every day. It provided me with a temporary lengthening and release of my muscles, and as I became more comfortable with the feeling, I was able to pull my muscles even farther. But of course the reason I craved that feeling every day is that the fix was only temporary. Less than 24 hours after stretching, my muscles had tightened right back up again.

Virtually everyone I meet who has tried stretching to relieve their chronic pain reports that it hasn't helped them at all. Why? First, stretching does not reeducate the nervous system. No amount of pulling on the muscles will create a lasting change in the resting level of muscle tension that is being set by the brain and the gamma loop. This must be reset through an active process of relearning driven by slow, conscious movement and the integration of sensory feedback from the muscle.

Second, pulling on an already tight muscle activates the stretch reflex and makes the muscle contract even further. You may find some relief from gentle stretching, but as we've already discussed, the increased muscle length is temporary and your muscles will rebound within a short period of time. Stretching will not only do little for your pain, it will likely increase and prolong your pain by triggering your stretch reflex and making your muscles tighter.

When I finally stopped stretching and started practicing Clinical Somatics exercises, I felt like I had a brand-new body. The difference was profound. Instead of feeling tight and uncomfortable all the time, I began to feel loose, comfortable, and completely relaxed. I reduced my level of resting muscle tension by reeducating my nervous system. If you like to stretch on a regular basis, I challenge you to start practicing Clinical Somatics exercises (which you'll start learning in chapters 9, 10, and 14) and see how different you feel.

Massage

Massage therapy has become overwhelmingly popular, and rightfully so; in addition to feeling good, it has a number of health benefits. If you've had a massage lately, you may have found yourself faced with a never-ending list of different varieties, including acupressure, Ayurvedic, deep tissue, hot stone, lymphatic, Shiatsu, sports, and Thai. Each one is a distinctive technique that applies pressure to lengthen tissues, relieve pain, relax the nervous system, and stimulate the circulatory system.

Developed in Eastern and Middle-Eastern cultures, massage is one of the oldest types of physical therapy, likely predating recorded history. Hippocrates defined it as "the art of rubbing." Massage gained popularity in Europe during the Renaissance. In the second half of the nineteenth century, Dutch massage therapist Johann Georg Mezger named the basic massage strokes and codified them into the method we know today as Swedish or classic massage.

The most significant health benefit of massage is that it provides the sensation of touch, which is critical in both early childhood development and overall adult health. Levels of somatotropin, or human growth hormone, correlate directly with the amount of physical contact you receive. Children especially need a great deal of growth hormone to develop fully. Two fairly shocking reports in 1915 revealed that at least 90% of infants in American orphanages died within one year of admission even though they had received adequate physical care. The few infants who survived suffered severe physical and mental retardation. As it turned out, the missing element in the infants' care was tactile stimulation—simple physical touch from another human being. When the orphanages brought on additional staff, each infant was held and played with every day, and mortality rates fell dramatically.

You need less of this hormone as an adult, but the small amount that you do need is critical for cellular healing and growth. A study of breast cancer patients showed that regular massage improved the patients' immune responses. Research also suggests the benefits of touch for conditions such as anxiety, autism, ADHD, cardiovascular disease, Alzheimer's disease, depression, aggressive behavior, stroke, and sleep disturbances.

Massage also cues relaxation in your nervous system. In 2012, researchers tested the effects of getting a Swedish massage twice a week for five weeks. They found that massage significantly decreased the release of both the stress hormone cortisol and the hormone arginine vasopressin, which raises blood pressure and constricts blood vessels. Massage also increases oxytocin levels (a hormone that decreases stress and anxiety and improves social bonding) and stimulates the circulatory system and lymphatic system, improving blood flow and eliminating wastes from the body.

One of the biggest benefits of massage is that it feels great, especially if you're in pain. Nerves that carry information about the sensation of touch to the brain are more heavily myelinated than the nerves that carry information about pain, so touch information travels faster than pain information. This is why you instinctively rub the skin around a painful area; the touch sensation temporarily drowns out the pain sensation, and you're given a brief moment of relief.

Massage also feels good because it temporarily reduces muscle tension. Pressing on tight muscles lengthens them in the same way that gentle prolonged static stretching does, and after an hour or so of this manual lengthening you may stand up feeling like your muscles are made of jelly. Unfortunately, within a few hours you'll likely experience what one of my clients called the "rebound effect." Your muscles begin to tighten up again as your stretch reflex regains normal function, and by the next day you're back to your original level of tension.

If your massage therapist applies a great deal of pressure, your stretch reflex may be activated immediately, making you feel tight and sore soon after a massage. A good rule of thumb is that if you feel pain during a massage, you're probably going to feel some soreness afterward as well. While it can be difficult or awkward in the moment, it's better to ask your massage therapist to press more gently than to suffer the consequences. It is absolutely not necessary to apply a painful amount of pressure to reap the benefits of a massage. Moreover, if you're in pain a deep massage can increase and prolong your pain by making your muscles tighter.

Lastly, massage temporarily softens connective tissues, which increases flexibility and range of motion. Tendons, ligaments, fascia (which surrounds, supports, and separates structures of the body), and scar tissue (which forms to heal an injury) are all made of collagen fibers arranged in varying patterns and densities. As muscles become habitually tighter and movement decreases, connective tissues also respond by tightening. Movement and heat can make these collagen structures more flexible and fluid.

Many in the massage community were surprised when research showed that myofascial release techniques have little to no lasting effect. Fascia does not respond well to manual stretching because it is not simply a collagen structure. It contains smooth (involuntary) muscle cells (like those in your organs) and is innervated by mechanoreceptors. Based on what we know now, the best way to make fascia looser and more flexible is to reeducate the nervous system through active movement, and the fascia will adapt over time.

For people with chronic pain, the most beneficial aspect of massage may be that it lowers stress, thereby reducing the sensation of pain and reactivity of the nervous system. A massage by itself is not enough to change deeply learned habitual movements or your resting level of muscle tension. The sensory awareness that can be gained through massage is valuable, but if it isn't followed by actual motor education in the form of voluntary movement, little lasting progress will be made. You must actively retrain your nervous system, and you can't do that with massage alone.

Chiropractic

Ancient Chinese and Greek cultures practiced techniques of spinal manipulation to ease back pain and improve health. Spinal manipulation began to gain popularity in the United States in the late nineteenth century, when Daniel David Palmer founded the Palmer School of Chiropractic in Iowa.

The theory of chiropractic is that joints become either restricted or hypermobile (abnormally loose) due to soft tissue injury caused by acute trauma or repetitive stress. Chiropractic care is focused on the spine and correcting vertebral subluxations, which occur when individual vertebrae become displaced or dysfunctional. Chiropractors work with a variety of musculoskeletal conditions, such as back and neck pain, bulging or herniated discs, headaches, whiplash, nerve sensation and pain, and other chronic pain conditions such as fibromyalgia.

When chiropractors perform spinal manipulations or "adjustments," they apply quick, controlled force to a joint to move it into proper alignment. Patients must remain fully relaxed so they don't resist the movement. The belief is that realigning joints restores mobility, alleviates muscle tightness and pain, and allows injuries to heal.

Chiropractic adjustments—or any movements that pop a joint back into alignment—usually provide an enjoyable sense of release and temporary relief from pressure or pain. Unfortunately—and if you've been paying attention you know what I'm about to say—simply manipulating the structure of the body does not change the way it functions. Within a few days or even just a few hours, your learned movement patterns and chronic muscle tension will typically pull your joints out of alignment again, and you'll be making an appointment for another adjustment.

While some people benefit from regular visits to their chiropractor, there are a number of potential adverse effects, including increased pain, headaches, dizziness, stroke, and even death. A review of medical literature published between 2001 and 2006 found that adverse effects occurred in between 30% and 61% of chiropractic patients. In 2014, the American Heart Association released a statement urging health care professionals, chiropractors, and patients to be aware of the risk of stroke resulting from chiropractic adjustments to the cervical spine.

A 2010 review published in the *International Journal of Clinical Practice* evaluated rates of death from chiropractic adjustments—usually caused by dissection of a vertebral artery—and concluded that the risks of the treatment outweigh the benefits.

If you choose to pursue chiropractic treatment, be sure to educate yourself on the risks involved. If your condition does not improve, it is probably not worth the potential adverse effects.

The Bottom Line

While stretching, massage, and chiropractic adjustments have some benefits, none of them address the underlying cause of pain, structural misalignment, and musculoskeletal degeneration. Your bones do not move unless your muscles make them move, and your muscles do not move unless directed by your nervous system. Your nervous system determines how you stand and move, how tight your muscles are, and ultimately what type of musculoskeletal pain and degeneration you experience.

The bottom line is that voluntary movement is necessary to reeducate the nervous system and change habitual motor patterns. On that note, let's talk about the only mainstream treatment for musculoskeletal pain that is based on voluntary movement: physical therapy.

Physical Therapy

While physical therapy often employs massage and other passive manipulation techniques, its focus is on the regular practice of active movements to improve function, reduce pain, and recover from injury.

Pehr Henrik Ling, who developed medical gymnastics and pioneered the use of massage in Western culture, was also fundamental in establishing physical exercise as an acceptable way to treat pain and illness. During the late nineteenth and early twentieth centuries, various forms of physical therapy became quite popular and professional schools were established. The polio epidemic in the United States during the 1940s and 1950s created great demand for physical therapists, and the profession grew exponentially.

Research provides clear evidence for the efficacy of physical therapy, not only for recovery from acute injury but also for chronic pain conditions. When people with back pain go through physical therapy treatment involving active exercises, they have greater reductions in pain, more improvement in function, less need for medication, and lower health care costs than people who receive passive therapy. Research also shows that the earlier someone has physical therapy, the better. The longer the pain condition goes on, the higher their health care costs and the more likely they are to require injections or surgery.

A physical therapist may prescribe exercises designed to improve strength, range of motion, mobility, and balance, depending on the patient's needs. Strength-building exercises are typically focused on the site of the injury. A person recovering from shoulder surgery, for example, will be taught exercises to build up strength in the muscles around the shoulder joint. This approach can be very effective in building strength and regaining function after an injury or surgery.

While there are many benefits to physical therapy, there are two main reasons why it may be less effective—or better used as a secondary treatment—for chronic pain patients. The first is that strength-building exercises are usually prescribed to correct imbalances in posture and movement. Lack of strength is typically not the issue for these patients, however. Most often, it is chronic tightness and damaging movement patterns. Strength-building exercises can make the targeted muscles tighter, which can sometimes increase muscle soreness and pain. People in chronic pain most often need chronically tight muscles to be released, not strengthened.

The second reason is that physical therapy usually does not address full-body movement patterns. Let's say a man has pain in his left knee, for example. He's probably standing and moving in such a way that undue pressure is being put on his knee, and muscles and connective tissues around it are pulling and pushing on the joint in unnatural ways. All of this pressure and imbalance creates inflammation and pain; over time this will lead to degeneration of the joint. Strength-building exercises will likely not eliminate his pain at this point. He must change the way he is moving his entire body, or he will damage his knee even further.

If this man gets to the point at which some or all of the cartilage in his knee has worn away, he'll likely have a knee replacement or a cartilage transplant. Either of these surgeries may help him a great deal in the short term by reducing his pain. However, if the movement pattern that caused his knee damage in the first place is not addressed, further damage can occur. He may experience loss of the new cartilage, pain in his knee or another area of his body, or the need for a second joint replacement.

Physical therapy has proven benefits for many patients, especially when it comes to rebuilding strength after an acute injury or surgery. But it doesn't address the chronic muscle tension and full-body movement patterns that contribute to most chronic pain conditions, recurring injuries, and joint degeneration. For most chronic pain sufferers, traditional physical therapy exercises will be most effective when pursued after their underlying muscle tension and movement patterns have been addressed.

Pain Medication

When you're in pain, any relief from the constant aching, throbbing, or burning can feel like a miracle. Relief provided by pain medication, however brief, can have profound positive effects on your emotional state.

You've already learned that when pain is experienced for a long time, neuroplastic changes can sensitize the nervous system, prolonging or increasing the sensation of pain even if the source has healed. You also learned in chapter 2 that early, strategic use of pain-blocking medication before surgery can prevent this sensitization from occurring. Medication administered during surgery has also been proven to help prevent the development of chronic pain after surgery. Since many surgical patients go on to develop chronic pain, these techniques should be used as often as possible to reduce the risk of chronic pain.

Pain medications work in various ways to block the sensation of pain. Nonopioid analgesics, the most common of which are acetaminophen and ibuprofen, work by blocking the production of prostaglandins, a group of lipid compounds that play a role in fever, inflammation, and pain. Acetaminophen prevents the production of prostaglandins in the CNS, while ibuprofen blocks production throughout the body. This is why ibuprofen can reduce inflammation at the site of an injury while acetaminophen can't.

Your adrenal glands produce the hormone cortisol as part of the fight-or-flight reaction when your body is under stress. Synthetic versions of cortisol called corticosteroids are powerful drugs that can be taken orally or injected directly into a joint or soft tissue to relieve pain and reduce inflammation.

While corticosteroid injections can be quite effective in providing temporary pain relief, they are counterproductive to long-term recovery. Pain patients who receive steroid injections have a lower rate of recovery than those who undergo physical therapy or do nothing at all. A 2010 review of 41 studies found that patients with tendinopathies who receive injections are 62% more likely to experience a relapse of their injury compared to those who have no treatment. Predictably, the more injections a patient receives, the lower their chance of a full recovery. Injections can also cause infection, increase pain, soften cartilage, and weaken or rupture tendons.

In chapter 2 we discussed opioids and how they block the sensation of pain by binding to opioid receptors. Like all pain medications, their effect is temporary, but opioids pose the added risk of addiction. The nervous system can become dependent upon opioids within just a week of regular use, and tolerance develops quickly, requiring the patient to take higher doses to get the same level of pain relief. Like many medications, opioids can have dangerous side effects when mixed with alcohol and some antidepressants, antihistamines, and sleeping pills— all of which are commonly taken by people trying to relieve their pain and related symptoms. Due to the associated risks, opioids are best used for short periods of time in conditions of acute pain when their dosage can be monitored by a health care professional.

Another risk of taking pain medication is that masking pain with drugs gives you the opportunity to do further damage to your body. An athlete who gets a steroid shot and then resumes playing risks worsening the injury, lengthening their recovery time, and increasing their chances of needing surgery. Nonathletes may take a daily dose of ibuprofen or prescribed opioid and then go about their daily lives, continuing to engage in the activities and movement habits that caused their pain or injury in the first place.

Pain medication can prolong and sometimes worsen your pain condition or injury. It gives you the misconception that you've found a solution, when in fact you may be making your condition worse by continuing activities that, without the drugs, would be too painful to undertake. Since much muscle and joint pain can be relieved or even eliminated by reeducating your nervous system, managing it with medication is not the best long-term solution for most people.

Surgery

We talked about the dangers of surgery and its lack of effectiveness for chronic pain conditions in chapter 1. I'd like to round out that discussion by making a couple of brief points.

First, there are cases of chronic pain for which surgery is absolutely the best course of treatment. When the structure of the body is damaged to the point that it cannot repair itself with rest and improved movement, surgery is probably the way to go. Joint-replacement surgeries in particular have become highly successful. But remember that surgery will not change your learned movement patterns. These will still be present after the surgery and will likely continue to damage your body, potentially demanding repeat surgeries. Surgeries that treat chronic musculoskeletal pain and degeneration should always be followed up with movement reeducation to address the original underlying cause of the condition.

Second, there are surgical techniques that target pain perception by working with or altering the nervous system. Electrical stimulators can be implanted near the spine to help manage and reduce pain. Surgeons can destroy portions of peripheral nerves, and can even sever pain pathways in the spinal cord and brain. These options should only be considered for extreme cases that have not improved with other treatments.

A Real Solution

Usually by the time clients come to me to learn about Clinical Somatics, they have tried every possible treatment for their pain. Some of the approaches have improved their condition for a period of time, but most have not helped at all. This is because no amount of external force, manipulation, drugs, or surgery will change the deeply learned, automatic messages being sent by your nervous system.

Thankfully, over the past hundred years or so, some curious, brilliant people figured this out. During the twentieth century, a series of movement educators and scientists began to explore the ways in which the habitual use of your body affects your health and functioning. In the next chapter, you'll hear their stories and learn what they discovered.

CHAPTER 7

The Evolution of Somatic Education

F.M. Alexander

Frederick Matthias Alexander was born in Australia in 1869. As a child he suffered from health problems including respiratory difficulties. Despite his difficulties with breathing and speaking, his lifelong love of the theater led him to pursue a career as an actor and reciter of poetry and other popular literature.

After reciting professionally for a number of years, Alexander's ongoing respiratory problems began to interfere with his work. Friends in the audience could hear him gasping for air as he spoke, and he would occasionally become hoarse during performances. Upon visiting a doctor, Alexander was diagnosed with irritated mucous membranes of the throat and inflammation of the vocal chords. He was advised to have surgery to fix these problems, but he declined.

Alexander tried resting his voice, but it didn't help. Since his hoarseness occurred only during performances and not during normal conversation, Alexander concluded that something he was doing during performances—something about the way he was using his voice—was causing him to lose function of his vocal chords. He set about to figuring out what it was.

Alexander knew that he was doing it subconsciously, so he would need a third-person perspective to give him an accurate assessment. He decided to observe himself in a mirror while speaking conversationally and while reciting. He noticed that as soon as he started reciting, he would habitually pull his head back, which compressed his larynx and caused him to gasp audibly as he breathed. Upon closer observation, Alexander noticed that these same habits were present during his normal speech, though to a much lesser extent.

Alexander hypothesized that the way he was moving and holding himself while reciting was directly causing his vocal problems. He wondered if one habit caused the others. Was his improper breathing the culprit? Was it the way he habitually pulled his head back? Or was it the way he compressed his larynx that was causing his voice to fail?

After months of experimenting, Alexander found that he was able to prevent himself to some degree from pulling his head back while reciting. This adjustment led to an improvement in his other two habits. As Alexander gradually changed his deeply learned patterns, he began to regain full use of his voice, and his tendency to become hoarse decreased. Doctors examined him and confirmed that the condition of his throat and vocal chords had improved considerably. Alexander's hypothesis was confirmed: The way he used his body while performing had directly affected the way his voice functioned.

Alexander experimented extensively with holding his head and neck in different positions as he spoke, trying to find a way to optimize the use of his voice. Over time, he realized that how he moved his head and neck directly affected the way he used his entire torso. He observed that any misuse of his head and neck distorted his posture and shortened his stature. This observation was an incredibly important discovery. He began to understand the larger patterns of tension involving his head, neck, and torso, and that the use of one part directly affected the use of the others. He later termed this relationship of the head, neck, and torso "primary control."

As Alexander continued to explore, he made more discoveries. Though he felt that he was making a great deal of progress in retraining himself, he noticed that when he performed he still tended to revert automatically into his old habits. The stress of performing always triggered these familiar movement patterns. He decided to experiment with what he called "inhibition." He practiced not responding at all to the stimulus of performing. As he became comfortable with not reacting automatically when under pressure, he was able to inhibit his old patterns of misuse.

Alexander realized that focusing on the goal of performing had caused him to rely on habitual patterns. By slowing down and concentrating on his reactions, he was able to teach himself to react differently. Alexander called this approach "means whereby." By focusing on the means whereby he was pursuing his goal—in other words, on the process rather than on the goal itself—he had much greater success in achieving his goal.

The endless hours he spent in front of a mirror gave Alexander another critical insight: His internal sense of how he used his body was quite different from what he saw in the mirror. He also observed that standing and moving in a way that he knew intellectually to be correct often felt wrong and difficult, experiencing firsthand how your proprioceptive senses adjust as your motor patterns become habitual. The mirror proved to be an invaluable tool in Alexander's exploration. Had he relied purely on his internal sense of how he was using his body, he would have made little progress in changing his movement patterns.

As Alexander's voice improved, he became quite well known in Melbourne, and many actors sought him out for vocal coaching. Word spread as he successfully helped one after another overcome similar performance and vocal issues. Local doctors heard about his success in working with functional disorders and began to refer patients to him. Alexander soon had a busy practice teaching clients how to retrain their posture and movement patterns, with the majority of his students seeking treatment of medical conditions rather than vocal coaching.

Demand for his work grew worldwide, and after years of people asking him to teach his methods, he launched a three-year teacher training course in 1931. Many doctors applied for the training, having witnessed the effects of Alexander's techniques in themselves and their patients.

While Alexander had predominantly worked with adults for many years, he had a great love of working with children. As knowledge of his work spread, parents began to send their children to study with him to help with conditions such as nervousness, inability to concentrate, speech difficulties, learning disabilities, flat feet, and rounded shoulders. With the help of teacher Irene Tasker and others, Alexander established the "little school," a division of his school devoted to teaching children. He strongly believed that his work should be promoted as education rather than reeducation—that learning proper use of your body early in life would prevent more serious functional disorders later on.

When Alexander first began his explorations, he believed that all illnesses or deficiencies were either mental or physical in nature. Over time, he realized that the mind and body are inextricably linked. Every human process and condition involves both the mind and body. Since the functions of all parts of the human organism are connected, change in one part will affect the whole, and any attempt to create change must work with the whole person to be successful.

Alexander was among the first to recognize that learned movement patterns cause a myriad of health problems. His work marked the beginning of what would come to be known as "somatic education," a general term describing education methods that improve physiological function by increasing sensorimotor awareness and changing habitual motor patterns. Alexander's exploration of proprioception, inhibition, and means whereby were fundamental in developing modern somatic education.

Alexander, known to his students as F.M., passed away in 1955 at the age of 86. His work continues to be taught in professional training programs internationally, and there are more than 2,500 registered teachers of the Alexander Technique worldwide. The method of education that Alexander developed inspired and contributed to the work of many other pioneers in the field of somatic education.

Elsa Gindler

Elsa Gindler was born in 1885 to a working-class family in Berlin, Germany. As a young woman she suffered from consumption, known today as tuberculosis. Her doctor recommended a period of rest and treatment in Switzerland during which her affected lung could heal. Gindler could not afford the treatment, so she decided to try to heal herself. By paying close attention to her internal sensations, she gradually improved her control of the muscles involved in breathing in an attempt to allow her infected lung to heal.

Incredibly, Gindler's experiment worked. As her health improved, her doctor called it a miracle, refusing to believe that such self-healing was possible. Like Alexander, Gindler had healed herself by focusing her attention inward and teaching herself to gain control of her physiological functioning.

Gindler became a physical education teacher, teaching a technique developed by Hedwig Kallmeyer called *Harmonische Gymnastik*, Harmonic Gymnastics. After some years of teaching this method she began to find it limiting, and she started to explore how to guide people through independent exploration of sensory awareness. She stopped using the word "exercise" and began calling her movements "experiments."

Gindler asked her students to focus their attention completely on their internal sensations as they moved. She understood the principles of attention and awareness—the more conscious attention you pay to a part of your body, the more sensation and motor control you develop. When retraining the nervous system, you must begin with this essential process of improving your internal awareness.

Gindler did not wish to offer professional training in her methods; she simply wanted to do research and lead people through explorations in small study groups. Luckily, her students traveled and spread the knowledge they gained from her work. Most notable was her student Charlotte Selver, who emigrated to the United States and introduced Gindler's work as "Sensory Awareness." Selver and Gindler's students influenced the work of many somatic educators and psychotherapists. Gindler's exploration of sensorimotor awareness was a great contribution to the development of somatic education as we know it today.

Gerda Alexander

Gerda Alexander (no relation to F.M.) was born in 1908 in Wuppertal, Germany, to parents who had a love of music and movement. She began dancing as soon as she could stand. As she grew older, she studied the work of Emile Jacques-Dalcroze, called Eurhythmics, a method that taught music and dance by having students focus on internal sensations rather than imitation of movement.

As a young woman, Alexander suffered from rheumatic fever that led to heart disease. Doctors told her that her dancing career was over and that she would spend the rest of her life in a wheelchair. Forced to rest for long periods of time, Alexander taught herself how to regulate her muscle tone and move with as little effort as possible so as not to strain her heart. Gradually, her health improved and in time she recovered completely. Contrary to her doctor's prognosis, she was able to dance again and began teaching Eurhythmics as well.

In 1929, as the Great Depression wrought worldwide havoc and the German government began to collapse, Alexander moved to Copenhagen, Denmark. There she began to explore ways to guide others through sensory experiments and movements that would allow them to improve their health and functioning. She was a proponent of holistic health, writing in her 1986 book *Eutony: The Holistic Discovery of the Total Person*, "The different functional systems in the living organism cannot be separated from each other. They interlock and influence each other without being aware of it."

In 1940, Alexander established a professional training school in Copenhagen, Denmark, where she instructed students in her technique of Eutony, a term derived from the Greek words for "good" and "tension." Alexander's philosophy about balancing tensions in the body and moving with ease, as well as her holistic view of human health, are central to somatic education.

Moshe Feldenkrais

Moshe Feldenkrais was born in 1904 to a Jewish family in the small town of Slavuta, Russia. He developed a passion for math and physics at a young age, and was intrigued by the burgeoning fields of neurology and psychology. By the age of 12 he was reading the works of Swiss psychotherapist and biologist August Forel.

At 14, Feldenkrais moved to Palestine to help build a Zionist society. There he worked, finished school, and became involved with Jewish defense groups, which introduced him to the martial art of jiujitsu. This sparked a passion for self-defense that would last his entire life. In particular, Feldenkrais became interested in unarmed defensive techniques that use the body in a natural way to defend oneself without a great deal of physical effort.

In 1930, Feldenkrais moved to Paris to study engineering. After graduating he began work as a research assistant in the laboratory of

Frédéric Joliot-Curie, son-in-law of Pierre and Marie Curie. During this time he met Jigoro Kano, the founder of modern judo. Inspired by Kano, Feldenkrais became Europe's first judoka black belt in 1936. He stayed in Paris until 1940, working with nuclear fission in the lab and studying and teaching judo.

Feldenkrais fled to England when the Germans invaded Paris in 1940. He continued his scientific work as an officer in the British Admiralty in Scotland, developing radar for antisubmarine warfare for five years. While in Scotland he taught judo and self-defense classes, and published a self-defense manual titled *Practical Unarmed Combat.*

Feldenkrais injured his left knee during a soccer match in 1929, and his right knee while working on a submarine in Scotland. He refused surgery even though the cruciate ligaments were damaged. Feldenkrais approached his knee injuries as an engineering problem, experimenting with moving and using his body in ways that would not put undue force on his knees. While working with the admiralty, he began to give lectures and teach movement classes in his experimental methods.

After the war, Feldenkrais moved to London, where he delved into research on all areas of human functioning. He studied the work of F.M. Alexander, Elsa Gindler, Gerda Alexander, American physician William Bates, and Russian philosopher George Gurdjieff. In 1949, he published *Body and Mature Behavior*, his first book on his own method of sensorimotor education.

Feldenkrais's predecessors had relied mainly on experience-based research to develop their methods of sensorimotor education. Feldenkrais strove to combine science and experience, and did a great deal of research into human development, learning, and the functioning of the nervous system. He realized that scientists understood "so little about the functioning of the nervous system as a complete unit, that we have little right to expect any theory to be near the truth."

Feldenkrais wanted to develop a theory that would explain the physical dysfunction and degeneration he saw in his students and himself. He was especially interested in the way that humans move within gravity and the functions of antigravity reflexes. He understood how the vestibular system allows you to constantly sense where you are in relation to gravity and how automatic reflexes allow you to stand upright. He observed that many adults develop learned motor patterns that overpower their reflexive responses, resulting in maladaptive postural patterns that put a great deal of strain on the body.

Feldenkrais's experience in engineering and physics gave him a unique perspective on human functioning. He observed that the structure of the human body, with a high center of gravity balancing on two thin legs and two relatively small bases of the feet, was ideally suited for movement rather than static standing, which requires a heavy, broad base. Standing perfectly upright with all parts stacked vertically is fairly effortless for humans, but a great deal of effort is required to maintain any posture in which someone's center of gravity is not directly on top of their base.

Since the reaction to gravity is almost always subconscious—because it's either reflexive or habitual—Feldenkrais knew that to unlearn these involuntary patterns, gravity must be taken out of the picture. To prevent the automatic triggering of antigravity muscular patterns, nearly all of the movements he taught were performed lying down.

Despite his background in concrete sciences, Feldenkrais saw beyond what could be scientifically proven. He became interested in the work of Paul Schilder, an Austrian physician and psychiatrist who proposed that habitual reactions involved emotional states, reflexive responses, and learned muscular patterns, all of which were intertwined; triggering any of them would cause the entire habitual reaction to occur. In other words, Schilder believed that experiencing an emotion includes a physical reaction, and performing a physical action generates a corresponding emotional state.

Feldenkrais witnessed a great deal of anxiety, fear, and neurosis in his students. He saw the effects of the withdrawal response. This protective reflex causes you to contract your flexor muscles when you're frightened or feel defensive, bending the joints in your arms and legs and making you curl up into the fetal position. Repeated activation of this response, whether from traumatic events or chronic fear and stress, leads to rounded posture due to habitual contraction of the abdominal muscles. Feldenkrais noticed that his more introverted students tended to have rounded posture, while his extroverted students tended to stand up straight.

Feldenkrais observed that when people attempted to correct learned motor habits such as standing with rounded posture, they usually ended up hiding their faulty habits with new ones instead of going through a process to unlearn the faulty habits. He set out to create a system that would allow people to address and correct dysfunctional movement patterns. By combining theories of physiology, psychology, and neuroscience, he created a method to improve health and functioning through learning rather than physical manipulation or pharmaceutical treatments.

By 1951, Feldenkrais had moved to Israel to direct the Israeli Army Department of Electronics. Three years later he moved to Tel Aviv and committed himself fully to teaching his somatic techniques. He set up a studio where he taught group movement classes in the method he called Awareness Through Movement. Later in life, he estimated that he had created over a thousand exploratory self-care exercises. The movements combined explorations of sensory awareness with F.M. Alexander's means whereby approach of focusing on the process of one's movements.

Feldenkrais's refined method was highly effective in improving posture and voluntary motor control. And while he was adamant that he developed his techniques solely for the purpose of sensorimotor education and not to resolve any specific pathologies, his students experienced healing from many functional disorders.

Feldenkrais began to give private instruction in addition to his group movement classes. This hands-on work, which he called Functional Integration, consisted of two techniques. The first used the principles of means whereby to give sensory feedback to the student, who would remain completely passive while Feldenkrais gently moved them through a range of motion, asking them to focus on their internal sensations. This technique allowed the student to become aware of subconscious patterns of muscular tension.

The second technique, which Feldenkrais's student Thomas Hanna later termed "kinetic mirroring," proved to be a major advancement in the field of somatic education. The principle of kinetic mirroring came from judo, the practice of which was deeply ingrained in Feldenkrais's approach to movement. In judo, you learn not to fight against your opponent's resistance but instead to move with it.

Feldenkrais instinctively used this approach when working hands-on with his students. When he felt that a tight muscle was creating resistance, he would move the student's joint or limb in the opposite direction, thereby shortening the tight muscle. (Notice that this is the opposite of stretching, where you lengthen a tight muscle.) The student would remain completely passive while Feldenkrais kept them in this position for a short period of time. After slowly bringing the student out of the position, Feldenkrais would find that the tight muscle had begun to relax. It was a wonderful, if somewhat accidental, discovery, and the technique became the main method by which Feldenkrais would teach his students how to relax their chronically tight muscles.

It was only later, as Feldenkrais continued his research of neurophysiology, that he came to understand exactly why kinetic mirroring worked. Let's say that your biceps muscles are contracted about 25% all the time as a result of weight training. It's impossible for you to completely relax your biceps voluntarily, and you're more comfortable with your elbows bent than straight. When you remain passive and allow someone else to bend your elbow, bringing your biceps into a position that is more than 25% shortened, that person is effectively doing the work of your muscles; your biceps are being brought into their desired shortened length without having to do any work. Your nervous system gets the feedback that the muscles are shortened and stops sending the message to contract.

In this situation, your nervous system works like a thermostat set to keep a room at 70 degrees. If it senses that the temperature has reached 71 degrees, it sends a message to the furnace to shut off. Likewise, when your nervous system gets the message that your muscle is shortened, your motor neurons temporarily stop firing and your muscle tension is reduced.

For decades, Feldenkrais traveled around the world to share his work with students. Feldenkrais left a legacy that is carried on by over 6,000 Feldenkrais practitioners all over the world. His understanding of antigravity reflexes and of humans' instinctive physical responses to fear as well as his development of kinetic mirroring helped to establish a scientific basis for somatic education.

Thomas Hanna

Thomas Hanna was born in 1928 in Waco, Texas. He spent his life pursuing the kind of freedom that can only come from developing self-knowledge and becoming truly self-reliant.

After Hanna graduated from Texas Christian University in 1949, he decided to pursue his interests in theology and the philosophy of religion—despite being a self-proclaimed atheist. After receiving a bachelor's degree in divinity and a doctorate in philosophy from the University of Chicago, Hanna traveled the world, teaching, writing, pursuing research, and doing social work. He served as supervisor of an orphanage in Brussels, and directed a club for refugee students at the University of Paris. He was drawn to helping people who, like him, were searching for freedom. During his travels, his continued study of philosophy led him into the fields of psychology, psychotherapy, and physiology, which he felt were all deeply connected.

In 1965, Hanna became chairman of the philosophy department at the University of Florida. Here he continued his research by studying neuroscience at the university's medical school. He learned that every psychological process occurs in tandem with changes in the physical systems of the body. In other words, your thoughts and emotions change your body as well. It became clear to him that issues of the psyche cannot be fully addressed without addressing the physical body, and vice versa. He began to refer to the connected mind and body as a "soma," an ancient Greek term that describes "the living body in its wholeness."

While studying neurology in Florida, Hanna wrote *Bodies in Revolt: A Primer in Somatic Thinking*, a survey of somatic philosophy. After reading the book, an acquaintance told him about the work of Moshe Feldenkrais. Intrigued, Hanna read Feldenkrais's *Body and Mature Behavior*, and attended his month-long workshop in Berkeley, California in 1973.

During the workshop, Feldenkrais demonstrated his hands-on techniques with a man who had suffered from cerebral palsy since the age of three. The man, then 53, had little control of his movements, and even his voice and breathing were spastic. Feldenkrais asked him to lie down and instructed him to be as relaxed as possible.

Feldenkrais began to press against the man's rib cage, gently holding for a short period of time and then changing position. After about 20 minutes of this kinetic mirroring, the man's breathing became slow and smooth, his chest and abdomen rising and falling rhythmically.

Feldenkrais then proceeded to work with the man's right hand, which was clenched involuntarily into a fist. Soon the man was able to move his pinky finger independently of his other fingers. Feldenkrais moved up to the man's face and began gently working his tongue and jaw. After several minutes, Feldenkrais asked the man to speak, and the words that came out were clear and unstrained. Within just half an hour, Feldenkrais had helped this man begin to unlearn years of habitual muscular patterns that a medical practitioner would have considered permanent.

Hanna knew in this moment that he wanted to learn how to do what Feldenkrais had done. At the time, Hanna was the director of the Humanistic Psychology Institute (now the Saybrook Institute) in San Francisco, and he was able to bring Feldenkrais to the school as a Distinguished Visiting Professor for three years. Here Feldenkrais led his professional training program in the United States from 1975 to 1978, teaching his hands-on method of Functional Integration and his Awareness Through Movement exercises for the first time.

Using Feldenkrais's methods, Hanna began to work with people who suffered from functional disorders and chronic pain conditions. He coined the term "somatic education" to describe his methods, which worked with both the mind and body to improve health and functioning. Hanna founded the Novato Institute of Somatic Research in Novato, California in 1975.

Like other somatic educators, Hanna observed that most adults are quite out of touch with their physical bodies and have lost a great deal of voluntary muscle control as a result. Because movement is necessary to stimulate the sensory nerves in the muscles and joints— so you can't sense muscles that you don't move—Hanna understood that widespread loss of sensation and control was the cause of most functional disorders and chronic pain. He used the term "sensory-motor amnesia" to describe the condition of the nervous system in which learned, habitual motor patterns have led to involuntary muscle contraction and loss of sensation.

According to Hanna, the modern lifestyle is one of the main causes of sensorimotor amnesia. Survival no longer depends on physical abilities as it did when humans lived as hunter-gatherers.

Our ancestors' varied movements and active daily lives have been replaced by repetitive tasks and sedentary lifestyles. As a result, most people have lost the sensorimotor awareness that comes with frequent, natural, and efficient movement.

Since this loss of awareness and control occurs gradually, most people remain completely unaware that it is occurring until they find themselves in pain or with actual damage to their bodies. As Hanna wrote in his book *The Body of Life*, "the 'normal' life that most humans lead is a life of unconscious self-destruction." You don't mean to harm yourself, but the natural processes of sensory adaptation and developing muscle memory make it difficult to avoid.

This self-destruction occurs in different ways and at different rates for each person, but the effects tend to be cumulative and rarely reverse themselves without intervention. Most people appear to break down as they age, and it makes many people fear growing old. Even worse, it creates the expectation that you too will begin to fall apart when you reach a certain age.

Hanna worked tirelessly to dispel what he called the "myth of aging," which he said is "firmly embedded in modern medicine." Our doctors believe it, as medical school offers them no other explanation. You, too, have probably accepted it as fact for most of your life: As you age, you will cease to be able to do the things you used to do. At some point the structure of your body will begin to break down. You will stop doing the things you used to, feel less energetic, lose flexibility, become stiffer in posture and movement, and wake up feeling achy. But by subscribing to this myth, you perpetuate it.

Hanna's study of neurophysiology taught him that the changes you experience in your body as you age, instead of being the result of inevitable structural breakdown, are for the most part a result of learning and adaptation. Supported by research showing that cortical learning occurs throughout people's lifetimes, Hanna taught his clients that what they had learned could be unlearned. As he showed them how to regain sensation and motor control, they experienced what seemed to be miraculous recoveries from back pain, disc problems, sciatica, scoliosis, stooped posture, arthritis, frozen shoulder, and many other functional disorders.

Hanna observed that many of his clients' issues were the result of their reactions and adaptations to stress. Feldenkrais had recognized the effects of the withdrawal response, which causes people to adopt a rounded posture when they're frightened or experiencing negative stress. Hanna saw some of his clients exhibit this posture, but observed that other clients tended to arch their backs or bend to one side.

While Feldenkrais's understanding of how the withdrawal response led to rounded posture was quite accurate, he had no explanation for what caused arched or side-bending postures. Feldenkrais had spent so much of his life focused on defense—he wouldn't enter a hotel without first finding the escape routes—that he believed the withdrawal response was the cause of all somatic pathologies.

But Hanna studied the work of endocrinologist Hans Selye, particularly his "general adaptation syndrome," a consequence of long-term stress in which your immediate fight-or-flight response becomes a prolonged, chronic state. When your stress response is activated repeatedly, blood pressure stays elevated, breathing is shallow, certain hormone levels are increased, cells atrophy, and your neuromuscular responses to stress become so automatic that they continue to occur subconsciously even when the stressful stimulus is no longer present.

Selye's work showed that not all stress is caused by negative stimuli, however. Intense positive emotions and experiences can put body systems under as much stress as negative ones. Selye coined the term "eustress" to describe positive stress, in contrast to negative stress or "distress."

Eustress explained the contracted back muscles and arched posture that Hanna observed in some of his clients. The muscles in their backs had become chronically tight due to repeated activation of the action response, which is the "fight" part of the fight-or-flight response. When you experience the kind of stress that makes you want to spring into action, you stand up straight, contracting your back muscles in preparation for movement.

While eustress and distress reactions explained the arched backs and rounded postures Hanna saw, there was a third pattern that didn't seem to be related to stress. Many of Hanna's clients had a posture that was tilted to one side or the other, sometimes so severely that the spinal curvature would be diagnosed as scoliosis.

Hanna realized that this side bending, like the other two postural patterns, was the result of an automatic nervous system response that had become learned and habitual. The flexor reflex makes you contract one side of your body to protect it from damage or prevent it from feeling pain. This differs from the withdrawal response, which makes you contract the flexor muscles into the fetal position.

The flexor reflex is triggered when you have pain or an injury on one side of your body. When this reflex becomes habitual, chronic muscular contractions on one side of the body pull your spine into a C-curve. Sometimes you instinctively balance yourself by bending to the opposite side, causing an S-curve.

During his years at the Novato Institute, Hanna explored movement techniques that would directly address the learned, habitual muscular tension that was the underlying cause of his clients' postural distortions, functional disorders, and chronic pain. He researched the pandicular response, an automatic nervous system response exhibited by vertebrate animals that prevents the buildup of chronic muscle tension.

If you've ever seen a dog or cat arch their back when they get up from a nap, or watched a baby stretch their arms and legs as they wake up, you've witnessed the pandicular response (Illustration 9). The response contracts and releases muscles, sending feedback about the level of muscle tension to the brain. This resets the resting level of muscle tension and restores voluntary control of the muscles. Essentially, pandiculation "wakes up" your sensorimotor system.

Illustration 9: Pandicular response in a cat
(Nevodka © 123rf.com)

Fetuses have been observed pandiculating in the womb, showing how deeply ingrained the response is and how critical it is to your musculoskeletal functioning. Unfortunately, as your motor patterns become habitual and you become less active, your natural pandicular response can't counteract all the learning that occurs in your nervous system. And as you lose sensorimotor awareness and control, your primal pandicular response can become inhibited.

Hanna developed hands-on movements and self-care exercises that use the pandicular response. These "voluntary pandiculations" are highly specialized eccentric contractions—the actions of muscles that are engaged while they lengthen under load. Picture what your biceps are doing as you lower a dumbbell, for example (Illustration 10). The muscles are slowly lengthening, but are still engaged as long as you hold the weight.

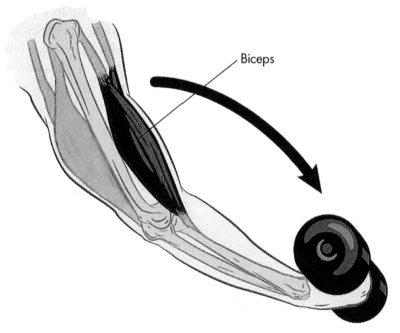

Biceps

Illustration 10: An eccentric contraction
(adapted from lukaves © 123rf.com)

A voluntary pandiculation must be performed very slowly and consciously so that your nervous system is able to sense and integrate the biofeedback that the movement provides. The opposing muscles should not engage during the pandiculation. And the resistance, or load, must be applied so that the actively lengthening muscles are fully engaged throughout the movement's range of motion.

In a hands-on pandiculation, the practitioner provides resistance to the muscles that are actively lengthening. These movements can be performed in any position relative to gravity because the practitioner can adjust the direction of the resistance as the student moves through the range of motion. Other exercises that Hanna developed are self-pandiculations, in which gravity provides the only resistance. This means you must be in specific positions relative to gravity to pandiculate muscle groups correctly.

Hanna's voluntary pandiculations proved to be groundbreaking. It was the first active technique that a somatic educator had employed to any significant degree. Previous somatic educators had focused on passive movement techniques that improved function by increasing sensorimotor awareness and relaxing the nervous system. Hanna found, however, that voluntary movement was the most efficient and effective way to unlearn chronic, involuntary muscular contraction and retrain posture and movement patterns.

Pandiculation quickly reduced muscular tension, and since this was accomplished through learning rather than manipulation, the effects were typically long-lasting. Hanna would first teach pandiculations that focused on contracting and releasing small groups of muscles. Once his students began to reduce their involuntary muscle tension, he taught them larger movements that integrated their muscular releases into natural, efficient, full-body movement patterns.

Hanna codified his methods into three standard lessons based on the three postural patterns he observed in his clients, an approach he called "Clinical Somatic Education." Following each hands-on lesson, Hanna gave his students simple self-care exercises so they could learn how to take care of themselves rather than rely on a practitioner. While earlier methods of somatic education were relatively free-form, Hanna's was systematized and easy for people to practice at home.

In 1990, after years of requests to teach his methods, Hanna began his first professional training program. Tragically, after teaching the first semester of the three-semester program, he was killed in a car accident. His students worked with the clients who were on his long waiting list, and went on to create training programs for future students.

Hanna wrote a number of books on somatic education and theory, including the classic *Somatics: Reawakening the Mind's Control of Movement, Flexibility, and Health*. Hundreds of people attended his movement workshops or traveled across the country to do hands-on lessons. He created a method of education that has helped thousands of people get out of pain, freeing them from the prisons of their stiff, unmoving bodies, and giving them the tools they need to take care of themselves and be truly self-reliant.

A Systematized Approach

F.M. Alexander, Elsa Gindler, Gerda Alexander, and Moshe Feldenkrais were driven to question conventional medical wisdom by a personal need to learn what caused their dysfunctions. They spent their lives learning how to increase sensation and improve control of their bodies. As science caught up with human experience, it became clear that these pioneers of somatic education had made groundbreaking discoveries about the effects of voluntary control on the functioning of the human nervous system.

In their methods we see the process by which each individual solved his or her personal challenge.

- The Alexander Technique uses subtle shifts in the movement of the head, neck, and pelvis to improve posture and function, an approach that enabled F.M. Alexander to regain use of his voice.

- Elsa Gindler's focus on internal awareness and control allowed her to recover from tuberculosis, and she taught her students how to improve their health by the same method.

- Moving with minimal effort and muscular tension enabled Gerda Alexander to regain full function without straining her heart; these principles became the basis of Eutony.

- Feldenkrais approached his problem from a scientific point of view, using his background in engineering and physics to heal his injured knees. His combination of scientific knowledge and personal experience led him to create the most effective method of somatic education that had been developed up to that point. Feldenkrais's lifelong study of defense gave him a myopic point of view, however. He believed that all dysfunction was the result of fear and anxiety, and he had difficulty explaining functional issues that were not caused by the withdrawal response.

Hanna benefited from his predecessors' discoveries, and since he did not need to satisfy any needs other than curiosity, he was able to approach the work more objectively. Developing his techniques 30 years after Feldenkrais and 70 years after F.M. Alexander, Hanna also had access to newer research in the fields of neuroscience and physiology. As a result, Hanna's method of Clinical Somatic Education proved to be the most comprehensive and effective approach to alleviating musculoskeletal disorders by changing learned posture and movement patterns.

All of the somatic educators faced the challenge of how to teach their techniques to others. While F.M. Alexander, Gerda Alexander, and Feldenkrais established professional training schools, their methods of education relied on personal experience, and the lack of an underlying system made it challenging for them to train others. Feldenkrais in particular was a truly gifted practitioner, but had difficulty teaching his hands-on work because he did not fully understand all of the underlying neuromuscular processes that were at work. The experiential, free-form nature of these early methods is one of the reasons that the field has not yet become mainstream. The movement techniques and their effects were too difficult for students to replicate on their own.

In contrast, Hanna created a highly systematic approach, so teaching his techniques is quite straightforward. While his widow Eleanor Criswell and some of his students have dedicated their lives to teaching his work, there are still only an estimated 200 certified practitioners in the world, so Clinical Somatic Education is not yet well known. When people discover how effective it is, they wonder why they've never heard of it before.

None of the somatic educators believed that their students should rely on them as any sort of master teacher or guru, but should instead learn to rely on themselves. They believed that not only is each individual capable of taking care of their own health, but that it is their responsibility to do so. As Gerda Alexander said in an interview for *Yoga Journal* in 1986:

"It is better to help people stand on their own two feet, in every sense of the word. It is important, in treatment, not to give and do more than is necessary, so that the other can rely on himself. It is not that I am the great master and give you help. Rather, I can introduce you to my work for your own self-discovery."

This is a tenet of somatic education: The teacher is merely the guide, giving the student the tools with which to increase their sensorimotor awareness, to discover the underlying cause of their pain or condition, and to improve their physiological functioning. Because the goal is to retrain your nervous system, it requires the first-person sensation of being in your body that only you can experience, and active movement that only you can perform.

In the next chapter, we'll talk about the principles of Thomas Hanna's Clinical Somatic Education, and what to expect when you learn and practice the exercises.

CHAPTER 8

Clinical Somatic Education

At this point you might be thinking, "Okay, I get it! My pain is most likely the result of the way I'm habitually using my body—so how do I get out of pain and stop doing damage to myself?" The answer: learn and practice Clinical Somatics exercises. The approach to sensorimotor education that Thomas Hanna developed is so effective and potentially life-changing that it should be taught in every school, sports program, medical practice, and retirement home throughout the world.

But beware: The word "somatic" has gained common use recently in both holistic health care and Western medicine. A quick internet search on the term returns a long list of modalities ranging from psychotherapy to voice work to self-massage. To find educators trained in Thomas Hanna's method you must look for someone who is certified in Clinical Somatic Education or Hanna Somatic Education. These practitioners have been professionally trained in Thomas Hanna's method of sensorimotor education.

The Principles of Clinical Somatic Education

1. **Chronic musculoskeletal pain, dysfunctional posture and movement, and physical degeneration are most often caused by learned muscular patterns.**

   Your nervous system controls your muscles, and your muscles move your skeleton. Your body does not move in any way unless your nervous system tells it to do so. Chronic pain, chronic muscle tension, postural distortions, joint degeneration, and stress fractures are most often the result of how your nervous system tells your body to stand and move.

   It's important to be aware that other issues such as nervous system disease, genetic makeup, metabolic or immune system function, diet, activity level, and even bacterial or viral infection can also cause musculoskeletal dysfunction or pain. Once these possible causes have been ruled out, it is fairly safe to assume that learned, habitual motor patterns are the cause of the issue, and they must be addressed to relieve pain and improve function.

2. **Active movement is necessary to create lasting change in learned muscular patterns.**

   While therapies that use only passive techniques are usually relaxing and enjoyable, the results of these therapies typically do not last more than a few days. An example of a passive movement is a therapist lifting up their client's arm while the client remains relaxed. Massage, chiropractic, and most other bodywork modalities are passive. An example of an active movement is a student lifting their own arm. Active movement is necessary to form new neural pathways and achieve lasting change in the functioning of the nervous system.

   Clinical Somatics uses a combination of both passive and active movement techniques. The passive movements calm your nervous system and increase your internal awareness, while the active movements create lasting change by reducing your resting level of muscle tension and retraining learned motor patterns.

3. The underlying cause of a problem must be addressed.

Most pain treatments, whether they be medication or a form of bodywork, address only the symptoms of the problem. These treatments either focus on relieving the sensation of pain or use spot work, an approach that assumes that the problem is occurring in the area of the body where the pain is being felt. Since these treatments address only symptoms, their results typically don't last.

Clinical Somatics addresses the underlying cause of pain by working with your nervous system to address full-body patterns of posture and movement. No part of the human body moves independently. Even a simple movement like picking up a cup requires adjustments and shifts throughout your entire body. When pain or breakdown occurs in one part of your body, it is most often a symptom of a dysfunctional full-body pattern. For the problem to go away for good, the entire pattern must be addressed.

Clinical Somatics addresses the underlying cause of pain by working with the core of your body first. Just as you must have a solid foundation before building a house on top of it, you must first work with the function of the core of your body, where all posture and movement patterns begin, before moving outward to your extremities.

4. Clinical Somatics educators work with students rather than on students.

In Clinical Somatics, the student is not simply a body to work on or manipulate. The student is a person whose thoughts, reactions, emotions, and experiences have created a set of habitual patterns that led to their dysfunction. The educator and student work together in partnership. Verbal communication throughout each lesson allows the educator to understand what the student is experiencing and adjust movements based on their feedback.

5. Students should learn how to be self-sufficient instead of dependent.

Many treatments and therapies for pain are based on some sort of dependence, whether the student must return for sessions or continue to take medication. Clinical Somatics gives you a way to take care of yourself. In fact, the method is founded on the belief that people should take care of themselves instead of relying on others to maintain their health.

At every private lesson or group class, the educator teaches new self-care exercises. These movements are slow and gentle, and most people find them relaxing and enjoyable. When working one-on-one with an educator, you will typically have between three and six lessons, though if you're working through a particularly complex issue or are in a great deal of pain, you may have more. After completing the series of lessons, you should have a deep enough understanding of the method that you are able to continue to make progress on your own.

Clinical Somatics is intended to equip you with the tools you need to continue to improve self-awareness, assess how you feel on a daily basis, and unlearn damaging patterns. This learning process not only helps you regain awareness and control, but it also helps teach you how to guide yourself through the learning process without an educator.

What to Expect in Lessons and Classes

A series of individual lessons or group classes is a learning process, and that process is different for every student. Some people experience significant changes in their pain or functioning very quickly, while for others it takes longer. It's important to focus on your learning process rather than your end goal. If you focus on your end goal, you'll inevitably rush through the exercises, and your nervous system will not be able to learn effectively. You must be completely focused on your movement and your internal sensations to allow your nervous system to integrate the feedback you're giving it and create lasting change.

Clinical Somatics is not a therapy, but an educational experience. You should come to lessons or classes expecting to be a student, and should be prepared to do your homework—the self-care exercises—every day for about 20 to 30 minutes. The exercises are taught through a process designed to get you to experience for yourself how your body should feel and move. This allows you to make long-lasting changes to your posture, movement patterns, level of muscle tension, and reactions to stress.

If you engage in other types of treatment or therapy while practicing Clinical Somatics exercises, you may not experience optimal results.

Some types of bodywork may actually make your muscles tighter, and some may confuse your nervous system while you're attempting to make changes in learned patterns. It's generally best if you go through the Clinical Somatics learning process without interference from passive, manipulative techniques like deep tissue massage or chiropractic adjustments. You should also avoid workouts that involve intense stretching or strengthening.

Clinical Somatics exercises are slow and gentle and appropriate for students in any physical condition. You need not be physically fit or aerobically active, and all movements can be modified so that you can do them comfortably. While most are practiced lying down, a few proprioceptive exercises designed to change your postural habits are practiced sitting or standing in front of a mirror. By combining your internal sense of posture with the objective view that you see in the mirror, you can determine if what you sense is correct.

Often when a student comes in for their first lesson or class, their proprioception is quite "off." They may sense that their shoulders are pulled back when they're actually rounded forward, or that their hips are even when one is higher than the other. Altered proprioception can be a significant roadblock in making changes to posture and movement. Even if a great deal of muscular release is achieved by doing Clinical Somatics exercises while lying down, students tend to go back to their old habits once they stand up because they instinctively want to stay balanced.

It can feel wrong or uncomfortable to sit and stand in a new way. People who have tight back muscles and arched backs will feel as though they're slouching when they begin to release their back muscles. People who hold one hip higher than the other will feel off balance when their obliques are released and they begin standing and walking with their hips even. Proprioceptive training practiced while sitting and standing is essential to create and maintain new posture and movement patterns.

In your lessons or classes, your educator will teach you self-care exercises that you'll practice at home. You should practice these for 20 to 30 minutes every day. It's fine to do more than 30 minutes, but it is typically not necessary. The most important aspect of the self-care exercises is not how many repetitions you do, but how you do them.

Practice the exercises in a quiet, private space where you won't be interrupted by family members, pets, television, or background noise.

Focus all of your attention on what you feel as you do the movements. It's important to remember that the exercises are exploratory, so you should allow yourself to feel something new and learn something new each time you do them.

Continuing the Learning Process

By the end of a series of lessons or classes, you may experience a significant reduction in your pain. This does not mean that your learning process is over, however.

You spend your entire life developing habitual motor patterns, and for a long time they don't cause you pain. Finally, you begin to feel soreness or pain. The habits that are causing this discomfort have been present for many years. While it may take a relatively short time to get out of pain, the habits are still present, and it can take years to fully unlearn these damaging patterns.

While some people keep up with their Clinical Somatics exercises just enough to keep themselves out of pain, others go further with the process and continue to improve their posture and movement for the rest of their lives. A regular practice of Clinical Somatics exercises is extremely enjoyable and rewarding. It's a process of continually discovering new sensations and new abilities in your body, and becoming aware of how wonderful your body is supposed to feel.

Regular practice of Clinical Somatics exercises is necessary not only to change deeply learned patterns, but also to release the tension you build up each day. Practicing the exercises daily is like brushing your teeth. Just as teeth get dirty every day, your nervous system keeps building up residual muscle tension as a result of stress and repetitive activities.

Clinical Somatics exercises have a very calming effect, a result of both decreasing muscular tension and reducing the reactivity of the nervous system. With continued regular practice, you'll react less to stress and experience less anxiety, thereby reducing your experience of pain.

Practicing Clinical Somatics exercises regularly with the intention of taking control of your health requires a shift in thinking for many people. Because you've been trained to let the experts tell you how to eat, drink, exercise, and medicate, assuming responsibility for taking care of yourself can be daunting.

Developing an awareness of your internal sensations and regaining full voluntary muscular control is critical to your health because it allows you to assess and correct yourself more quickly and effectively than if you were to wait for painful symptoms to appear. The human nervous system is a highly complex, extremely powerful tool, and learning how to harness its potential gives you an enormous capacity to prevent pain and injury, and improve the quality and even the length of your life.

In the next five chapters, we'll examine the most significant factors that contribute to your unique motor patterns: stress, reactions to injuries, handedness, repetitive daily activities, personality, automatic imitation, and athletic training.

CHAPTER 9

Stress and Posture

If you have any type of chronic or recurring pain, you may have noticed that it tends to become worse with stress. Stress increases your overall muscular tension and triggers specific, reflexive muscular contractions designed to protect your body from threats. Stress also makes you revert to old, deeply learned motor patterns. So even if you've begun to retrain your patterns, stress can make you slip back into old habits and put you back in pain.

We've already talked about how chronic stress causes changes in brain chemistry, damages brain cells, and leads to conditions such as anxiety and depression, which can worsen your experience of pain. In this chapter we'll discuss the direct effects of stress on neuromuscular functioning: how the stressors you endure and the way you perceive them affects your muscle tension, posture, and learned motor patterns.

When you encounter an acute physical stressor, your automatic fight-or-flight response is triggered, inducing many physiological changes that prepare you to defend yourself. The blood vessels to your muscles dilate to supply extra fuel, and your muscle tension increases so that you can act swiftly and with strength. When the stressor is gone, blood flow slows and your muscle tension returns to normal.

When you experience chronic psychological stress, however, the same stress response is constantly activated by the ever-present worries in your mind. Your neuromuscular system never gets a chance to recover or return to normal. Your heart rate remains elevated and your muscles retain a higher than normal level of tension.

Not surprisingly, studies show that people with anxiety have higher resting levels of muscle tension, react to stress with stronger muscle contractions, and return to their baseline level of tension more slowly than control subjects. As a result of their muscle tension, levels of lactate in the blood are higher in anxiety patients. But what is quite interesting is that this feedback loop goes both ways. You can actually make yourself anxious by injecting lactate into your bloodstream. So not only does anxiety increase muscle tension, but chronic muscular contraction and increased lactate levels can cause anxiety, creating a vicious cycle.

This stress response can make you feel more pain even if you don't have a clinical anxiety disorder. Your level of psychological stress and the way that you process it exists on a spectrum. A moderate amount of worry triggers the stress response to a lesser degree than a diagnosable anxiety condition would. It's surprisingly easy to get used to an increased level of muscle tension and heart rate and to be completely unaware that your baseline level of stress is elevated.

Perfectly healthy people experience increased muscle tension when they feel stress. One study found that simply having to complete word and math problems in a research lab increased the muscle tension of test subjects. In another experiment, subjects were given a picture and asked to tell a story about it. While they told their stories, their muscle tension increased because they experienced a little bit of anxiety, just as most of us would when performing in front of other people. When they finished, half of the subjects were praised for doing a good job on the task. Their muscle tension dropped back to normal levels. The other half of the subjects were criticized for their poor performance, and their muscle tension remained higher than normal—until they were reassured by a different researcher that they had actually done a good job.

Mental activity alone, not just psychological stress, is enough to increase muscle tension. Edmund Jacobson, a physician and psychologist, conducted a number of studies in the 1920s and 1930s using electromyography (EMG) to observe the correlation between thought and muscle tension. He developed a technique called "progressive relaxation" to guide his subjects through a process of contracting and releasing their muscles one by one. As the subjects' muscular tension decreased, their mental activity decreased as well. Once relaxed, it was quite easy to see the elevations in muscle tension that occurred when the subjects were instructed to think about specific things.

When you perceive stress, not only does your overall level of muscle tension rise, but the withdrawal response and the action response cause you to contract your muscles in predictable patterns, depending on whether you perceive the stress to be negative or positive. The withdrawal response contracts your abdominal muscles, making you curl up into the fetal position to protect your internal organs from attack. The action response serves the opposite purpose; it makes you contract your back muscles and stick out your chest, preparing you to move and fight. Like all automatic human responses, these evolved to help you survive.

While you're born with these automatic responses, experience and learning can affect the degree to which they're activated. If you hear a gunshot, your withdrawal response will be triggered automatically. When you realize that it was just a car backfiring, and you start to hear that same car backfire every day, you'll soon become desensitized to the sound. Your withdrawal response will be activated to a much lesser degree or not at all. This adaptation is generally a good thing. You adjust your reaction as a result of learning that the stressor is not dangerous, protecting the systems of your body and mind from the negative effects of the withdrawal response.

On the flip side, if you perceive a stimulus to be more stressful than it actually is, you may become oversensitized and your automatic responses can increase in frequency and intensity. As you might imagine, this is not a good thing, as it can put a great deal of unnecessary strain on your body and mind.

Moshe Feldenkrais observed the effects of the withdrawal response on posture. His clients who experienced distress on a regular basis and had chronic fear and anxiety were most often the ones with stooped postures, rounded shoulders, and sunken chests.

Thomas Hanna identified the action response as the cause of the opposite posture. His clients who experienced a great deal of eustress, like those in high-profile jobs who were expected to constantly perform, tended to stand with their backs arched and have chronically contracted back muscles. Hanna concluded that most back and neck pain occurred when people experienced the withdrawal or the action response so frequently that the muscular patterns became habitual.

The Withdrawal Response and Rounded Posture

You're walking down the street and hear a gunshot behind you. Within just 14 milliseconds, your jaw muscles begin to contract. At 25 milliseconds, your upper trapezius muscles contract, raising your shoulders and bringing your head forward. At 34 milliseconds, the muscles of your eyes and brow contract, squeezing your eyes shut.

These lightning-fast neural impulses continue down your body, making your elbows bend, arms rotate inward, abdominal muscles contract, inner thigh muscles and hamstrings tighten, and knees and ankles roll inward. The withdrawal response pulls your extremities inward and brings you into a crouched position, protecting the most vulnerable parts of your body from attack (Illustration 11).

Illustration 11: The withdrawal response
(Joydeep © Wikimedia Commons and Antonio Guillem © 123rf.com)

Organisms throughout the animal kingdom—amoebas, earthworms, sea anemones, squirrels, meerkats, sloths, coyotes, monkeys, bears, and of course humans—all exhibit some form of the withdrawal response when danger is sensed. This primitive response occurs automatically and is critical to your survival. In humans and some mammals with more complex nervous systems, the intensity of the response is determined by experience, expectation, and baseline stress level.

For millennia the withdrawal response helped humans survive as a species. But for those of us living in industrialized societies, it's not doing us any favors. Your life is no longer threatened on a regular basis, but the never-ending demands of work, family life, financial responsibilities, and social expectations are constantly present, and you subconsciously perceive these stressors to be life-threatening.

These types of distress activate your withdrawal response, contracting your abdominal muscles and bringing you into the rounded posture you probably associate with aging. When this posture becomes habitual, you experience back and neck pain as well as a host of other physiological dysfunctions including shallow breathing, high blood pressure, and digestive issues. As Moshe Feldenkrais said, "Should the environment change too sharply, the reflex reaction may be the doom of the species as surely as it has served it."

When you experience chronic distress, the muscles involved in the withdrawal response are constantly activated. And you know what happens when you repeat a muscular contraction over and over: The pattern of muscular contraction originally caused by the withdrawal response becomes habitual, and your nervous system learns to keep those muscles partially contracted all the time. Now, even if the cause of your chronic stress is reduced or eliminated completely, the learned patterns of muscular contraction will remain and continue the vicious cycle of increasing your stress.

Hyperkyphosis

The abdominal muscles are central to the withdrawal response. When they're chronically contracted, as shown in Illustration 12, the head and rib cage are pulled forward and held there as if you're doing a stomach crunch. Chronic contraction of the abdominals results in hyperkyphosis, the rounded posture associated with aging. Hyperkyphosis occurs when the natural kyphotic curve in the thoracic portion of your spine becomes exaggerated.

Illustration 12: An example of hyperkyphosis
(Undrey © 123rf.com)

People with hyperkyphosis have significantly more neck pain and disability than people with normal posture, and the further forward they hold their head, the greater their pain. For every 15 degrees you move your head forward, your head gains 10 to 12 pounds of weight because of the increased strain on your cervical spine. Your suboccipital muscles (Illustration 13), just below the base of your skull, must contract even further if you want to lift your head up to face forward instead of looking down at the ground. Pain can result simply from all of these muscles being chronically contracted. Disc problems and nerve pain may develop from the increased compression of the cervical spine.

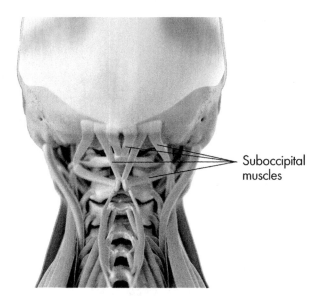

Illustration 13: Suboccipital muscles
(Sebastian Kaulitzki © 123rf.com)

Hyperkyphosis can also cause lower back pain. When your abdominals contract and the weight of your head and rib cage are pulled in front of your center of gravity, you quite literally will fall forward if you don't do something to balance yourself out. So as your abdominals gradually become habitually contracted, your lower back muscles must work harder and harder to keep you upright in gravity. A person with hyperkyphosis may complain only of a sore back, but all attempts to treat the back muscles directly will have little effect until the underlying cause—the habitual abdominal contraction—is addressed. The sore back muscles will never be able to release as long as they have to compensate for the chronically contracted abdominal muscles.

In addition to causing pain, disc degeneration, and nerve compression, hyperkyphosis has negative effects on many other functions of the body. Tight abdominals limit the ability to take a full breath, which demands that the diaphragm contract downward and push the contents of the abdomen forward. If the abdominals are tight, this action can't occur and breathing becomes shallow and strained. Chronic tightness and compression in the front of the body also put pressure on all the internal organs, contributing to high blood pressure, digestive problems, frequent urination, constipation, and impotence.

The withdrawal response causes problems in your extremities as well. Headaches, bruxism (teeth grinding), temporomandibular joint disorders, and tinnitus (ringing in the ears) can develop due to constant contraction of your neck and jaw muscles. The withdrawal response also contracts the inner thigh muscles, rotating your thighs inward; this places stress on your knees and ankles and makes the arches of your feet collapse. Hip flexors, quadriceps, and hamstrings can become tight and sore from holding your body in a flexed position.

The effects of the withdrawal response tend to be more obvious in the elderly, simply because they've been alive longer and have had more exposure to stress. However, developing rounded posture as you age is not inevitable. The way that you perceive and cope with stress throughout your life determines how the systems of your body react. Learning how to deal with stress in a constructive way can prevent you from automatically triggering your withdrawal response and suffering the negative physical effects.

Thanks to the advent of personal computers, smart phones, and other electronic devices, many people in their twenties and thirties, teens, and even children have also developed hyperkyphosis. Spending hours upon hours sitting at a computer keeps you in the withdrawal response posture: hips and knees flexed, arms rotated inward, head and rib cage forward. It takes a great deal of conscious attention, as well as proper seating, to prevent this posture from becoming habitual.

You need only walk around a shopping mall to observe the effects of smartphones and a sedentary lifestyle on young people. It always makes me sad to see a lovely teenager in the prime of life who has already begun to round forward as if they're 80 years old. It's virtually impossible to use a smartphone without tilting your head downward and contracting your biceps and pectoral muscles. When you consider that the average person between the ages of 11 and 18 spends more than eight hours a day using some form of electronic media, it's easy to see how rounded posture can become a habit.

A study of over 800 Australian teenagers found that computer use was associated with habitual postural deviations such as increased head and neck flexion (meaning that their heads tilted forward and down). This flexion was consistent whether the teens were looking straight ahead, looking downward, sitting in a slumped position, or standing up. At their young age, these postural habits were already so deeply learned that their heads and necks remained flexed even when they weren't at the computer.

The study also found associations between small variations in posture and increased neck and shoulder pain. Slight changes in habitual posture can be enough to cause pain, even in young people who are typically quite resilient and feel little pain. This is why paying attention to how you use your body is so important. You won't know what seemingly meaningless movement habit might be causing or contributing to your pain until you learn to regain control of your chronically contracted muscles.

In addition to new technology and changes in daily activities, our competitive, industrialized society puts ever-increasing demands on children and teenagers, subjecting them to the same social constructs and pressure to succeed that adults face. As a result, their stress responses—most often their withdrawal responses—are triggered far more often than in past generations.

There are still other factors that contribute to rounded posture. Fatigue, which in and of itself is often stressful, makes you want to curl up in a ball and go to sleep. Chronic lack of sleep alone can cause someone to slouch and adopt the withdrawal response posture.

People who are quite tall often develop rounded posture as a result of functional needs like working at a counter top built for average-height people. Very tall people have to almost constantly bend over or look down in order to function in an average-height world. They also tend to round forward in order to shorten their stature so that they can more easily interact with people who are shorter than they are.

Abdominal surgery or injury also often results in withdrawal response posture, as people instinctively want to protect the painful area by contracting the muscles around it. Athletic training that demands a great deal of core strength, such as swimming or gymnastics, can cause even the most elite athletes to have rounded shoulders and sunken chests. Even simply being cold on a regular basis can contribute to withdrawal response posture. Notice what happens next time you feel really cold: You'll bring your arms in toward your body, round your shoulders and raise them up, and, if you're sitting or lying down, you'll contract your abdominals and curl up into the fetal position to stay warm.

If you have rounded posture, Clinical Somatics exercises can release the chronic tightness in your abdominal and pectoral muscles. To learn two simple exercises that will help you to straighten rounded posture, go to: **somaticmovementcenter.com/posture-exercise**

The Action Response and the Arched Back

In the first few months of life you're entirely helpless, unable to crawl or even sit up by yourself. You've spent nine months curled up in the fetal position and have yet to gain control of the extensor muscles of your neck and back. Around three months of age, you finally succeed in lifting your head off the ground when lying on your stomach. A few months later, the muscles in your lower back are activated, allowing you to crawl, sit up, stand, and eventually walk.

Once you're using the extensor muscles of the neck and back, the cervical and lumbar curves in your spine begin to develop. These are called lordotic curves, and they curve in the opposite direction of the kyphotic curves of the thoracic and sacral portions of the spine (Illustration 14).

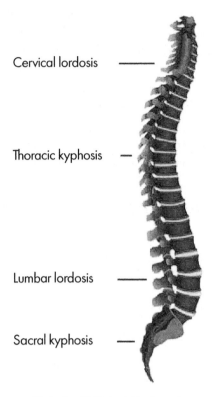

Cervical lordosis ———

Thoracic kyphosis —

Lumbar lordosis ———

Sacral kyphosis —

Illustration 14: Natural spinal curvature
(adapted from Vonuk © 123rf.com)

The natural kyphotic and lordotic curves are essential to the spine's ability to absorb shock, allowing it to function like a big spring. If you didn't have these curves, your vertebrae would be stacked on top of each other in a straight line, and compressive forces would cause a great deal of damage and pain.

In infants, the contraction of the back and neck muscles in response to the instinctive desire to become mobile is called the Landau reflex (Illustration 15). But even after you learn how to stand, walk, and run, your extensor muscles automatically contract every time you want to get up and go; this is the action response. You arch your back, lift your head, pull your shoulders backward, stick out your chest, straighten your knees, and rotate your legs outward.

Illustration 15: The Landau reflex
(Sylvie Bouchard ©123rf.com)

Your action response is also triggered by eustress, or positive stress like giving a presentation or meeting your new boss. Whenever you want to make a good impression and be on your game, you instinctively contract your back muscles so that you stand up straight, look taller, and appear confident. This posture prepares you both physically and psychologically for action (Illustration 16).

Illustration 16: An example of action response posture
(Denis Ismagilov © 123rf.com)

You probably subconsciously associate this upright, often arched posture with confidence, strength, youth, and beauty. It's no coincidence that the military trains soldiers to stand up straight and stick out their chests—this action response posture shows the enemy that you're ready for a fight. And people find it much more pleasing to look at someone who stands erect rather than rounded over; imagine watching a dancer or ice skater who was slouching as they performed.

So far, the action response sounds pretty great. It prepares you for action and automatically makes you look and feel more confident—all in a completely natural way. When your action response is triggered once in a while, it is great. But when it's activated constantly by a high-stress job or practiced repetitively as part of physical training, the pattern of muscular contraction becomes learned. So even after you retire from your stressful job or quit dancing, your back muscles remain habitually tight, causing soreness, pain, and often nerve compression or structural damage to intervertebral discs.

When the extensor muscles of the back are chronically contracted, they typically pull the lumbar spine into hyperlordosis, an exaggerated arching of the lower back that compresses the discs between the lumbar vertebrae, often causing them to bulge or herniate. People with tight lower back muscles may experience sciatica due to compression of the sciatic nerve as it exits the spine between the lumbar vertebrae. Tight lower back muscles also compress the sacroiliac joint, causing pain and inflammation and occasionally shifting the sacrum and ilium bones out of alignment.

Once the action or withdrawal response has become habitual and you're subconsciously holding yourself in a dysfunctional posture most or all of the time, pain becomes pretty much inevitable. Research shows that people who stand with a flattened lower back (due to contraction of the abdominal muscles) or an arched back are more likely to experience pain than people who stand with ideal posture. Luckily, this pain can be alleviated and eliminated by unlearning the damaging postural patterns.

To learn an exercise that gently releases the lower back muscles, go to: **somaticmovementcenter.com/back-pain-exercise**

Aging and the Dark Vise

Everyone experiences the action and withdrawal responses throughout their lifetime in varying frequencies and to different degrees, depending on the stressors you encounter and the ways you perceive them. Each time you repeat the action or withdrawal response posture, a small degree of it is retained in your muscle memory. Over time, your reactions to stress contribute to patterns of posture and movement that are completely, uniquely yours.

The muscular contractions of the action and the withdrawal responses work against each other. The action response cues the nervous system to automatically release the flexors to allow unhindered contraction of the extensors. The withdrawal response has the opposite effect, automatically releasing the extensors so that the flexors can curl the body into the fetal position.

As you age, you tend to lose mobility as these opposing muscular patterns fight against each other. Both the abdominal muscles and the lower back muscles pull the rib cage down toward the pelvis, compressing your spine and shortening your stature. Your trunk, which once bent and twisted freely, becomes stiff and unmoving. You only need to watch a young person walk next to their grandparent in order to observe the muscular rigidity that occurs with age. Notice how the young person moves with ease, their trunk twisting and limbs swinging freely, while their grandparent moves quite stiffly.

Thomas Hanna called this gradual locking down of the body the "dark vise." As you age, you tend to tighten up like a vise grip, pulling yourself inward and downward toward your center. Your muscles and connective tissues tighten, movement becomes constricted, and you wake up feeling stiff and achy.

To add insult to injury, all of this chronic muscular contraction has another adverse effect: chronic fatigue. As you learned in chapter 4, muscles require energy in order to contract. The more muscle tension you have, the more energy you expend, and the more tired you become. Even a full night's sleep doesn't feel refreshing because your muscles have stayed partially contracted throughout the night, using energy while you sleep.

Staying Aware of Your Reactions to Stress

You can't avoid the action response or the withdrawal response completely, nor would you want to—they still come in handy sometimes. But you should become acutely aware of when these responses are triggered and the effects they have on your posture, movement, and pain. Because while getting locked into the dark vise is not inevitable, it will happen to you unless you're very self-aware and take conscious action to prevent it.

Research consistently shows the correlation between stress and pain. But even more important than the type or amount of stressors you encounter is the way that you deal with them. Everyone perceives and copes with stress differently due to their personality and past experiences. A stressful occurrence that might trigger the action response in one person could trigger the withdrawal response in someone else, and another person might not perceive the occurrence to be stressful at all. Becoming aware of your reactions to stress and learning how to modify them is one of the most important things you can do to prevent pain caused by muscular tension and postural responses.

CHAPTER 10

Why You Bend
to the Side

Imagine that you've slipped on your icy front steps and sprained your ankle. On top of the fact that you don't have an exciting mountain climbing story to tell, you have to wear an ankle brace and use crutches for at least a month so your torn ligaments can heal. You have to put all your weight on your uninjured side, and you instinctively contract and immobilize the injured side to protect it. Over the next four weeks, you become adept at hobbling around on your one good leg. This unnatural way of moving starts to become habitual, and even after your ankle is fully healed, you find yourself standing with your weight shifted to one side and the other hip hiked up.

Now imagine that you have chronic pain in your right shoulder. Your doctor says you have a torn rotator cuff, a result of years of wear and tear from weight lifting. As the pain increases, you use your shoulder less in order to avoid the pain, and develop the tendency to hold your right arm against your body to limit the movement in your shoulder. After surgery and months of physical therapy, your pain is finally gone, but your learned movement pattern remains. The muscles that hold your shoulder in place and pull your arm in toward your body are chronically contracted, and you hold your right shoulder an inch lower than your left.

The ways you adjust your posture and movement in reaction to an injury or chronic pain are largely subconscious. You contract certain muscles to protect the painful or injured area, and modify your motor patterns to avoid the pain. Your pain-processing system works with your proprioceptive and vestibular systems to adjust posture and movement automatically so that you can minimize your pain and prevent further injury.

The Flexor Reflex

When one side of your body is injured or feels pain, like when you step on a nail or touch a very hot pan, an automatic nervous system response called the flexor reflex is triggered. The flexor muscles on the injured side of your body contract to pull the affected area away from the source of pain. Then the crossed-extensor reflex kicks in, activating the extensor muscles on the opposite side of your body so that your weight remains balanced and you don't fall over.

The flexor reflex is extremely helpful during acute pain or injury because it helps you avoid pain and further damage to your body. When it's activated constantly by chronic pain or a prolonged healing process from an injury, however, you can easily develop permanent motor patterns. What begins as a protective postural mechanism becomes a habitual motor pattern, causing misalignment, dysfunctional movement, and further pain.

The heightened emotional state during and after an injury also contributes to the pattern getting locked in. Much like never forgetting a marriage proposal even though it only occurs once, a strong emotional reaction to an injury or event can cause a pattern of muscular contraction to become deeply learned immediately.

Your reflexive, protective response to injury will always be experienced on one side unless the injury or pain is directly in the center of your body, like in the abdomen or along the spine. After abdominal surgery, for example, you might stand with rounded posture to protect your abdomen, which has effectively gone through trauma. Likewise, if your spine is injured, your back muscles will tighten up to limit movement.

Thomas Hanna observed the effects of the flexor reflex in his students: tilted and often rotated posture, uneven hips and shoulders, and different patterns of muscular contraction on each side of the body. Many of these clients had sciatica or pain in their hip, knee, and ankle joints, while others had frozen shoulder, bursitis, or carpal tunnel syndrome.

Some of Hanna's students had even been told by doctors that one of their legs was longer than the other. This perceived difference in leg length was caused by tight waist muscles hiking one hip up higher than the other. When Hanna taught his clients how to release their oblique muscles, their hips evened out and, miraculously, their legs were the same length.

Handedness

In addition to injury, an important factor in determining how you use the two sides of your body is your handedness. Whether you are right- or left-handed plays a large role in the movement patterns you develop. It determines how you sit at your desk and use your computer, the side on which you carry your babies, the leg you use to kick a ball, and the side you tend to lean on.

You refer to your sides as being "dominant" and "nondominant," but in reality, both sides of your body play equally important roles in your ability to carry out complicated motor tasks. If you're right-handed, you tend to use your right side to perform tasks requiring precision and dexterity, while your left side plays the critical role of providing support and balance.

You develop patterns of habitual muscular contraction on both sides of your body. On the dominant side, the tension is the result of repetition of voluntary movements. On the nondominant side, it's the result of automatically stabilizing your body and balancing your weight, which allows you to carry out voluntary movements.

There are countless examples of repetitive activities—brushing your teeth, talking on the phone, sitting on the couch, and sleeping in bed—that involve using each side of your body differently. Let's examine a situation that most people can relate to: carrying a bag on one shoulder.

You likely started carrying a bag to school when you entered kindergarten. You probably chose which side to carry it on based on whether you are right- or left-handed. The more often you carried your bag on that same shoulder, the more comfortable it became. And without knowing it, you automatically adjusted your entire posture to keep that bag on your shoulder. If you were carrying the bag on your right side, you pulled your right shoulder backward and held your right arm still to prevent the bag from slipping off your shoulder. This subtly twisted your entire torso to the right. You also shifted your rib cage to the left and put more weight on your left leg to balance the weight of the bag.

Believe it or not, you make these postural adjustments every time you carry a bag on one side, even if it's small and lightweight. You make similar adjustments every time you carry anything on one side. Try standing up and holding a bag on one shoulder as you typically do. Then try holding it on the other shoulder. You might feel uncoordinated, and it might even feel like it's impossible to hold it on that side comfortably.

When I ask my students to try carrying their bags on their other shoulders, they usually look at me and say, "But ... I can't." The postural adjustments involved in carrying a bag on one shoulder are so deeply learned that it can feel physically impossible to do the opposite.

You might ask yourself—why is this such a big deal? To a certain extent, it's not. Virtually everyone is right- or left-handed, and as a result you develop motor patterns in which you use the two sides of your body differently. This is a natural part of the way that humans move, and it allows you to perform complex tasks.

But as you already know, when a motor pattern becomes habitual, you tend to become increasingly unaware of it. This lack of awareness allows you to fall deeper and deeper into that pattern.

Carrying a bag on the same shoulder every day of your life can cause the postural adjustments involved to become so deeply learned that without realizing it, you stand and move that way all the time: one shoulder pulled up and back, spine twisted to one side, rib cage and weight shifted to the other side. At some point, the pattern becomes dysfunctional enough that it begins to cause problems. You could feel run-of-the-mill muscle pain, but you could also feel something more serious like a pinched nerve or joint pain due to cartilage being worn away.

It's entirely human to use the sides of your body in different ways. Unfortunately, when your motor patterns become strengthened by a great deal of repetition or when a reaction to an injury worsens your movement patterns, you can find yourself out of balance to the point that you're in pain and causing damage to the structure of your body. It's very important to notice when you're overdoing one-sided movements, and to teach yourself to use the sides of your body more evenly so that you can avoid pain and recurring injuries. We'll talk about how to do this in chapter 15.

Idiopathic Scoliosis

Scoliosis is lateral curvature of the spine (bending to one or both sides). While the natural lordotic and kyphotic curves in the spine help absorb shock, scoliosis is different: There's no natural lateral curve in the spine, and any bend greater than 10 degrees may be diagnosed as scoliosis. While some cases are present at birth or caused by diseases such as cerebral palsy or muscular dystrophy, a 2014 review published in *American Family Physician* found that approximately 85% are classified as idiopathic. In other words, the cause of most scoliosis cases is unknown.

The same review found that between 2% and 4% of teenagers have scoliosis. According to a retrospective study done at Johns Hopkins University, the rate of scoliosis increases to more than 8% in adults over the age of 40. And a 2005 study of 75 healthy adults over the age of 60, with no previous diagnosis of scoliosis or spinal surgery, found the rate of scoliosis to be 68%. This increasing prevalence with age is a strong indicator that learned motor patterns, reactions to physical trauma, and handedness play a role in developing the condition.

According to the review in *American Family Physician*, 85% to 90% of adolescent scoliosis cases involve a thoracic curve that is convex to the right, and around 90% of the population is right-handed. This suggests that the way people habitually use the sides of their bodies due to their handedness can influence the direction of their scoliotic curves.

Scoliosis can be the result of a structural deformity, but most of the time it's caused by muscles pulling the spine out of alignment. Chronic muscular contraction on one side of the spine pulls the vertebrae into a C-shaped curve; contraction on both sides causes an S-curve (Illustration 17). If the curve is greater than 20 to 25 degrees, a brace may be prescribed. If the curve progresses to more than 45 degrees, spinal fusion surgery will most likely be recommended.

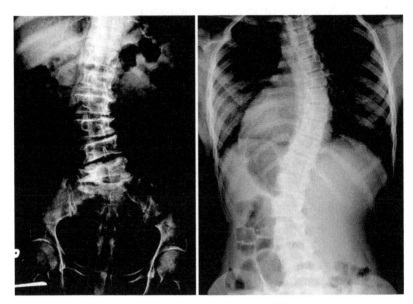

Illustration 17: Left: a C-curve; right: an S-curve
(Puwadol Jaturawutthichai © 123rf.com and draw05 © 123rf.com)

Roughly 66% of adults with scoliotic curves between 20 and 55 degrees experience back pain. Many people with scoliosis also develop pain in other parts of their bodies due to their postural misalignment, which puts uneven stress on the hips, knees, neck, and shoulders. Arthritis, disc and nerve compression in the spine, and difficulty breathing are also common in scoliosis patients.

About 38,000 scoliosis patients in the United States undergo spinal fusion surgery each year. In this procedure, metal rods, hooks, wires, and screws are attached to the spine to force it into a straight position. Then doctors attach pieces of bone, which grow together and create the actual fusion of the spine.

Patients who undergo this type of surgery lose 20% to 60% of their spinal flexibility. The unfused parts of the spine are subject to a great deal of strain, leading to a high rate of disc degeneration and osteoarthritis. A 2008 study published in *Spine* examined 32 spinal fusion patients and found that 75% of them experienced degeneration in their sacroiliac joint after surgery. And sadly, a 2001 study of idiopathic scoliosis patients found that 40% of them experienced no reduction in their pain levels following scoliosis surgery.

In 2008, researchers did a large-scale review of spinal fusion surgery studies, and found that while rates of complications in spinal fusion surgeries vary, they are quite high across the board—up to 89% of patients experience some type of complication. And a large population-based review of lumbar spinal fusion surgeries in Washington state found that in at least 23% of cases the vertebrae did not actually fuse. Even though the vertebrae are usually held in place by hardware, patterns of contraction in the back muscles cause micromovements that prevent continuous bone growth. Muscular contractions can be so strong that metal rods inserted along the spine can actually break, causing a great deal of pain and requiring repeat surgery. Given the high risk of complications and the lack of evidence supporting spinal fusion as an effective treatment, the 2008 review concluded that the surgery can be used to slow or halt progression of spinal curvature, but that it's not an ideal long-term solution.

Attempting to improve a functional spinal curve by using manual force will have little to no effect on the messages sent by the nervous system that cause muscles to contract. A broken bone is a structural issue, and it must be set in place in order to heal. But when your skeleton is pulled out of alignment by your muscles, it's a functional issue; the misalignment is caused by the way that your nervous system is functioning. Idiopathic scoliosis patients who learn how to release the chronic muscular contraction that is causing their curvature typically experience reduction or elimination of pain as well as gradual straightening of their spine.

To learn an exercise that helps to alleviate idiopathic scoliosis, go to: **somaticmovementcenter.com/scoliosis-exercise**

Noticing Postural Patterns

Now that you've learned about the effects of the withdrawal response, action response, and flexor reflex, you'll likely find it difficult not to notice them in everyone you see (the Baader-Meinhof effect). You'll see strangers who are hunched over, their backs and shoulders rounded and their heads sticking forward. You'll be able to tell who among your friends has back pain simply by observing their tight, arched lower backs. You may even look in the mirror and see that one of your shoulders or hips is higher than the other. Don't worry—these are all functional issues that can be alleviated and eliminated with Clinical Somatics exercises.

Stop and think for a few minutes about motor patterns you've developed over the years. As you go through your day, notice your posture, muscle tension, and how you might be using the sides of your body differently as you do the following activities:

- Working on a computer

- Driving your car

- Using your phone

- Sitting to read or watch television

- Sleeping

Do you think that any of your posture or movement habits might be causing muscle tension and contributing to your pain?

CHAPTER 11

Personality and Posture

Look at the photo of two young boys shown in Illustration 18. The one on the left looks relaxed and confident, happy to be the center of attention and to have his picture taken. You can see how he feels by observing his body language: He stands with his pelvis pushed forward and his hands on his hips, opening up his chest and abdominal area. His relaxed stance and easy smile show that he has no worries and does not feel defensive.

Illustration 18: Personality and posture
(Zurijeta © 123rf.com)

In contrast, the boy on the right looks shy and nervous. He's forcing a smile, clearly trying to put on a brave face even though he wishes he could get away from the camera. His upper back is rounded, his chest concave, and his shoulders raised, all of which are reflexive postural reactions to feeling afraid. If confronted by a bully, this boy would likely run the other way—unless his buddy on the left stepped in to defend him first.

How can you tell all this from a photo? Because posture, facial expression, and movement communicate the way you feel inside. Scientists have found that somewhere between 60% and 93% of all communication is nonverbal. This helps explain the desire to use multiple exclamation points and emoticons when sending emails and text messages. When you can't communicate face-to-face, written words aren't enough—you need symbols to convey your emotions.

Body language isn't limited to direct communication with others; it's intrinsically tied to your emotional state. Your feelings are constantly being conveyed through your posture and the way you move, even if you're alone and no one can see you.

If you want to trick someone or make a good impression, you might instinctively try to fake your body language, like the boy in the picture who's smiling despite feeling uncomfortable. In the boy's case, however, his smile is not convincing enough to counter his habitual posture. His withdrawal response has been triggered so many times that he's now stuck in that posture involuntarily most of the time.

Like any habitual motor pattern, you can change your body language through intentional practice and repetition. And by changing your body language, you can actually change the way you feel inside. In 2010, Amy Cuddy of Harvard University and Dana Carney and Andy Yap of Columbia University tested the effects of what they call "power posing," and the results of their research have fascinating real-world applications.

In the study, test subjects had to spend two minutes sitting in either high-power or low-power poses. High-power poses were expansive and open, meaning that the subjects expanded their bodies to take up more space and brought their limbs away from the center of their bodies (similar to the action response). Subjects in low-power poses took up less space and brought their limbs in closer to the center of their bodies (similar to the withdrawal response).

The study measured levels of cortisol and testosterone before and after power posing. Levels of the stress hormone cortisol are typically higher in people who feel powerless, and lower in those who feel powerful. Testosterone is linked to assertiveness, and people with high levels of testosterone typically feel powerful and act confidently.

The high-power posers experienced a spike in testosterone levels and a drop in cortisol levels, while the low-power posers experienced a drop in testosterone and a rise in cortisol. These hormone changes were accompanied by emotional shifts; the high-power posers reported feeling more powerful and were more likely to take a gambling risk after striking their poses than the low-power posers. Incredibly, spending just two minutes in a posture has immediate effects on the way you feel, your behavior, and even your hormone levels. If two minutes in a posture can create such a powerful change in your hormones, emotions, and actions, imagine the effects of spending a lifetime in a certain posture.

Power posing even affects how you perceive pain. Researchers from the University of Toronto and the University of Southern California explored how adopting a dominant or submissive pose affects your pain tolerance. Their findings were quite clear: After holding a dominant pose for just 20 seconds, test subjects showed an increased tolerance for pain.

Power posing helps you feel less pain because it gives you a sense of control. Studies show that when you feel like you have control over a situation, your tolerance for pain increases. Likewise, when you feel like you're not in control, your tolerance for pain is reduced. Power posing also increases testosterone levels, which further increases your tolerance for pain.

So your motor patterns affect the way you feel inside and how you behave, especially once the patterns have become habitual. Can you then predict which habitual posture a person will develop based on their personality? To some degree, the answer is yes. In a study comparing personality and posture, researchers from McGill University and the San Diego University for Integrative Studies found striking correlations between posture and extroversion.

The researchers separated their test subjects into groups based on four different habitual postures, shown in Illustration 19: ideal, kyphosis-lordosis (in which the kyphotic and lordotic curves are exaggerated), swayback (in which the lumbar curve is decreased and the hips are in front of the ankles), and flat back (in which the lumbar curve is flat). The study showed that 96% of the subjects who had ideal posture and 83% of the subjects who had kyphosis-lordosis posture were extroverts. The introverts, on the other hand, were far more likely to stand with either a swayback or flat back.

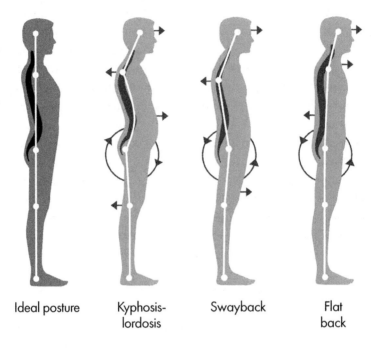

Ideal posture   Kyphosis-   Swayback   Flat
lordosis   back

Illustration 19: Habitual postures
(adapted from elenabsl © 123rf.com)

These results are quite remarkable, especially when you look at the position of the lower back and pelvis in these postures. Extroverts tended to hold their pelvis upright or tipped forward, resulting in a natural or enhanced arch in their lower back. In other words, the people who were more confident and outgoing had adopted the powerful posture of the action response.

The introverts, in contrast, had a strong tendency to contract their abdominal muscles and tuck their pelvis under—the submissive posture of the withdrawal response—flattening the natural lumbar curve and bringing them into flat back or swayback posture.

The study also found that the people who adopted the three nonideal postures had more muscle tension than those who had ideal posture.

This should come as no surprise because as you've already learned, your muscles have to stay contracted to keep you in unnatural postures. Predictably, people with the three nonideal postures also experienced more back and neck pain than those with ideal posture.

Your personality—the unique combination of emotional and behavioral characteristics that make you who you are—causes you to adopt certain postures and movement patterns. As you repeat these patterns over and over, they become deeply learned habits. Over time, the learned patterns themselves contribute to the way you feel and behave. Your personality and your learned motor patterns work in tandem to keep you stuck in habitual ways of standing, moving, feeling, and acting. This means you can literally change your personality by changing how you use your body. You can become more resilient in the face of pain, feel more confident, and experience far less stress by releasing chronic muscle tension, changing your posture, and creating new movement patterns.

The Connection between Posture and Emotions

Try moving your body in the following ways to help you increase your awareness of how your posture can almost immediately affect your emotions.

1. Slouch. Let your chest collapse, tighten your abs, round your shoulders forward. How do you feel in this position? What emotions or sensations do you notice? Does this put strain on your neck, shoulders, or lower back? Do you feel pain in any area of your body in this posture?

2. Adopt a power pose. Put your hands on your hips and stick out your chest. Tilt your head slightly upward, and tilt your pelvis slightly forward so that your lower back arch is exaggerated. How do you feel in this position? What emotions or sensations do you notice? Does this put strain on your neck, shoulders, or lower back? Do you feel pain in any area of your body in this posture?

3. Consider how your thoughts and emotions may contribute to your habitual posture and movement. Throughout the day, start noticing when certain postural patterns are triggered and if they

affect how you feel. Do certain postures or movements make your tension or pain worse?

Noticing connections like this will help you become more aware of how your personality and posture work together. When you feel muscle tension, stress, or pain, try changing your posture to help yourself feel better.

CHAPTER 12

Automatic Imitation

You're interviewing for a new job and the competition is stiff. Your potential boss, Mr. Peterson, leans forward in his chair, gesturing passionately as he discusses the issues his company is facing. You lean forward, listening intently and responding with equally strong ideas and gestures. Mr. Peterson then leans back in his chair and asks you to explain your thoughts further. You lean back and go into detail about your plan to get the company back on track.

Liking what he's hearing, Mr. Peterson crosses his legs and leans on his right elbow. You settle into the same posture and continue to explain your plan. The two of you discuss the future of the company, each nodding along as the other talks. As you leave, Mr. Peterson thinks to himself, "I really liked that guy. He had great ideas and I felt like we were on the same page."

You've nailed the interview, thanks in large part to your instinctive use of imitation. Your strong desire to establish rapport with Mr. Peterson made you subconsciously mimic his body language. As a result, he felt a connection with you, was receptive to your ideas, and genuinely liked you.

While scientists have known about automatic imitation in animals since the mid-eighteenth century, it wasn't until recently that the underlying mechanism of the behavior became clear. In the 1990s, Italian neuroscientist Giacomo Rizzolatti and a group of researchers at the University of Parma discovered specialized brain cells called "mirror neurons" in monkeys.

In 2010, researchers found mirror neurons in parts of the human brain that are responsible for movement, vision, and memory. As in the monkeys, these cells are activated equally when you perform an action and when you observe another person performing the same action. Like pretty much everything that happens automatically in your nervous system, the way these neurons function helps you survive. Automatically imitating other people's postures and movements establishes a sense of affinity and facilitates communication, both of which are vital elements in forming relationships and creating a healthy group dynamic.

Automatic imitation also plays a role in your ability to perceive others' emotions, an essential skill in maintaining relationships and communicating. When test subjects are given facial injections of Botox, a medical grade of the botulinum neurotoxin, the facial muscles are paralyzed because the signals from the motor nerves are blocked. This impairs not only the subjects' ability to mimic facial expressions, but to perceive emotions as well. Sensory feedback from muscular contractions in facial expressions is critical to the ability to understand what others are feeling.

You tend to subconsciously imitate the people around you. You also tend to imitate people with whom you want to create rapport. As you initially develop motor patterns during childhood, you subconsciously imitate your family members' posture and movement. So if you think you get your posture from your mother, you could be right—but genetics doesn't have much to do with it.

Automatic imitation is so dependent on social relationships that animals even imitate their human owners. Recent studies show that dogs yawn contagiously when their owners yawn, and that they can't help imitating their owners' actions even when a food reward should compel them to do the opposite.

Teenagers often display a great deal of automatic imitation due to their strong desire to fit in and be accepted. Teenagers want so badly to be part of a group that their subconscious minds work overtime to create similarities between themselves and their peers. At this age, habitual postures learned from friends may override those learned from parents and siblings.

As an adult, new motor patterns are formed as you subconsciously imitate your partner. Mirror neurons fire when you merely observe someone you want to connect with, so simply spending time with your partner can lead to changes in your posture and movement. As you walk down the street, notice couples who walk at the same pace with the same gait and posture.

Noticing Automatic Imitation

Take a few moments to think about how your posture and movement patterns may have been shaped by family members, friends, and the people you spend the most time with. Does anyone close to you have a noticeable postural pattern, and have you mimicked it to any degree? Or, has someone close to you adopted your habitual posture, movements, or mannerisms?

As you go through your daily life, notice how you automatically mirror other people's body language while talking or spending time with them. When you're chatting with someone who's leaning on one side or crossing their arms, do you subconsciously do the same? You may be surprised by how much automatic imitation affects the way you stand and move.

CHAPTER 13

Athletic Training

You and the pitcher are staring each other down, motionless, trying to read each other's minds. You watch him shift his weight, wind up, and release the ball. A moment later, you hear the crack of your bat hitting the ball, and watch the ball soar off into center field. Your brain took in everything you saw about the pitcher's preparation, made the decision about what type of swing would be most likely to hit his pitch, and sent messages to your muscles to contract in a specific, complex sequence—all in less than half a second.

During a game, competition, or performance, there's little time for conscious decision-making; every reaction must happen instantaneously and accurately. That's why athletes practice so much. It's not just about being in the best possible physical condition. It's about training the entire neuromuscular system to be able to react automatically and with precision while under stress.

Athletes spend so much time consciously training with the goal of acquiring muscle memory so that their motor patterns become very deeply learned. And depending on what sport or discipline they practice, they may have to train themselves to move in ways that put excess strain on certain parts of their bodies.

Athletes' movement patterns are also shaped by stress, personality, and all of the other factors we've already talked about. When combined with the training required by their chosen sport, the result is that their patterns of habitual muscle tension can be more complex than those of nonathletes.

Sometimes athletic training will improve an individual's posture and movement, helping to correct imbalances and increase overall strength and flexibility. But in many cases, the great number of repetitions or the strain of heavy weights required by athletic training can enhance existing dysfunctional patterns.

For example, a beginning runner whose internally rotated hips have created a knock-kneed stance may have no pain at all until she starts to train for a marathon. Her movement patterns are then put to the test, and she quickly develops pain in her knees and ankles.

Likewise, a man who habitually stands with an arched lower back may have no issues until he decides to get in shape and start weight lifting. His back muscles become tighter with each repetition; soon his lower back aches constantly and the compression of his lumbar spine leads to bulging discs.

Some types of athletic training magnify your natural functions of handedness, demanding a great deal from your dominant side. Many sports require throwing, hitting, or kicking a ball with great force and precision, over and over again. Other disciplines, like gymnastics and dance, require jumping, balancing, and turning movements to be performed repeatedly on one side, shifting the body weight and creating imbalances in posture and strength. The sheer overuse of one side of your body is likely to lead to excess muscle tension, fatigue, and structural breakdown.

Young Athletes

Those who start their athletic training at a young age may be at increased risk of developing overuse injuries because their musculoskeletal system is not fully developed. Their bones are growing quickly, and sometimes their muscles and connective tissues have not become long or strong enough to support the size of their skeleton. One in three children who compete in sports suffers pain or an injury serious enough to make them miss a game or practice. Many of these injuries will stay with them for their entire lives, even if they switch sports or stop training altogether.

In addition to children's undeveloped physical structures, another part of the problem is that they specialize in sports far too early. If you have a child, encourage them to play more than one sport. Children who play two or three sports suffer fewer injuries than those who play just one, because they learn how to move in varied ways depending on which sport they're playing; this also gives rest to overused muscles during each off-season.

Common sense dictates, and research shows, that preseason conditioning, functional training, and education about proper body mechanics helps prevent injuries in young athletes. The emphasis should be on preparation for future success and health, rather than performance. If a quarterback needs to throw the football farther, his coach should first address how he's throwing the ball rather than focusing on the immediate goal of increasing yardage. Most likely, his passes will get longer as his technique and body mechanics improve. All great athletes know that improved performance comes primarily from improved technique, not simply from increased strength or speed.

Why You Become Injured

Numerous studies have shown strong correlations between body mechanics and incidence of sports injuries. Researchers at the Sports Injuries Research Centre in Limerick, Ireland, performed a two-year study with soccer players and found that back, knee, and ankle injuries, as well as muscle strains, were all linked to dysfunctional postural habits such as swayback, lumbar lordosis, kyphosis, scoliosis, and lower leg misalignment.

They even tested the athletes' abilities to accurately sense the alignment of their legs, and found that faulty proprioception was a predictor of ankle sprains. Other studies have had similar results, showing that misalignment of the pelvis and legs leads to anterior cruciate ligament injuries, and that athletes with poor lower back posture are more likely to suffer hamstring strains.

Training that creates and enhances damaging patterns is not the only reason athletes suffer injuries. Athletes are also at high risk for injury because they tend to play through the pain. The desire to be tough and keep going often prevents athletes from taking care of themselves and being proactive about their pain and injuries.

Also, the stress that athletes experience during competition sends endogenous opioids coursing through their bloodstream, dulling any pain they might experience. Many athletes ignore subtle warning signs of an injury, like soreness or mild pain, until it gets bad enough to affect their performance. By that point, however, their injury has progressed to the point at which considerable rest and retraining will be necessary to allow the injury to heal and prevent it from reoccurring.

Unless you're on the brink of winning an Olympic gold medal or the Super Bowl, playing through the pain of an injury is probably not worth it. Taking a game or a season off is difficult, but damaging your body permanently, being in chronic pain, and cutting your career short is far worse. If you notice a slight pain or strange sensation when practicing or competing, you can reduce the likelihood of sustaining a serious injury by slowing down, taking a break, and trying to figure out what is causing the pain. The worse you let it get, the more damage you'll do, and the more time you'll have to take off. Pushing past the pain may make you seem tough, strong, and brave, but it may lead to serious injury and reduced athletic performance over time.

At this point it might seem like I'm not in favor of athletic training, but quite the opposite is true. In addition to the endless physiological benefits that come from regular exercise, studies show that serious athletic training teaches discipline, increases life satisfaction, and improves your sense of well-being. Athletes and coaches simply need to have a stronger focus on training proper movement patterns. Everyone should put a higher value on injury prevention and recovery than on risky short-term performance gains. As the saying goes, train smarter, not harder.

The Benefits of Clinical Somatic Education for Athletes

Clinical Somatic Education has profound benefits for any type of athlete. Clinical Somatics exercises keep your muscles flexible and your joints moving freely, and are a much more effective method than static stretching for cooling down and releasing muscle tension after a workout.

Most importantly, Clinical Somatics exercises give you a high degree of awareness and control over your posture and movement. With regular practice, you'll develop the ability to use your body in an extremely precise way. Your heightened level of proprioception will allow you to sense when your movements are the slightest bit off, and change the way you're moving before your pain gets worse or you suffer an injury.

Noticing Your Athletic Movement Patterns

Do you or have you ever worked out or played sports? If so, go through the following exercises and reflect on the questions to see how the movement patterns from your athletic activities may be impacting your current patterns and pain.

1. **List every sport you've played and every kind of athletic activity you've done.**

   This includes general exercise, weight lifting, and training programs. If you're an extreme athlete, focus on your most recent sports and training programs.

2. **Practice each movement from your sport or athletic activity slowly.**

   Which movements do you or did you tend to do most often in each of your activities? Once you've identified them, slowly move your body through each one. Aim to take at least 10 seconds to complete the movement from beginning to end, as if you were a sloth.

   If you do push-ups, for example, do one very slowly. As you go through the movement, notice which muscles are contracting. Does the movement seem fluid and easy, or difficult and strained? Are some of your muscles tight or loose, and do your joints seem stiff, make noises, or pop? Notice how you feel as you slowly go through each movement.

3. **Reflect on every injury you've had, and anywhere in your body you currently feel pain.**

   Notice if any of the movements you just practiced triggered pain or reminded you of past injuries. See if you can figure out why you suffered from those injuries and which movement patterns currently contribute to your pain.

   Don't worry if you can't figure it all out right now. You'll learn much more as you continue to increase your awareness of your movements with Clinical Somatics exercises.

In the next chapter, you'll learn how muscle tension and motor patterns lead to specific types of pain, and how your patterns can actually damage the structure of your body. You'll also learn some simple exercises you can do at home to relieve some of the most common pain conditions.

CHAPTER 14

How Your Patterns Lead to Common Pain Conditions

Muscle Spasms and Cramps

You may have a friend who throws his back out every few months and has to spend several days lying flat on his back in bed. Or maybe you're the unlucky one who's had to call for help getting up off the floor. Muscle spasms are no fun at all, and they can be incapacitating when experienced in the back or neck.

Muscle spasms typically occur in muscles that are already being held chronically tight. When you get back spasms, it usually happens when you're doing something seemingly innocuous like reaching for a cup of coffee or bending over to brush your teeth. A small movement can put a little extra strain on your already tight back muscles, causing the stretch reflex to kick in, automatically contracting your back muscles even more in order to prevent the fibers from tearing.

Muscle spasms can last just a few moments, or they can go on for many days. Typically the pain will gradually decrease as the muscles slowly relax and return to their normal resting level of tension.

One factor that can hinder this process is your natural tendency to hold painful parts of your body stiff. You do this subconsciously to "splint" an injured body part and prevent further pain that might be caused by movement. Unfortunately, in the case of muscle spasms, you can increase your own pain by keeping the spasmodic muscles and surrounding muscles tight. This prevents the movement that is necessary for you to regain voluntary control.

In contrast to muscle spasms, muscle cramps are short-lived, intense, involuntary contractions. Dehydration and electrolyte imbalance were long thought to be responsible for cramping; however, there's little evidence for this theory. Cramping occurs most often in high-level athletes, and studies have found no electrolyte changes or body weight changes in these groups after performance. Research shows that repetitive muscle contraction, muscular fatigue, and the resulting loss of neuromuscular control are likely responsible. Scientists hypothesize that when proprioceptors in your muscles become overexcited, their relaxation phase is reduced, resulting in a strong, painful contraction.

Cramping can occur in nonathletes too. Women who wear high heels, for example, experience cramps in their calves and feet because those muscles are kept in a shortened, contracted state all day long. By the end of the day they're fatigued from the constant contraction.

How can you prevent muscle spasms and cramps? By reducing your resting level of muscle tension, relearning natural, efficient movement patterns, and allowing yourself time to rest when doing intense exercise.

To learn a simple exercise that reduces tension in the lower back muscles and helps prevent lower back spasms, go to: **somaticmovementcenter.com/back-pain-exercise**

Sciatica and Piriformis Syndrome

As you learned in chapter 2, the sciatic nerve is the largest and thickest in the human body. It's formed by nerves that exit the spine between the fourth lumbar vertebra and the third sacral vertebra; the nerves merge and run through the buttocks and all the way down each leg. It's responsible for much of the sensory and motor innervation of your legs and feet.

When your sciatic nerve is compressed, you may feel shooting pain, a burning sensation, tingling, numbness, or weakness in your legs and feet. Sciatica symptoms are generally caused when the roots of the nerves exiting the spine are compressed between the vertebrae by a bulging disc, or when the sciatic nerve is compressed after it has exited the spine.

In a small portion of the population, the sciatic nerve runs through a gluteal muscle called the piriformis instead of underneath it. For these people, chronic tightness in the piriformis can also compress the sciatic nerve, causing piriformis syndrome. The symptoms of sciatica and piriformis syndrome are the same; the distinction is made based on where the nerve compression occurs.

Sciatica and piriformis syndrome are most often caused by chronically tight lower back and gluteal muscles that compress the spine and the sciatic nerve. The symptoms typically clear up once the muscle tension is released and the dysfunctional movement patterns are retrained.

To learn two exercises that you can do to alleviate sciatica and piriformis syndrome, go to: **somaticmovementcenter.com/sciatica-exercise**

If you're experiencing nerve sensations like tingling, numbness, burning, shooting pain, or weakness elsewhere in your body, you may have radiculopathy (nerve compression) occurring in a different part of your spine. Like sciatica and piriformis syndrome, many cases of radiculopathy are caused by chronic muscle tension that compresses the spine. You can get a good idea of where your nerve compression is occurring by looking at the dermatome map in Illustration 20. A dermatome is an area of skin innervated by a single spinal nerve. To use the map, identify where you feel nerve sensation on your body, and find it on the diagram. The corresponding spinal nerve, labeled in the diagram, is the likely source of nerve compression.

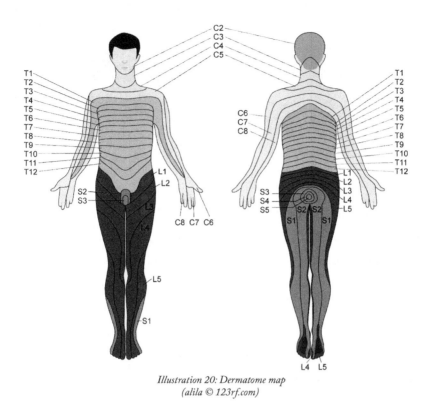

Illustration 20: Dermatome map
(alila © 123rf.com)

Thoracic Outlet Syndrome

If you feel shooting pain, numbness, weakness, or tingling in your arms or hands, you might have thoracic outlet syndrome. It's a condition in which the bundle of nerves and blood vessels responsible for sensation, motor control, and circulation in the arm is compressed. The bundle of nerves, called the brachial plexus, travels through the scalene muscles of the neck, between the collarbone and first rib (the area known as the thoracic outlet), under the pectoralis minor muscle, and around the humerus. If the bundle is compressed at any point along its path, you may feel the symptoms of thoracic outlet syndrome (Illustration 21).

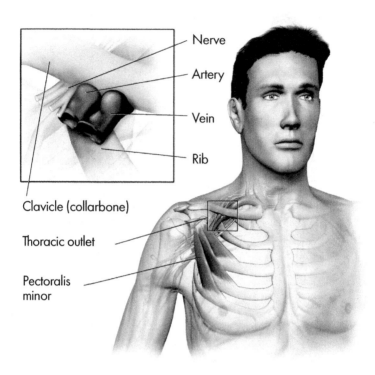

Nerve

Artery

Vein

Rib

Clavicle (collarbone)

Thoracic outlet

Pectoralis
minor

Illustration 21: Thoracic outlet syndrome
(BruceBlaus © Wikimedia Commons)

Chronic muscle tightness in the neck, chest, and front of the shoulders leads to the compression that causes most cases of thoracic outlet syndrome. This syndrome often occurs in people who repeatedly contract these muscles, like musicians, electricians, computer workers, and athletes like swimmers and baseball players. Thoracic outlet syndrome also occurs when people have had an injury like a broken arm and must keep their arm in a sling for a long period of time. The neck, chest, and shoulders become tight due to both lack of use and instinctive protecting of the injured area.

To learn two exercises that release chronic muscle tension in the chest and shoulders, helping to alleviate thoracic outlet syndrome, go to: **somaticmovementcenter.com/thoracic-outlet-exercise**

Iliopsoas Syndrome

The psoas (SO - as) muscle, formally called the psoas major, attaches the lumbar vertebrae to the lesser trochanter of the femur. The psoas muscle is often grouped with the iliacus muscle; together they're referred to as the iliopsoas (Illustration 22). Due to its location deep within the core of the body, the iliopsoas is difficult to feel with your hands and to sense internally.

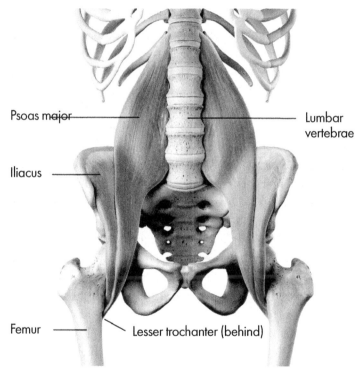

Psoas major — Lumbar vertebrae

Iliacus —

Femur — Lesser trochanter (behind)

Illustration 22: The iliopsoas
(adapted from Sebastian Kaulitzki © 123rf.com)

The iliopsoas performs several important actions:

- It flexes the hip, meaning that when it contracts it brings the knee in toward the stomach. If you spend a lot of time sitting, your iliopsoas is likely tight as a result of spending so much time in a shortened state.

- It rotates the hip laterally, allowing you to stand like a ballet dancer with your feet pointed outward. Dancers often have a great deal of tightness in their iliopsoas.

- It adducts the hip, bringing the leg in toward the center of the body. If you squeeze your knees together, you're engaging your adductor muscles.

- Because of its attachments to the lumbar vertebrae, the iliopsoas contributes to lateral tilting of the pelvis (hiking the hips up one at a time) and lateral flexion of the spine (bending the spine to one side).

"Iliopsoas syndrome" is a convenient way to refer to the symptoms that often result from chronic tightness in the iliopsoas: pain in the lower back, hips, buttocks, pelvis, or groin, popping or snapping of the hip joint, radiating pain down the leg, or limping. A tight iliopsoas can also contribute to functional leg length discrepancy, idiopathic scoliosis, instability in the core of the body, and limited flexibility in the lower back.

The most common condition resulting from chronic tightness in the iliopsoas is lower back pain. When your iliopsoas is tight and you're standing up, the contraction brings your lower back into hyperlordosis, or a greater than normal degree of arching. This compresses the lumbar vertebrae and brings all of the lower back muscles into a shortened state. The result is muscular tension and pain, disc problems, sciatica, and a tendency to throw the lower back into spasm.

It's safe to say that most people, from office workers to professional athletes, have some chronic tightness in their iliopsoas. In addition to overuse and limited movement, physical and emotional trauma have been linked to iliopsoas tension. Because it is deep within the core of your body, the iliopsoas instinctively tightens up when you feel stress or fear. This is part of the withdrawal response that you learned about in chapter 9. For some people, learning to let go of the tension in their iliopsoas is an intense emotional process. It's totally normal if you feel strong emotions when doing the following iliopsoas exercise, or any somatic exercises, because your nervous system is releasing old patterns that are linked to your emotions, stressful experiences, and basic survival instincts.

To learn an exercise that releases chronic tightness in the iliopsoas, go to: **somaticmovementcenter.com/iliopsoas-exercise**

Functional Leg Length Discrepancy

Leg length discrepancy, which can be found in at least 70% of the population, means that the legs are unequal in length. Some cases are anatomical (or structural), meaning that there is a measured difference in the length of the bones of the leg, or a difference in the structures of the hip, knee, or ankle joints. Other cases are functional, meaning that an imbalance in the muscles, tendons, and ligaments of the hip and leg makes one leg seem longer than the other.

Whether anatomical or functional, unequal leg length can create a great deal of uneven stress on the structure of your body. Leg length discrepancy is associated with lower back pain, lumbar scoliosis, pain and arthritis in the hips and knees, tightness in the iliotibial band, patellar tendinitis, Achilles tendinitis, stress fractures, and misalignment of the knees and ankles.

Functional leg length discrepancy is not always painful, but it is bothersome and often misdiagnosed as a structural issue. Most cases are caused by muscles that have become chronically, involuntarily contracted. Tight muscles in the waist and lower back can laterally tilt your pelvis, hiking one side up higher than the other. Tight gluteal muscles and hip rotators can also contribute to one leg appearing to be longer than the other.

The most common treatment for leg length discrepancy is to put a lift in the shoe of the shorter leg. This theoretically evens out the length of the legs, relieving the uneven stress on the joints, bones, and soft tissues. In cases of functional leg length discrepancy, however, a lift does not address the cause of the problem and can actually make symptoms worse by allowing the muscular imbalances to become more pronounced.

To release the chronically tight muscles that cause functional leg length discrepancy, go to:

somaticmovementcenter.com/leg-length-exercise

Plantar Fasciitis

The plantar fascia is a thick band of connective tissue that runs along the underside of the foot, from the heel bone to the metatarsals. Its function is to support the arch of the foot by carrying tension when the foot bears weight. When too much is demanded of the plantar fascia, either as a result of repetitive movements, constant strain from tight muscles, or excessive body weight, the tissue can become inflamed and degenerate.

Plantar fasciitis is most often experienced by runners and people who are overweight. But since only a portion of these folks ever feel plantar fasciitis pain, we know that overuse is only part of the problem. Habitual posture and movement patterns that cause chronic tightness along the back of the legs and bottom of the feet are the other main contributing factor. Improper footwear, which I'll talk about in chapter 15, can also be a culprit.

To learn exercises that you can do to alleviate plantar fasciitis, go to: **somaticmovementcenter.com/plantar-fasciitis-exercise**

Carpal Tunnel Syndrome

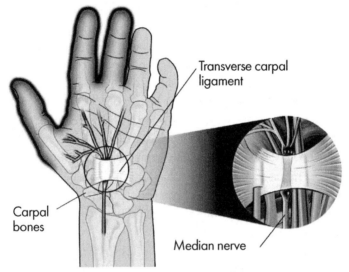

Illustration 23: Carpal tunnel syndrome
(adapted from Alessandro Innamorati © 123rf.com)

The median nerve, which innervates portions of the forearm and hand, passes between the carpal bones and transverse carpal ligament of the wrist (Illustration 23). When this nerve is compressed you experience carpal tunnel syndrome, a condition characterized by shooting pain, burning, tingling, numbness, and weakness in the hand or wrist. Carpal tunnel syndrome typically occurs in people who do repetitive tasks with their hands, such as computer workers, massage therapists, and assembly line workers.

The joints of your extremities, like the wrists, are designed to do less work than the joints closer to the center of your body. In a reaching movement, for example, most of the range of motion should come from a bending or twisting of the spine. Then the shoulder blade will slide to allow more movement, and lastly the arm and hand joints will articulate as needed to complete the task. People who experience carpal tunnel syndrome typically have chronic tension in their torso and shoulder in addition to the wrist and hand, and have developed movement patterns in which they overuse their wrist joint and underuse the core of their body. They demand far more movement from their wrist than the joint is equipped to do, and irritation, inflammation, and pain occur as a result.

To learn exercises that alleviate carpal tunnel syndrome, go to: **somaticmovementcenter.com/carpal-tunnel-exercise**

Temporomandibular Joint Disorders

The temporomandibular joints (TMJ) connect the mandible, or jawbone, to each side of the skull. They open and close the jaw, and allow the jaw to slide from side to side as well as forward and backward.

TMJ disorders include many problems in and around the jaw, most often caused by dysfunctional motor patterns and chronic tension in the muscles that move the jawbone. Many people with TMJ disorders have habitual patterns of muscular tension and pain in their neck and shoulders as well.

Stress is a major factor in developing tightness in and around the jaw. Stress causes you to clench your jaw and grind your teeth, even in your sleep. Learning to keep the jaw relaxed and identifying the sources of stress that trigger the pattern often allow TMJ issues to resolve swiftly.

To learn simple exercises you can do to alleviate temporomandibular jaw disorders, go to: **somaticmovementcenter.com/tmj-exercise**

Headache

Over 45 million Americans suffer from chronic headaches. Headaches are one of the most frustrating pain conditions because the causes are so varied and can seem completely mysterious. In fact, over 150 different recognized types have been established by the International Classification of Headache Disorders. It's estimated that the cost of missed work and medical bills related to headaches totals about $50 billion per year.

There are no nociceptors in the brain tissue itself, so headaches are felt in areas surrounding the brain: the head and neck muscles, blood vessels, eyes, ears, sinuses, and the membrane lining the outer surface of the skull. According to the National Headache Foundation, 78% of all headaches are classified as tension headaches, which can be brought on by habitual muscular contraction as well as stress, anxiety, or injury. Tension headaches typically feel dull and aching, as if a band is tightening around your head.

The second most common type of headache is migraine, which causes severe pain and is often accompanied by vision changes or nausea. Migraine headaches can be hereditary; two genes have been identified that are present in about half of migraine sufferers. It's believed these headaches are brought on when the trigeminal nerve, the largest of the cranial nerves, releases irritating chemicals that cause blood vessels on the surface of the brain to swell. Migraine pain is often felt in the eyes or temples. Migraines can be triggered by many controllable factors like lack of sleep, certain foods, missing a meal, stress, caffeine withdrawal, alcohol, and medications.

After muscle tension and migraine, there's a seemingly never-ending list of other causes of headaches: sinus pressure, viral infection, stress, premenstrual symptoms, stroke, high blood pressure, dehydration, caffeine withdrawal, alcohol consumption, allergies, celiac disease, heavy metal poisoning, carbon monoxide poisoning, and brain conditions such as infection, tumor, and aneurysm. In addition, medication-overuse or "rebound" headaches can occur when people take pain medication more than three times per week. Yes, that's right—the exact medication that's supposed to relieve your headaches can actually cause them.

If you suffer from chronic headaches, it will help both you and your doctor immensely if you begin to keep a headache journal. Spend a few weeks writing down everything you eat and drink, your sleep patterns, exercise habits, and sources of stress. Record everything about the headaches you experience: when they come on, how long they last, and what they feel like. Notice if relaxing activities, like soaking in a hot tub or going on vacation, reduce your headache symptoms. If they do, stress and muscular tension are probably contributing to your headaches.

You'll likely have to go through a process of experimentation and elimination to discover which factor or factors are causing your headaches. While it might take some time, it's worth it. Just because headaches are common doesn't mean you have to live with them.

To learn exercises that release muscle tension in the shoulders, chest, neck, and face, relieving tension headache pain, go to:

somaticmovementcenter.com/headache-exercise

When Function Changes Structure

Your body can only withstand so much. When a damaging movement pattern continues for a long period of time, your structure begins to break down. Constant compression, limited movement, and unnatural movement patterns cause soft tissues to tear, intervertebral discs to thin or rupture, cartilage in your joints to wear away, and stress fractures to form in otherwise healthy bones. The following structural issues are most often caused by functional problems—the way you're using your body.

Tendinosis

Tendons are a type of connective tissue that serve the important function of connecting muscles to bones. They're made up of densely packed collagen fibers arranged in parallel along with a small amount of a protein called elastin, which allows tendons to return to their normal length after contracting or stretching.

When tendons are injured, inflammation will occur and cause pain. This condition is called tendinitis; the suffix "–itis" refers to an acute, or sudden-onset, condition. Most tendon pain, however, is actually caused by degeneration rather than acute inflammation. This means that most tendon pain is actually "tendinosis," indicated by the suffix "–osis," which refers to a chronic condition. In these cases, inflammation is not present, and the color of the tendon has turned from a healthy shiny white to a dull gray or brown. The tough collagen fibers have become soft, developed microtears, and have begun to lose their ability to bear tension.

So if painful inflammatory substances aren't present in tendinosis, why is it painful? Research shows that degenerating tendons contain high levels of the amino acid glutamate, and it's likely that this is at least partly responsible for the pain.

Dysfunctional movement patterns and general overuse of joints are the main causes of tendinosis. Demanding too much of a tendon, or making it move in a way it's not designed to, will gradually break down and weaken its collagen fibers.

Tendon pain, whether it's "–itis" caused by inflammation or "–osis" caused by degeneration, can be quite frustrating because tendons can take a long time to heal. Tendons have limited blood supply, so the healing and rebuilding process can take much longer than it does with muscle or skin.

When you're trying to heal a painful tendon, it's always a good idea to take a break from the activity that's causing the pain so that the joint has a chance to rest. You also need to address your full-body patterns of movement that are putting excess strain on the joint. By retraining your movement patterns and increasing your activity level gradually, you should be able to resume your normal activities without pain. And by learning new movement patterns that don't put unnatural strain on your tendons, you'll be able to prevent future damage.

Bursitis

In every joint there are bursae, small sacs of connective tissue filled with synovial fluid, which reduces friction in joints. Bursae look like little water balloons. They sit between bones and tendons, cushioning the joint and allowing tendons to move easily over bone. When you overuse a joint, new bursae can actually grow to provide extra protection.

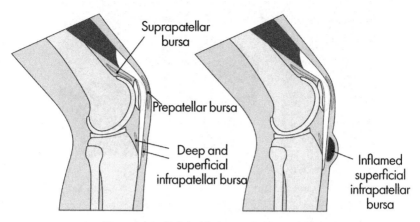

Illustration 24: Left: healthy knee; right: knee with bursitis
(Aksana Kulchytskaya © 123rf.com)

Bursitis occurs when a bursa gets inflamed and causes pain (Illustration 24). When you repeat the same movement over and over, the tendon rubs repeatedly against the bursa, and after a while the bursa can become irritated. The inflammatory process increases the amount of synovial fluid inside the bursa, and the increased pressure from the fluid causes pain. Muscles around the painful joint will often tighten up to splint the injury, limiting range of motion and compressing the joint—leading to even more pain. Bursitis can occur in any joint, but most often develops in the shoulder, elbow, hip, or knee.

Like tendinosis, bursitis most often results from overuse. Take a break from the activity that's causing the pain and damage so the joint has a chance to rest. You also need to retrain your full-body patterns of movement that are putting excess pressure and strain on the joint.

Adhesive Capsulitis (Frozen Shoulder)

Every joint is protected by a joint capsule, a sleeve of dense connective tissue that encases the cartilage and synovial fluid. In adhesive capsulitis, the joint capsule of the glenohumeral (shoulder) joint gradually becomes thicker and tighter, restricting movement and causing pain (Illustration 25).

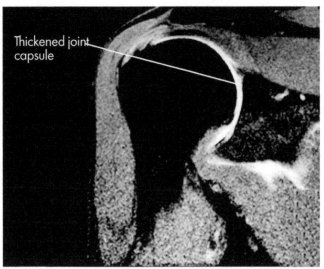

Illustration 25: Frozen shoulder
(RSatUSZ © Wikimedia Commons)

Adhesive capsulitis is often directly related to lack of movement, as it typically occurs in people who have undergone surgery or had an injury for which they had to keep their arm immobilized. Connective tissue adapts to the amount of movement demanded from it, becoming tighter with less movement and looser with more. This adaptation can lead to a vicious cycle: As connective tissues get tighter, movement becomes more difficult and sometimes painful, limiting movement further and causing the tissues to tighten even more.

To learn exercises that alleviate frozen shoulder, go to: **somaticmovementcenter.com/shoulder-exercise**

Disc Degeneration

Spinal problems are among the most common issues resulting from dysfunctional movement habits. Made up of 24 articulating vertebrae, plus the fused sacral vertebrae and bones of the coccyx, the spine is a miraculous feat of engineering. It allows you to bend forward and backward, side to side, and twist from right to left. The vertebral column protects the spinal cord while bearing a great deal of weight and absorbing shock as you run, jump, and lift heavy objects.

The discs that sit in between each vertebra are incredibly strong and resilient. Each is made of a tough outer layer of collagen fibers, called the annulus fibrosus, surrounding a soft core of a gel-like substance called the nucleus pulposus. The two structures work together to distribute pressure across the disc; this provides essential cushioning between the vertebrae and allows for bending, twisting, shock absorption, and weight bearing.

As you build up habitual muscle tension in your back, neck, and trunk, you put increasing pressure on your spine, and your intervertebral discs suffer the consequences. The more the discs are compressed, the looser and weaker the fibers of the annulus fibrosus become. When compression is constant, a disc will begin to bulge or protrude from its normal boundaries. Sometimes it will press on a nerve root or the spinal cord, causing pain or another nerve sensation. If the bulge doesn't press on nerve tissue, you may not feel anything at all.

If a disc is put under a great deal of strain from constant compression or a sudden increase in pressure, it can rupture, or herniate, allowing the contents of the nucleus pulposus to leak out. While this sounds like permanent damage, injured discs can actually heal if given the chance. The inflammatory process automatically kicks in to repair the disc, and if compression on the spine is reduced and muscular patterns are improved, a ruptured disc can heal and resume its normal size and function.

To learn a simple exercise that releases muscle tension in the lower back, relieving pressure on the lumbar spine, go to:

somaticmovementcenter.com/back-pain-exercise

Osteoarthritis

Constant compression and imbalanced movement patterns also affect the cartilage in joints throughout the body. Cartilage is a connective tissue that provides padding and protection in between bones. Most cartilage does not have a blood supply of its own, so it relies on the pumping action from joint movement to diffuse blood and other nutrients through joint fluid. Too much compression and too little compression both spell trouble for cartilage; it needs a moderate amount of movement, involving regular loading and unloading of weight, to remain healthy.

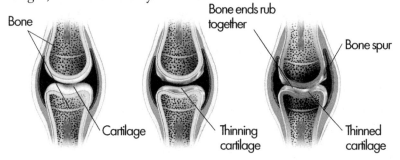

Illustration 26: Left: Healthy joint; center and right: joints with osteoarthritis (guniita © 123rf.com)

Your cartilage constantly grows, maintains, and rebuilds itself throughout your life. Due to the indirect way it receives nutrients, however, the process is fairly slow. If cartilage repair can't keep up with the rate at which you do damage, cartilage cells can wear away completely. The cells that produce new cartilage, called chondrocytes, are unable to migrate outside of their designated area, so once an area of cartilage is completely worn away, it's gone for good.

The painful condition of osteoarthritis results from a loss of healthy cartilage (Illustration 26). Without the essential padding in between bones, joints become quite stiff and painful. Muscles surrounding these painful joints tighten reflexively, worsening the condition by limiting range of motion. Bones that rub together without the protection of cartilage can wear away, change shape, and develop growths called osteophytes, or bone spurs. Osteoarthritis occurs most often as a result of the way you use your body, so in most cases it is preventable.

Acute Injury

There are times when you can't prevent the damage that is done to your body. Injuries can come out of the blue, like when you strain a muscle, sprain an ankle, or dislocate a shoulder. Just as a chain will break at its weakest link, the parts of your body that are already compromised as a result of continuous dysfunction are the areas most likely to get injured when your body is under acute stress.

Repeated strain on a bone can cause a hairline fracture to form; if the damaging movement continues, the stress fracture will continue to grow. Once a stress fracture is present, a sudden increase of pressure on the bone can be enough to break it completely.

When muscles and tendons are stretched beyond their limit, their fibers will tear, causing what is known as a strain. A strong, unexpected force can cause a strain in any part of the body, but most often strains will occur in muscles and tendons that are tight due to habitual movement patterns.

Ligaments, the straps of connective tissue that connect bones to other bones, can also be torn. Both tendons and ligaments are made of collagen fibers, but ligaments have a denser structure. As such, they provide less stretch and rebound than tendons and are more prone to tearing. Injuries to ligaments are called sprains, and they're generally more serious than tendon strains. Like tendons, ligaments have limited blood supply, so healing takes a long time. While the structure of tendons allows them to regain their original length and strength after healing, ligaments can become loose after being injured, making joints unstable and increasing the risk of dislocation and damage to cartilage.

Whiplash, one of the most common acute injuries that results in chronic pain, typically occurs in a car accident when the head is first thrown backward and then forward from the impact. This sudden, extreme degree of movement can cause strains, sprains, and serious damage to the cervical vertebrae, discs, facet joints, temporomandibular joint, and spinal cord.

While this structural damage itself can be quite serious, the most common cause of long-term pain from whiplash is actually muscle spasm. At the moment of impact, the neck muscles automatically contract in an attempt to stabilize the head. After the injury, the muscles of the neck—and often the shoulders and back as well—will remain contracted to splint the injury. This chronic contraction results in muscle pain and compression of the injured structure, potentially causing nerve pain, limiting blood flow, and slowing the healing process of injured discs and connective tissues.

Addressing the Cause of Pain

If you've experienced any of the conditions we've covered in this chapter, you've likely been to your doctor, received a prescription for medication or physical therapy, and maybe visited a massage therapist or chiropractor. Most of the time, these approaches don't have much lasting effect because they don't address the underlying cause of the pain—damaging motor patterns, which can only be changed through a process of active relearning.

In the next chapter, we'll talk about how to change habits in your daily life that might be causing or contributing to your pain.

CHAPTER 15

How to Keep Yourself out of Pain

I've seen some students, despite their best efforts in diligently practicing Clinical Somatics exercises, prolong their pain with damaging habits. Sometimes their workout routine, stress level, attitude, and even mundane things like their footwear or desk chair keep them in pain. If you spend 20 minutes a day practicing Clinical Somatics exercises to release painfully contracted shoulder and neck muscles, but you spend eight hours a day working at a desk in a position where you contract those same muscles constantly, it's going to take longer to change your patterns and get out of pain.

This chapter contains a list of things you can do in your daily life to reduce or prevent pain. Consider each one individually, and do one at a time. Once you've seen results and made that change habitual, try making another change. Don't overwhelm yourself by attempting to address all of your habits at once. Retraining your nervous system and healing from chronic pain takes time, so be patient with yourself as you learn new ways of using your body.

Relax and Move Naturally

When you're in pain, you tend to adjust your normal movement patterns. This might mean putting more weight on the nonpainful side of your body or holding parts of your body stiff as you move. These compensatory patterns quickly become learned habits, and often lead to further pain. For example, someone who has pain in their right knee will tend to put more weight on their left side, a habit that over time may lead to problems with the left hip, knee, or ankle.

When you're in pain, try to move as normally as you can. This is easier said than done, but I strongly encourage you to try. This means keeping your weight distributed evenly between both feet and relaxing your entire body as much as possible, allowing your joints to move freely. Try not to hold any part of your body stiff, and check in with yourself periodically so that you stay aware of how you're standing and moving.

Try this exercise:

- Stand up. Starting with your head and neck and moving downward, relax all of the muscles in your body. Let your arms hang limply by your sides. You may feel a little wobbly or unstable—that's fine.

- Now, staying totally relaxed, start walking very slowly. Let your head face forward, your neck and shoulders relax completely, and your arms hang limply by your sides. Release all tension in your spine. Let your whole body feel loose.

- Does this feel different than how you normally walk?

- If so, are you now aware of the unnecessary tension that you tend to hold in your body as you walk around?

- If you gradually speed up your walking pace, can you maintain this feeling of being totally relaxed?

Reminding yourself to relax and move naturally will not only help prevent compensatory patterns from developing, but will also help muscular pain go away faster. When you experience a muscle spasm, for example, you tend to instinctively tense the spasmodic muscle and surrounding muscles even more to splint the injury and prevent movement that could worsen the pain. Generally, preventing movement of a spasmodic muscle will only serve to keep it tight. If you're experiencing a spasm, by imagining that you're not in pain and letting yourself move naturally—but slowly and gently—you allow the muscle to gently contract and release as you move, and you'll gradually regain voluntary control.

Keep Moving

There are countless benefits to regular exercise. It improves cardiovascular fitness, muscle strength, bone density, brain function, and mental health, and reduces the risk of developing cancer and heart disease.

A great deal of research has shown that regular exercise reduces rates of chronic pain, and there are a number of reasons for this. Regular movement maintains flexibility of muscles and connective tissues. Exercise improves circulation, which speeds up the healing process and keeps joints healthy by increasing blood flow in and around them. Exercise also increases proprioceptive awareness, improves posture, and creates the opportunity for you to focus on your body mechanics.

If you sit all day at your job and get no exercise, you'll likely spend little time thinking about the way you stand and move. Even if you have an active job, it's difficult to think about improving your body mechanics when you're focused on a task at work. Exercise gives you the opportunity to get out of habitual postural and movement patterns because during your workout you can focus completely on how you're using your body.

Lastly, exercise triggers the release of endorphins and has even been shown to increase confidence. By putting you in a positive state of mind, exercise decreases stress, anxiety, and negative thought patterns, thereby reducing the unpleasantness of pain.

But here's the catch: What if exercise worsens your pain? Or what if your exercise of choice seems to have caused your pain or injury in the first place? If you find yourself in this situation, start by moving slowly and gently. Try doing a different type of exercise so that you'll be less likely to use your body in the habitual way that caused your pain. Going for a slow walk, practicing tai chi, or going for a swim can all be good low-impact options. Don't worry that you're not doing your normal high-intensity workout. The most important thing is to find a way to keep moving without injuring yourself or increasing your pain.

Cross-training, or practicing different types of exercise on a regular basis, is the best way to keep up with regular exercise while reducing your risk of pain and overuse. You should incorporate both aerobic exercise and strength or resistance training into your weekly workout schedule. I also recommend practicing forms of exercise that use your muscles in different ways. For example, if you love weight lifting, do a short yoga routine a few times a week to elongate your muscles and improve your balance. If you're a hard-core long-distance runner, try swimming so that you can keep up your cardio fitness while taking strain off your legs and giving all the muscles in your body a gentle resistance workout.

Move Smarter, Not Harder

Habitual muscular tension and stress can lead you to use more force than necessary to perform the simplest of everyday activities. You grip the steering wheel as you drive to work and keep your whole upper body tense as you work at your computer. All of this unnecessary tension can cause you to feel more pain.

You likely even overuse your muscles when you exercise. Many athletes hold excess tension throughout their bodies when they move. Not only can this result in injury, but it's quite inefficient as far as energy usage; chronically tight muscles constantly burn fuel unnecessarily.

You probably think of muscle tone as being desirable. You want your muscles to look tight so you appear fit and so your body doesn't get loose and saggy. It's important to understand, however, that muscle tone does not directly determine strength, nor is it evidence of strength. Weight training makes your muscles bigger, because the size and number of your muscle fibers increases. But just because you get stronger doesn't mean you have to retain excess muscle tension.

Building up residual muscle tension so that your muscles look tight and toned reduces your ability to use your muscles through their full range of motion. If your muscles are 30% contracted all the time, you might be strong within the upper 70% of your range of motion. But it will be difficult for you to use your muscles in the lower 30% of their range of motion—the range that allows you to fully relax your muscles and extend your joints.

After a certain point, lifting heavier weights will not make you healthier. In fact, pushing yourself to lift weights that are too heavy for you makes you adopt poor body mechanics, strains your body, increases risk of injury, and makes it difficult for you to use your muscles through their full range of motion.

When you're trying to build strength, you should always start with light weights and focus on your body mechanics. Contract and release your muscles slowly, moving through your full range of motion. As you get stronger, you can gradually work with heavier weights; just make sure you can maintain proper body mechanics while doing so. And every time you work out, take the time to warm up with light weights, focusing on using your body correctly and moving through your full range of motion. Your body is like a rubber band—it will go much farther and not break if you move slowly and gently before pushing it to its limits. Following this approach, you will gain far more control over your muscles, reduce your risk of injury, and ultimately be able to perform at a higher level than you would otherwise be able to.

Try this experiment: Go through your day using as little muscular effort as possible to perform every movement. Stay as relaxed as possible while brushing your teeth, driving your car, walking, and doing tasks at work and around the house. You'll be forced to use good body mechanics instead of muscular force to carry out the movements. You'll reduce your resting level of muscle tension and feel more relaxed overall. You may be surprised at how impactful this simple experiment can be.

Don't Fixate on Your Pain

When you're in pain, it's difficult to think about anything else. Pain is generally so unpleasant and potentially dangerous that when you're feeling it, your first instinct is to find a way to make it stop.

Fixating on your pain often leads to stress and anxiety, increasing your level of muscle tension, triggering reflexive postural patterns, and worsening your perception of pain. It can be very challenging, but I encourage you to take deep breaths, relax, and do your best to forget about the pain—even if it's just for a few moments at a time.

Fixating on your pain often leads to subconscious behavioral habits like stretching or massaging tight muscles just to get some temporary relief. These habits do nothing to change nervous system function, so they won't help you get out of pain. They may actually make your pain worse by intensifying your mental focus on the pain, increasing the sensitivity of your nervous system, and making your muscles tighter by activating your stretch reflex.

My simple advice to students who have habits like subconsciously stretching or massaging a tight muscle is to "stop messing with it." Every time you have the urge, just stop, take a deep breath, and relax. Better yet, you can substitute your habit with a Clinical Somatics exercise that will actually relieve your tension and retrain your nervous system without overstretching your tight muscles or aggravating a painful area.

Improve Your Proprioception

If your proprioception—your internal sense of your posture and movement—is off, you might feel like you're standing and sitting straight when in fact you aren't. Here are a few simple exercises you can do to begin improving your proprioception.

Standing Posture Exercise

Stand normally, arms hanging by your sides, and just relax—don't try to stand with perfect posture. Wear fitted clothing and no shoes. Have someone take photos of you from the front, back, and both sides. While you're standing there, and before you look at the photos, close your eyes and have your friend ask you the following questions:

- Do you feel like your weight is more on the balls of your feet or your heels?

- Does it feel like there is there more weight on one foot than the other?

- Do you feel like your knees are locked and pushed back, fairly straight, or slightly bent?

- Does one knee feel different from the other?

- Do you feel like you're arching your back and sticking out your belly, or tucking your pelvis under and contracting your abdominals?

- Does it feel like one hip is higher than the other?

- Do you feel that your shoulders are rounding forward, fairly neutral, or being pulled back so that you're sticking out your chest?

- Does it feel like one shoulder is higher than the other?

- Do you feel like your head is sitting right on top of your spine, pulled back, or jutting forward?

- Imagine a line running up the side of your body and going through these five points: ankle, knee, hip, shoulder, and ear. Does this feel like a straight line? Or does it feel like any of these body parts are in front of or behind the line?

Once you've answered all these questions, you can open your eyes and look at your photos. You'll find out if what you see in the photos matches up with what you were feeling. You may want to ask your friend what they see, because your friend's interpretation of the photos will be more objective than yours.

Sitting Posture Exercise

Sit on a stool or chair with a flat seat, and move forward so you're not leaning back in the seat. Let your thighs be parallel to the ground or sloping downward so that your knees are lower than your hips. Make sure your ankles are directly under your knees or in front of your knees.

Close your eyes, and very slowly and gently roll your pelvis forward and backward until you find a place in the middle where you feel like you're sitting straight up and down. Ask your friend to take a photo of you in this position. Then look at the photo, and find out if what you see in the photo matches up with what you were feeling.

Set a Relaxation Alarm

Set an alarm on your phone or watch to go off every 10 minutes throughout the day. Pick the happiest, least annoying alarm sound you can. Each time the alarm goes off, take a moment to close your eyes, take a deep breath down into your belly, and let go of all the muscular tension you're holding on to subconsciously. Notice where in your body you tend to hold tension.

After each alarm, see how long you can stay relaxed as you go back to your normal activities.

You'll likely be surprised at not only how much tension you're holding on to subconsciously, but also at how quickly you're able to train yourself to stay relaxed instead of holding on to unnecessary stress and muscle tension.

Switch Sides

We've talked about the effects of handedness on habitual motor patterns, and how simply using the sides of your body in different ways can lead to pain and structural damage. Exploring the ways that you use the sides of your body differently will help you become more aware of your learned patterns and allow you to change them. To begin this process, try the following activities. One by one, perform each movement with the side you typically use, and then use your other side.

- Brush your teeth

- Brush your hair

- Rest your weight on one side

- Balance on one leg

- Carry a bag on your shoulder

- Use a computer mouse

- Throw a ball

- Kick a ball

- Bend forward and pick up a small, light object

At first, you may feel like you're physically incapable of performing these simple tasks with your nondominant side. When you feel like this, slow down and analyze the movement as you perform it with your dominant side. How are you moving, what postural adjustments are you making, and what muscles are you engaging in order to carry out this task with your dominant side?

Once you have a sense of the body mechanics involved in the movement, try doing it with your nondominant side. Go back and forth from side to side until the movement starts to feel natural on your nondominant side. This process will increase your awareness and control of your nondominant side and train you to use your body in a more balanced way.

Improve the Ergonomics of Your Daily Life

Ergonomics, the practice of designing and arranging things so that people can use them efficiently and safely, is typically talked about in the context of work environments. But good ergonomics is important in every situation, not just at work, if you want to avoid injuries and pain. The ways in which you adapt to your physical surroundings as well as the equipment and furniture you use play a large role in developing dysfunctional muscular patterns. Good ergonomics helps you reorganize your environments to better suit your body, rather than reorganizing your body to suit your environments.

Consider the ergonomics of your home and other spaces you use on a regular basis while doing the following activities.

Driving

Adjust your seat so the seat back and head rest are supportive. You should be able to sit straight up and down with your shoulders relaxed and not rounded forward. When you're driving, try to use both arms equally to control the steering wheel. Check in with yourself every few minutes so that you can adjust your posture and release any unnecessary muscle tension.

Using Your Phone

If you spend a lot of time talking on the phone, you should use a headset or keep the phone on speaker. Holding a phone to your ear requires you to keep your arm in a bent position and tilt your head to the side. Neck pain is a common complaint among folks who spend a lot of time talking on the phone.

If you spend a lot of time using your phone to text or surf the internet, be aware of your posture. Is your head tilted downward, your arms bent, your shoulders rounded forward, and your chest contracted? If so:

- Take frequent breaks so your muscles can relax.

- Use your phone less. If you need to work, use a desktop computer so that you can sit up straight. If you're using your phone for fun, either rest it on something so you don't have to hold it, or find another activity to keep you entertained.

Working at a Computer

Whether you use a computer at work, at home, or both, take the time to create an ideal setup.

- Your computer screen should be at eye level, not below, so you can look straight ahead rather than downward while you're working.

- Your screen should be directly in front of your chair so you don't have to twist or turn to work.

- The screen should be an appropriate distance away so that you don't have to strain your eyes or lean forward to see what you're working on. Remember, you can zoom in on documents and websites instead of craning your neck forward.

- Your wrists should be in a neutral, relaxed position when typing. Your keyboard should be at the height of or slightly above your elbows.

- Your chair should have a high enough back so you feel fully supported and don't need to use any effort to sit up straight.

- The seat of your chair should be flat rather than tipped backward.

- You should be able to stretch out your legs under your desk so your hamstrings aren't constantly contracted.

- While working at your computer, you should be in a relaxed, neutral position. Check in with yourself periodically throughout the day and remind yourself of what that feels like.

- If you aren't comfortable sitting to do your work, consider a standing desk or an adjustable-height table. Consider switching between sitting and standing to work throughout the day so you don't develop damaging postural habits by staying in the same posture all day long.

Sitting on the Couch

When you're at home, consider the ergonomics of the areas where you spend the most time. For example, if you spend time every day relaxing on the couch, either watching television, reading, or using electronics, notice the way you sit or lie on the couch. Do you tend to lean to one side or the other? If so, try to switch sides, or find a comfortable neutral position in which you can relax.

When watching television, make sure you can look straight ahead at the screen rather than having to turn your head to see. Also consider the couch itself: the higher the back, the easier it will be for you to sit up straight without straining your neck. You can use pillows behind your back and neck to create the ideal supportive setup.

Sleeping Position

Aside from where you work, the place where you likely spend the most time is your bed, so you should put some thought into your ideal mattress, pillow, and sleeping position. Having inadequate support or sleeping in unnatural positions can cause or worsen muscle tension and pain.

The main thing to consider is the alignment of your spine while you're sleeping. You spend six to eight hours every night in this position, so imagine standing in that same position all day. When you're sleeping, your spine should be aligned from your tailbone all the way up to the top of your head.

If you sleep on your back, you should use either a very thin pillow or no pillow at all. Lying on your back and using a thick pillow is equivalent to standing with your head jutting forward all day. If you have back pain, consider sleeping on your back with a pillow under your knees; this will take the pressure off your lower back and allow your spine to rest in a neutral position.

If you sleep on your side, use a pillow that allows your neck to be straight. Formed pillows that provide shaped support for your neck and head are wonderful for side sleeping. Mattress firmness is quite important for side sleepers. Your hips and shoulders must be able to sink down a bit so that your spine remains straight, as shown in Illustration 27. Appropriate mattress firmness depends on body weight; the heavier you are, the firmer your mattress should be to provide the right amount of support. Side sleepers may find that putting a small pillow between their knees improves overall alignment and reduces lower back pain. If you tend to sleep only or mostly on one side, you should try going back and forth so that you spend equal time sleeping on both sides.

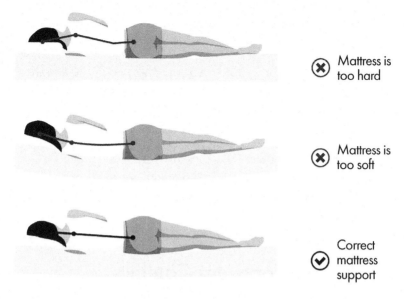

Illustration 27: Correct side-sleeping position
(elenabsl © 123rf.com)

If you sleep on your stomach, I strongly encourage you to start sleeping on your back or your side. Stomach sleeping causes tension and pain because your neck is turned to one side or the other, contracting muscles in your neck and shoulders. Lying on your stomach also puts pressure on your lower back. It may take some time to train yourself to sleep on your back or your side, but it will be worth it in the long run.

In general, sleeping on your back is the healthiest way to sleep. Sleeping on your back allows your body to be in a completely neutral position, with your spine straight, your limbs extended, and your muscles relaxed. Unfortunately, many people find it difficult to sleep this way. Lying on your side or your stomach feels more conducive to sleeping, largely because you feel more protected in those positions.

If you want to train yourself to sleep on your back:

- Lie on your back for a while when you first get into bed at night. Start without a pillow under your head for a few minutes. If using no pillow is uncomfortable or painful, try gradually decreasing the thickness of your pillow (you can use a folded towel if you don't have a thin pillow). Gradually increase the time you spend on your back, and let yourself relax as much as possible. Over time, you may start falling asleep on your back without even trying!

- Lie on your back for a while when you wake up in the morning, or if you wake up in the middle of the night. The more time you spend lying on your back and relaxing, the more mentally and physically comfortable it will become.

- Use a weighted blanket. These are often recommended for anxiety sufferers, but a weighted blanket can help anyone feel safer and more protected, and make it easier to fall asleep on your back.

Choose Your Footwear Carefully

Humans evolved wearing no shoes at all, and your feet are designed to hold your body weight with no additional support. It might not feel like that if you're accustomed to wearing thick-soled sneakers, arch support inserts, or high heels, however. This is because your posture, movement patterns, and the resting level of tension in the muscles of your feet and legs have adapted to your footwear.

Consider the fit of your shoes. If they're too tight or restrictive, you might get bunion pain or cramping in the muscles of your feet. If your shoes are too loose, the way that you walk and run will be affected and you may experience hip, knee, or ankle problems. Your shoes should be roomy enough that your feet truly feel comfortable, yet fitted enough that your feet don't slide around inside your shoes as you walk and run.

The soles of your shoes should be flexible. You should be able to hold your shoe by the heel and toe and fold it in half. A flexible sole allows the muscles of your feet to do their job, and allows you to move in a way that is most similar to being barefoot.

In general, the soles of your shoes should be as thin as is comfortable for you. Here's why: If you wear thick-soled sneakers, having extra cushioning under the heel allows you to strike the ground harder than you would if you were barefoot. Heel-striking puts unnecessary strain and pressure on your feet, ankles, and knees, and contributes to poor overall body mechanics. Thin-soled shoes tend to promote better full-body movement patterns.

That being said, humans evolved to walk and run on dirt and grass rather than concrete. If you're walking or running long distances on concrete, you may find that you're more comfortable wearing sneakers with some cushioning. Ultimately, the amount of cushioning in your sneakers is not the most important thing—it's your walking and running form. If you do wear sneakers with thick soles, make sure they're flexible, and consider having your walking or running form analyzed to ensure you're not heel-striking.

Some of you may not like to hear this, but you knew it was coming: Don't wear high heels. Any shoe that has a raised heel shifts an unnatural amount of weight onto the ball of the foot, especially onto the big toe joint. For this reason, high heels are one of the main causes of bunion pain. Raised heels also keep the Achilles tendon and the muscles of the foot and calf in a shortened state for long periods of time, leading to chronic tightness, muscle cramps, and plantar fasciitis.

Lastly, I recommend varying your footwear from day to day, especially if you spend a lot of time on your feet. This will help prevent you from developing poor body mechanics and habitual tension in the muscles of your feet and legs.

Take some time to go through your closet and take stock of your footwear. Find the shoes that are comfortably fitted with thin, flexible soles and no raised heels; these are the shoes you should be wearing the majority of the time. Remember, your natural movement patterns should not be altered by the shoes you wear.

Stop Trying to Look Tough

We touched on this subject in chapter 13, but it's important to note that athletes are not the only ones guilty of hurting themselves by toughing it out. Many people keep quiet about their pain because they don't want to be viewed as weak or they worry that their family and friends are sick of hearing them complain. Unfortunately, the result of ignoring your pain is that you may be making the problem worse.

Please stop ignoring or hiding your pain. Acknowledge it, and resolve to find a way to address it. It takes a tough, intelligent person to know when to rest and take care of their body. Remember, this is the only body you get for your entire life. Don't make yourself suffer now or in the future just because you're worried about looking tough.

Make Self-Care a Priority

Make it your most important priority to take care of yourself. This can be difficult for many of us: Other things seem more important or urgent, like getting work done and taking care of your kids, and it's easy to put yourself last. You do not need to feel guilty about taking time to take care of yourself. Good self-care practices will allow you to be more productive at work and to be a better parent and spouse.

If you're in pain, one aspect of your self-care must be getting yourself out of pain and keeping yourself out of pain. You should practice Clinical Somatics exercises every day so you can continue to improve your posture and movement and keep your muscles loose. Just like eating healthy and exercising, the results are cumulative. You will reap far more benefits from Clinical Somatics exercises when you practice them regularly.

Another aspect of self-care for every person must be physical exercise. Get moving in whatever way is enjoyable and accessible for you. Regular exercise increases energy, reduces pain, reduces stress, improves mood and mental health, promotes better sleep, increases muscle strength and endurance, strengthens the immune system, and reduces the risk of developing lifestyle-related diseases.

Another mandatory aspect of your self-care routine is taking time to relax. This may include different activities for different people: taking a hot bath, watching your favorite TV show, reading a book, socializing with friends, or spending some quiet time alone. Whatever makes you feel relaxed, do it regularly. Reducing your overall stress level will reduce your muscular tension and pain, improve your mood, improve your relationships, make you more productive, and increase your life span by reducing the risk of stress-related diseases.

If you catch yourself making excuses for why you don't or can't take care of yourself, I invite you to let them go. When you make excuses, you prevent yourself from living the happiest and healthiest life possible. No one else can do it for you—you are the only one who can take care of yourself. For many of us, that means tearing up your list of excuses and making a commitment to take care of yourself as best as you possibly can.

Build self-care into your schedule and make it nonnegotiable. Print out your weekly schedule, including work, activities, and self-care, and post it somewhere so you hold yourself accountable to it. You can improve your quality of life, prevent future health problems, and lengthen your life by making self-care a priority.

Don't let your excuses keep you stuck and in pain.

Expect to Get Better

You know from our discussion of the placebo effect in chapter 2 that if you expect to get better, you generally will. But the opposite is also true: If you expect to get worse, you generally will. When you're in pain, it can be difficult to believe you'll get better. But finding a way to have a positive attitude is one of the best things you can do for yourself.

The increase in pain from negative expectations is referred to as nocebo hyperalgesia, and research has shown how this effect occurs at a neurobiological level. Brain-imaging studies show increased activation of a pain pathway known as the medial pain system when subjects expect that a stimulus will be painful. So it's important to understand that having a negative expectation doesn't just mean that you'll report your pain as being worse—it means you'll actually experience more pain.

Researchers have found they can predict which surgical patients will experience greater postoperative pain based on presurgical assessment using the Pain Catastrophizing Scale. The scale measures how fixated the patients are on their pain, to what extent they magnify their pain and expect that it will get worse, and their feelings of helplessness. The more patients catastrophize about their pain before the surgery, the more pain they experience afterward.

Over the course of your life, you develop habitual ways of thinking just as you develop habitual ways of standing and moving. It's easy for you to get stuck in old thought patterns. It can be difficult to get objective feedback on how you think and even more difficult to listen to the feedback rationally, learn from it, and change. But as a friend of mine says, "Don't believe everything you think." Just because you think something doesn't mean it's true. You need to remain open-minded so you can learn new things and get new results.

Your habits make you comfortable, and changing your deeply learned thought and motor patterns takes effort and willpower. If you find yourself thinking negatively about your pain, stop yourself and try to think about your situation in the opposite way. Instead of telling yourself, "My back is just going to get worse and worse. I'll never be able to hike again," practice thinking, "My back is going to get better! This pain is going to go away and I'll be so excited to go hiking again!"

With practice, positive thinking will become easier and even habitual. And remember, positive thinking won't just improve your attitude—it will actually reduce your experience of pain on a neurobiological level. It will also change your behavior. If you think you can get better, you'll be more diligent about practicing self-care exercises daily because you'll believe they will work.

Don't Expect Change to Happen Overnight

It's tempting to believe in fast results and miracle cures. But if you've ever tried any diet or exercise plan that promises results in a short amount of time, you've learned from experience that lasting change rarely comes quickly or easily.

This is especially true when it comes to getting out of pain and changing deeply learned motor patterns. You've spent your entire life developing the habitual patterns that now cause your pain, so it's unreasonable to expect that they can be permanently changed and that your pain will go away in a few days or weeks. Embarking on a process to change habitual patterns is like beginning a journey without knowing exactly where it will take you or when you'll arrive.

Like any learning process, you'll get out of it what you put into it. Practicing Clinical Somatics exercises every day for 20 to 30 minutes is ideal, though there is no harm in practicing for longer periods of time. Just keep in mind that your learned motor patterns, your proprioception, and the tissues of your body can only change so fast. Doing more will not necessarily get you better or faster results, and slow change is best, in general. Your progress will have more to do with how you practice the exercises and how well you're able to integrate what you've learned from the exercises into your daily life.

You may find it helpful to keep a journal or log of how you feel every day. Each day you can note whether or not you did your Clinical Somatics exercises and rate your pain on a scale of 0 to 10. You can also make notes about what might have affected your pain that day, such as activities you did, your sleep pattern, and your mood. Keeping a log like this can help you track your progress, notice patterns in your pain, and identify which exercises and self-care routines are most helpful for you.

You can go to this link to download a Clinical Somatics exercise tracking log: **somaticmovementcenter.com/exercise-tracking-log**

Keep in mind that your improvement will probably not follow a straight upward path. There will be days when you feel great and other days when you don't. You may be pain free for months and then have an old pain suddenly return or a new pain emerge.

Making changes in your posture and movement, even when they're changes for the better, can cause some soreness or discomfort simply because you're using your body in an unfamiliar way. Going through a process of change is rarely a smooth journey. You'll encounter some bumps in the road, but the most important thing is that you're heading in the right direction.

Don't Wait

The longer you let your pain persist, the more damage you can do to your body and the more sensitized your nervous system can become. The best thing you can do for yourself is to stop simply managing your pain and find a way to address it in a constructive way. Don't wait—do it today!

CHAPTER 16

Moving Forward

Simply understanding how to change your learned motor patterns may not be enough. To get out of pain, you need to shift your attitude. You must expect to improve over time instead of gradually breaking down as you age. You must understand that you're supposed to feel wonderful and comfortable in your body throughout your life.

Next, you must accept responsibility for your health and be willing to do the work that keeps you healthy. Many doctors and patients pursue treatment that offers an easy fix, even if that fix is only temporary and comes with side effects. That approach is "easier" than putting in the time and energy to take care of your health for the long term. But there are very few quick fixes or miracle cures. You must learn to be self-sufficient, and appreciate how incredible it is to be able to take steps to improve your health instead of hoping that others will fix your problems for you.

If you're like many people, you don't become motivated to take care of yourself until your health begins to decline. Most pain and disease conditions exist on a spectrum, and you must get to a certain threshold in order to be diagnosed and treated. By that time, your condition has already progressed to the point at which a great deal of time and treatment will be required to alleviate or eliminate it.

It's much simpler, easier, and cheaper to take a preventive, proactive approach to your health than to wait until something bad happens. You know you need to eat well and exercise in order to prevent obesity, diabetes, and heart disease, but do you actually practice these habits? Now it's time to recognize that you must maintain your sensorimotor awareness and practice Clinical Somatics exercises throughout your life to prevent pain, recurring injuries, and musculoskeletal degeneration.

In his book *Man's Supreme Inheritance,* F.M. Alexander writes, "The great phase in man's advancement is that in which he passes from subconscious to conscious control of his own mind and body." Practicing Clinical Somatics exercises will help you regain conscious control of your mind and body and give you the freedom to change old habits that have been keeping you in pain. It will also give you tools to create new habits that will allow you to perform better in sports and in all of your daily movements.

Like Alexander and Hanna, I imagine a world in which people don't suffer needlessly from lifestyle-related chronic diseases and pain. A world in which patients take control of their own health and heal themselves as much as possible. A world in which people put their well-being first, and expect their quality of life to keep getting better over time. With each person that takes responsibility for their health, we get one step closer to that world.

That world starts today. It starts right now, right here, with you. Learn to master your muscle memory, transform your health, and live your best possible life.

I invite you to get started right away with the following exercises:

Clinical Somatics Exercises

I recommend you download and print your free Clinical Somatics exercise tracking log: **somaticmovementcenter.com/exercise-tracking-log**

Place it where you will see it every day; this will remind you to do your exercises, which will help you increase your awareness and understanding of your body.

In addition, it's a great tool to help you track the intensity of your pain from day to day so you can see your results and celebrate your successes as you learn to relieve your own pain.

Here is the complete list of Clinical Somatics video lessons that come free with this book:

- Straighten rounded posture:
  somaticmovementcenter.com/posture-exercise

- Release the muscles of the lower back, alleviate hyperlordosis, alleviate lumbar disc problems, and prevent lower back spasms:
  somaticmovementcenter.com/back-pain-exercise

- Alleviate idiopathic scoliosis:
  somaticmovementcenter.com/scoliosis-exercise

- Alleviate sciatica and piriformis syndrome:
  somaticmovementcenter.com/sciatica-exercise

- Alleviate thoracic outlet syndrome:
  somaticmovementcenter.com/thoracic-outlet-exercise

- Release the iliopsoas:
  somaticmovementcenter.com/iliopsoas-exercise

- Alleviate functional leg length discrepancy:
  somaticmovementcenter.com/leg-length-exercise

- Alleviate plantar fasciitis:
  somaticmovementcenter.com/plantar-fasciitis-exercise

- Alleviate carpal tunnel syndrome:
  somaticmovementcenter.com/carpal-tunnel-exercise

- Relieve temporomandibular joint pain:
  somaticmovementcenter.com/tmj-exercise

- Relieve tension headaches:
  somaticmovementcenter.com/headache-exercise

- Alleviate frozen shoulder:
  somaticmovementcenter.com/shoulder-exercise

How to Learn More

I hope you move forward with the knowledge you gained in this book by learning Clinical Somatics exercises so that you can prevent, alleviate, and eliminate your pain and improve your overall health. If you want to have one-on-one lessons or attend group classes, seek out your nearest certified Clinical Somatic Educator or Hanna Somatic Educator.

If there are no certified educators near you, I offer online courses that teach advanced Clinical Somatics self-care exercises. These online courses teach the exercises one by one through video demonstrations, audio classes, and written descriptions. The courses are a wonderful way to learn the exercises at home. They give you the tools you need to develop a regular practice, improve your posture and movement, and keep yourself out of pain for the rest of your life.

To learn more and register for the courses, go to:

somaticmovementcenter.com/learn-somatics-exercises

Acknowledgments

Thank you to Tom Corson-Knowles and Amy Loerch for guiding me through the editing and publishing process and making this book the best it could be.

Thank you to my parents, stepparents, and sisters, for always supporting me and encouraging my creativity. I couldn't ask for better role models.

Thank you to my lululemon family, past and present, for your inspiration, motivation, and never-ending positive energy.

Thank you to my daughter, for always reminding me what's really important.

Thank you to Kevin, for your constant love and support.

References

Introduction: Why You're in Pain

Friedrichsdorf, S.J., et al. "Chronic Pain in Children and Adolescents: Diagnosis and Treatment of Primary Pain Disorders in Head, Abdomen, Muscles and Joints." *Children* 3, no. 4 (December 2016): 42.

Maciałczyk-Paprocka, K., et al. "Prevalence of Incorrect Body Posture in Children and Adolescents with Overweight and Obesity. *European Journal of Pediatrics* 176, no.5 (2017): 563–572.

Chapter 1: How Pain Affects Your Life

American Pain Foundation. *Voices of Chronic Pain Survey Voices: A National Study Conducted for American Pain Foundation.* David Michaelson & Company, LLC, 2006.

Apkarian, A.V., et al. "Chronic Back Pain Is Associated with Decreased Prefrontal and Thalamic Gray Matter Density." *Journal of Neuroscience* 24, no. 46 (November 17, 2004): 10410–10415.

Apkarian, A.V., et al. "Chronic Pain Patients Are Impaired on an Emotional Decision-Making Task." *Pain* 108, no. 1–2 (March 2004): 129–136.

Bair, M.J., et al. "Depression and Pain Comorbidity: A Literature Review." *Archives of Internal Medicine*, 163, no. 20 (November 2003): 2433–2445.

Baliki, M.N., et al. "Beyond Feeling: Chronic Pain Hurts the Brain, Disrupting the Default-Mode Network Dynamics." *Journal of*

Neuroscience 28, no. 6 (February 6, 2008) 1398–1403.

Blue Cross Blue Shield. "Planned Knee and Hip Replacement Surgeries Are on the Rise in the U.S." *Health of America Report*, January 23, 2019.

Brook, M., et al. "Trends in Lumbar Fusion Procedure Rates and Associated Hospital Costs for Degenerative Spinal Diseases in the United States, 2004-2015." *Spine* (August 2, 2018).

CBS News. "A New Hope for Back Pain Sufferers?" May 6, 2012. www.cbsnews.com/news/a-new-hope-for-back-pain-sufferers

Centers for Disease Control and Prevention. National Center for Chronic Disease Prevention and Health Promotion. "Division for Heart Disease and Stroke Prevention at a Glance." 2016. www.cdc.gov/chronicdisease/resources/publications/aag/heart-disease-stroke.htm

Centers for Disease Control and Prevention. "National Diabetes Statistics Report, 2017: Estimates of Diabetes and Its Burden in the United States." 2017. www.cdc.gov/diabetes/pdfs/data/statistics/national-diabetes-statistics-report.pdf

Centers for Disease Control and Prevention. Opioid Overdose. "Prescription Opioid Data." www.cdc.gov/drugoverdose/data/prescribing.html

Centers for Disease Control and Prevention. "Vital Signs: Overdoses of Prescription Opioid Pain Relievers—United States, 1999–2008." *Morbidity and Mortality Weekly Report* 60, no. 43 (November 4, 2011): 1487–1492.

Columbia University. National Centre on Addiction and Substance Abuse. *Addiction Medicine: Closing the Gap between Science and Practice.* June 2012. www.centeronaddiction.org/sites/default/files/Addiction-medicine-closing-the-gap-between-science-and-practice_1.pdf

Columbia University. National Centre on Addiction and Substance Abuse. *Missed Opportunity: National Survey of Primary Care*

Physicians and Patients on Substance Abuse. April 2000. eric.
ed.gov/?id=ED452442

Courtney-Long, E.A., et al. "Prevalence and Most Common Causes
of Disability Among Adults—United States, 2005." *Morbidity
and Mortality Weekly Report* 64, no. 29 (July 31, 2015): 777–783.

Deyo, R.A., et al. "Trends, Major Medical Complications, and
Charges Associated with Surgery for Lumbar Spinal Stenosis in
Older Adults." *Journal of the American Medical Association* 303, no.
13 (April 7, 2010): 1259–1265.

Deyo, R.A., J. Rainville, and D.L. Kent. "What Can the History and
Physical Examination Tell Us about Low Back Pain? *Journal of
the American Medical Association* 268, no. 6 (1992): 760–765.

Farina, K.L. "The Economics of Cancer Care in the United States."
American Journal of Managed Care: Evidence-Based Oncology
(March 16, 2012). www.ajmc.com/journals/evidence-based-
oncology/2012/2012-2-vol18-n1/the-economics-of-cancer-care-
in-the-united-states-how-much-do-we-spend-and-how-can-
we-spend-it-better

Grachev, I.D., B.E. Fredrickson, and A.V. Apkarian. "Abnormal
Brain Chemistry in Chronic Back Pain: An In Vivo Proton
Magnetic Resonance Spectroscopy Study." *Pain* 89, no. 1
(December 15, 2000): 7–18.

Harvard Health Publishing. "Painkillers Fuel Growth in Drug
Addiction." *Harvard Mental Health Letter.* January 2011. www.
health.harvard.edu/newsletter_article/painkillers-fuel-growth-
in-drug-addiction

Institute of Medicine of the National Academies. Committee on
Advancing Pain Research, Care, and Education. *Relieving Pain in
America: A Blueprint for Transforming Prevention, Care, Education
and Research (2011).* National Academies Press, June 29, 2011.
www.nap.edu/catalog/13172/relieving-pain-in-america-a-
blueprint-for-transforming-prevention-care

Lucas, A.J. "Failed Back Surgery Syndrome: Whose Failure? Time
to Discard a Redundant Term." *British Journal of Pain* 6, no. 4
(November 2012): 162–165.

Mariotto, A.B., et al. "Projections of the Cost of Cancer Care in the United States: 2010–2020." *Journal of the National Cancer Institute*, 103, no. 2 (April 20, 2011): 117–128.

Martin, B.I., et al. "Expenditures and Health Status Among Adults with Back and Neck Problems." *Journal of the American Medical Association* 299, no. 6 (February 13, 2008): 656–664.

Mazer-Amirshahi, M., et al. "Rising Opioid Prescribing in Adult U.S. Emergency Department Visits: 2001-2010." *Academic Emergency Medicine* 21, no. 3 (March 2014): 236–243.

National Institutes of Health and Friends of the National Library of Medicine. "Prescription Pain Medicines—An Addictive Path?" *NIH Medline Plus*, 2, no. 4 (Fall 2007): 22.

Nguyen, T.H., et al. "Long-Term Outcomes of Lumbar Fusion Among Workers' Compensation Subjects: A Historical Cohort Study." *Spine*, 36, no. 4 (February 15, 2011): 320–331.

Pain News Network. "2017 CDC Survey Results." www.painnewsnetwork.org/2017-cdc-survey

Peter D. Hart Research Associates. "Americans Talk About Pain: A Survey among Adults Nationwide." (August 2003). www.researchamerica.org/sites/default/files/uploads/poll2003pain.pdf

Roger, V.L., et al. "Heart Disease and Stroke Statistics—2011 Update: A Report from the American Heart Association." *Circulation* 123 (2011): e18–e209.

Suddath, Claire. "'Living with Pain,' in Health Special: Chronic Pain." *Time*, March 11, 2011. content.time.com/time/specials/packages/article/0,28804,2053382_2055269_2055261,00.html

Tsang, A., et al. "Common Chronic Pain Conditions in Developed and Developing Countries: Gender and Age Differences and Comorbidity with Depression-Anxiety Disorders." *Journal of Pain* 9, no. 10 (October 20118): 883–891.

US Substance Abuse and Mental Health Services Administration. Center for Behavioral Health Statistics and Quality. *Results from the 2010 National Survey on Drug Use and Health: Summary of National Findings.* 2011. www.samhsa.gov/data/sites/default/files/NSDUHNationalFindingsResults2010-

Van Zee, A. "The Promotion and Marketing of OxyContin: Commercial Triumph, Public Health Tragedy." *American Journal of Public Health* 99,no. 2 (February 2009): 221–227.

Vivolo-Kantor, A.M., et al. "Vital Signs: Trends in Emergency Department Visits for Suspected Opioid Overdoses—United States, July 2016–September 2017." *Morbidity and Mortality Weekly Report* 67, no. 9 (March 9, 2018): 279–285.

Wolford, M.L., K. Palso, and A. Bercovitz. "Hospitalization for Total Hip Replacement Among Inpatients Aged 45 and Over: United States, 2000–2010." National Center for Health Statistics Data Brief, no. 186 (February 2015).

Chapter 2: How and Why You Feel Pain

Apkarian, A.V. "Human Brain Imaging Studies of Chronic Pain." In *Translational Pain Research: From Mouse to Man*, edited by L. Kruger and A.R. Light. Boca Raton, FL: CRC Press, 2010.

Apkarian, A.V., M.C. Bushnell, R.D. Treede, and J.K. Zubieta. "Human Brain Mechanisms of Pain Perception and Regulation in Health and Disease." *European Journal of Pain*, 9, no. 4 (August 2005): 463–484.

Arnstein, P.M. "The Neuroplastic Phenomenon: A Physiologic Link between Chronic Pain and Learning." *Journal of Neuroscience Nursing* 29, no. 3 (June 1997): 179–186.

Assefi, N.P., et al. "A Randomized Clinical Trial of Acupuncture Compared with Sham Acupuncture in Fibromyalgia." *Annals of Internal Medicine* 143 (2005): 10–19.

Associated Press. "Runner Finishes on Broken Leg." August 9, 2012. www.espn.go.com/olympics/summer/2012/trackandfield/story/_/id/8251820/2012-london-olympics-us-runner-manteo-mitchell-finishes-4x400-meter-relay-broken-leg

Bear, M.F., B.W. Connors, and M.A. Paradiso. *Neuroscience: Exploring the Brain*, 3rd ed. Baltimore, MD: Lippincott Williams & Wilkins, 2007.

Beecher, H.K. "Relationship of Significance of Wound to Pain Experienced." *Journal of the American Medical Association* 161, no. 17 (August 25, 1956): 1,609–1,613.

Boecker, H., et al. "The Runner's High, Opioidergic Mechanisms in the Human Brain." *Cerebral Cortex,* 18, no. 11 (2008): 2,523–2,531.

Borgens, R.B., and R. Shi. "Immediate Recovery from Spinal Cord Injury through Molecular Repair of Nerve Membranes with Polyethylene Glycol." *FASEB Journal* 14, no. 1 (January 2000): 27–35.

Braun, C.A., and C.M. Anderson. *Pathophysiology: Functional Alterations in Human Health.* Baltimore, MD: Lippincott Williams & Wilkins, 2007.

Cintron, L. "Preemptive and Preventative Analgesia for Chronic Postsurgical Pain." *Practical Pain Management* 17, issue 7 (2017).

Clement-Jones, V., et al. "Increased Beta-Endorphin but Not Met-Enkephalin Levels in Human Cerebrospinal Fluid after Acupuncture for Recurrent Pain." *Lancet* 2, no. 8201 (November 1, 1980): 946–949.

Cloud, J. "Beyond Drugs." *TIME,* March 11, 2011. www.content.time.com/time/specials/packages/article/0,28804,2053382_2055269_2055260,00.html

Coderre, T.J., et al. "Contribution of Central Neuroplasticity to Pathological Pain: Review of Clinical and Experimental Evidence." *Pain* 52, no. 3 (March 1993): 259–295.

Colt, E.W., S.L. Wardlaw, and A.G. Frantz. "The Effect of Running on Plasma Beta-Endorphin." *Life Sciences* 28, no. 14 (1981): 1,637–1,640.

Correll, G.E., et al. "Subanesthetic Ketamine Infusion Therapy: A Retrospective Analysis of a Novel Therapeutic Approach to Complex Regional Pain Syndrome." *Pain Medicine,* 5, no. 3 (September 2004): 263–275.

De Craen, A.J., et al. "Placebos and Placebo Effects in Medicine:

Historical Overview." *Journal of the Royal Society of Medicine*, 92, no. 10 (October 1999): 511–515.

De Mos, M., et al. "The Incidence of Complex Regional Pain Syndrome: A Population-Based Study." *Pain* 129, no.1–2 (May 2007): 12–20.

DosSantos, M.F., et al. "Immediate Effects of tDCS on the Micro-Opioid System of a Chronic Pain Patient." *Frontiers in Psychiatry* 3, no. 93 (November 2, 2012).

Egger, G. "In Search of a Germ Theory Equivalent for Chronic Disease." *Preventing Chronic Disease* 9 (2012): e95.

Eriksson, P.S., et al. "Neurogenesis in the Adult Human Hippocampus." *Nature Medicine*, 4, no. 11 (1998): 1313–1317.

Ferrero-Miliani, L., et al. "Chronic Inflammation: Importance of NOD2 and NALP3 in Interleukin-1 Beta Generation." *Clinical & Experimental Immunology* 147, no. 2 (February 2007): 227–235.

Goddard, G., et al. "Acupuncture and Sham Acupuncture Reduce Muscle Pain in Myofascial Pain Patients." *Journal of Orofacial Pain*, 16, no. 1 (2002): 71–76.

Guillemin, R., et al. "Beta-Endorphin and Adrenocorticotropin Are Secreted Concomitantly by the Pituitary Gland." *Science* 197, no. 4,311 (September 1997): 1,367–1,369.

Han, J. "Acupuncture and Endorphins." *Neuroscience Letters* 361 (2004): 258–261.

Hunter, P. "The Inflammation Theory of Disease." *EMBO Reports*, 13 (September 10, 2012): 968–970.

International Association for the Study of Pain. "IASP Terminology." May 22, 2012. www.iasp-pain.org/Education/Content. aspx?ItemNumber=1698&navItemNumber=576

IRIN. "A Selected History of Opium." August 24, 2004. www. irinnews.org/report/25857/afghanistan-selected-history-opium

Juhan, D. *Job's Body: A Handbook for Bodywork*, 3rd ed. Barrytown, NY: Barrytown/Station Hill Press, Inc., 2003.

Kidd, B.L. and L.A. Urban. "Mechanisms of Inflammatory Pain." *British Journal of Anaesthesia*, 87, no. 1 (2001): 3–11.

Kiefer, R., et al. "Complete Recovery from Intractable Complex Regional Pain Syndrome, CRPS-Type I, Following Anesthetic Ketamine and Midazolam." *Pain Practice* 7, no. 2 (2007): 147–150.

Levine, J.D., N.C. Gordon, and H.L. Fields "The Mechanism of Placebo Analgesia." *Lancet,* 2, issue 8,091 (September 23, 1978): 654–657.

Linde, K., et al. "Acupuncture for Migraine Prophylaxis." *Cochrane Database of System Reviews* 1, CD001218 (January 21, 2009).

Lu, H., et al. "Macrophages Recruited via CCR2 Produce Insulin-Like Growth Factor-1 to Repair Acute Skeletal Muscle Injury." *FASEB Journal* 25, no. 1 (January 2011): 358–369.

Lu, X., et al. "Polyethylene Glycol in Spinal Cord Injury Repair: A Critical Review." *Journal of Experimental Pharmacology* 10 (2018): 37–49.

Marinus, J., et al. (2011). "Clinical Features and Pathophysiology of Complex Regional Pain Syndrome." *Lancet Neural* 10, no. 7 (July 2011): 637–648.

McMurray, G.A. "Experimental Study of a Case of Insensitivity to Pain." *AMA Archives of Neurology & Psychiatry,* 64, no. 5 (November 1950): 650–667.

Melzack, R., and P.D. Wall. *The Challenge of Pain,* 2nd ed. London, England: Penguin Books, Ltd., 2008.

Mense, S. "The Pathogenesis of Muscle Pain." *Current Pain and Headache Reports* 7, no. 6 (December 2003): 419–425.

Mense, S. "Pathophysiology of Muscle Pain." Presented at Pain in Europe III, EFIC 2000, Nice, France, September 26–29, 2000. www.painstudy.ru/pe3/muscle_pain.htm

Moffet, H.H. "Sham Acupuncture May Be as Efficacious as True Acupuncture: A Systematic Review of Clinical Trials." *Journal of Alternative and Complementary Medicine* 15, no. 3 (March 2009 March): 213–216.

National Institute on Drug Abuse. *Opioid Overdose Crisis.* www.drugabuse.gov/drugs-abuse/opioids/opioid-overdose-crisis

PBS. Frontline. "Opium throughout History." (1998). www.pbs.org/
wgbh/pages/frontline/shows/heroin/etc/history.html

Pert, C.B., and S.H. Snyder. "Opiate Receptor: Demonstration
in Nervous Tissue." *Science* 179, issue 4,077 (March 9, 1973):
1,011–1,014.

Petersen-Felix, S., and M. Curatolo. "Neuroplasticity—An Important
Factor in Acute and Chronic Pain." *Swiss Medical Weekly* 132
(2002): 273–278.

Petrovic, P., et al. "Placebo and Opioid Analgesia—Imaging a Shared
Neuronal Network." *Science Magazine* 295 (March 1, 2002):
1,737–1,740.

Price, D.D. "Psychological and Neural Mechanisms of the Affective
Dimension of Pain." *Science* 288, no.5472 (June 9, 2000):
1,769–1,772.

Rainville, P., et al. "Pain Affect Encoded in Human Anterior
Cingulate but Not Somatosensory Cortex." *Science* 177 (August
15, 1997): 968–971.

Roth, S.M. "Why Does Lactic Acid Build Up in Muscles? And Why
Does It Cause Soreness?" *Scientific American,* January 23, 2006.
www.scientificamerican.com/article/why-does-lactic-acid-buil/

Safari, A., A.A. Khaledi, and M. Vojdani. "Congenital Insensitivity
to Pain with Anhidrosis (CIPA): A Case Report." *Iranian Red
Crescent Medical Journal* 13, no. 2 (February 2011): 134-138.

Salomons, T.V., et al. "Perceived Controllability Modulates the
Neural Response to Pain." *Journal of Neuroscience* 24, no. 32
(August 11, 2004): 7,199–7,203.

Sandroni, P., et al. "Complex Regional Pain Syndrome Type I:
Incidence and Prevalence in Olmsted County, a Population-
Based Study." *Pain* 103, no. 1–2 (May 2003): 199–207.

Sapolsky, R.M. *Why Zebras Don't Get Ulcers: The Acclaimed Guide to
Stress, Stress-Related Diseases, and Coping,* 3rd ed. New York, NY:
Holt Paperbacks/Henry Holt and Company, LLC, 2004.

Schmidt, C.E., and J.B. Leach. "Neural Tissue Engineering:
Strategies for Repair and Regeneration." *Annual Review of*

Biomedical Engineering 5 (2003): 293–347.

Scrivo, R. "Inflammation as 'Common Soil' of the Multifactorial Diseases." *Autoimmunity Reviews* 10 (2011): 369–374.

Seifert, F., and C. Maihofner. "Functional and Structural Imaging of Pain-Induced Neuroplasticity." *Current Opinion in Anaesthesiology* 24, no. 5 (2011): 515–523.

Simon, E.J., J.M. Hiller, and I. Edelman. "Stereospecific Binding of the Potent Narcotic Analgesic (3H) Etorphine to Rat-Brain Homogenate." *Proceedings of the National Academies of Sciences*, 70, no. 7 (July 1973): 1947–1949.

Stackhouse, S.K., D.S. Reisman, and S.A. Binder-Macleod. "Challenging the Role of pH in Skeletal Muscle Fatigue." *Physical Therapy* 81, no. 12 (December 2001): 1897–1903.

Stix, G. "Can Acupuncture Reverse Killer Inflammation?" *Scientific American.* "Talking Back" blog. March 3, 2014. www.blogs. scientificamerican.com/talking-back/can-acupuncture-reverse-killer-inflammation

Terenius, L. "Stereospecific Interaction between Narcotic Analgesics and a Synaptic Plasma Membrane Fraction of Rat Cerebral Cortex." *Acta Pharmacologica et Toxicologica (Copenh)* 32, no. 3 (1973): 317–320.

Tinazzi, M. et al. "Neuroplastic Changes Related to Pain Occur at Multiple Levels of the Human Somatosensory System: A Somatosensory-Evoked Potentials Study in Patients with Cervical Radicular Pain." *Journal of Neuroscience* 20, no. 24 (December 15, 2000): 9,277–9,283.

Torres-Rosas, R., et al. "Dopamine Mediates Vagal Modulation of the Immune System by Electroacupuncture." *Nature Medicine* 20, no. 3 (March 2014): 291–295.

Valance, A.K. "Something Out of Nothing: The Placebo Effect." *Advances in Psychiatric Treatment* 12 (2006): 287–296.

Vithoulkas, G., and S. Carlino. "The 'Continuum' of a Unified Theory of Disease." *Medical Science Monitor* 16, no. 2 (February 2010): SR7–15.

White, A., and E. Ernst. "A Brief History of Acupuncture."
Rheumatology 43, no. 5 (2004): 662–663.

Wilkinson, P.R. "Neurophysiology of Pain Part I: Mechanisms of
Pain in the Peripheral Nervous System." *CPD Anaesthesia* 3, no. 3
(2001): 103–08.

Woods, J. *The Discovery of Endorphins.* National Alliance of
Methadone Advocates. www.methadone.org/library/
woods_1994_endorphin.html

Wu, J.A. "Short History of Acupuncture." *Journal of Alternative and
Complementary Medicine,* 2, no. 1 (1996): 19–21.

Yeh, D.C. "Holistic Approach to Axonal Regeneration in Cases
of Spinal Cord Injury." *Journal of Biomolecular Research and
Therapeutics* 7, no.1 (2018).

Yilmaz, P. et al. "Brain Correlates of Stress-Induced Analgesia." *Pain*
151, no. 2 (November 2010): 522–529.

Young, D. "Scientists Examine Pain Relief and Addiction." *American
Journal of Health-System Pharmacy* 64, issue 8 (April 15, 2007):
796–798. www.ashp.org/news/2007/03/30/scientists_examine_
pain_relief_and_addiction

Chapter 3: Why Stress Makes Pain Worse

American College of Rheumatology. "2010 Fibromyalgia Diagnostic
Criteria—Excerpt." www.rheumatology.org/Portals/0/
Files/2010%20Fibromyalgia%20Diagnostic%20Criteria_Excerpt.
pdf

American Fibromyalgia Syndrome Association. "What Is
Fibromyalgia?" www.afsafund.org/fibromyalgia.html

Asmundson, G., et al. "PTSD and the Experience of Pain: Research
and Clinical Implications of Shared Vulnerability and Mutual
Maintenance Models." *Canadian Journal of Psychiatry* 47
(December 2002): 930–937.

Bear, M.F., B.W. Connors, and M.A. Paradiso. *Neuroscience:
Exploring the Brain*, 3rd ed. Baltimore, MD: Lippincott Williams
& Wilkins, 2007.

Bondy, B., et al. "Substance P Serum Levels Are Increased in Major Depression: Preliminary Results." *Biological Psychiatry* 53, no. 6 (March 15, 2003): 538–542.

Brown, E.S., A.J. Rush, and B.S. McEwen. "Hippocampal Remodeling and Damage by Corticosteroids: Implications for Mood Disorders." *Neuropsychopharmacology* 21, no. 4 (1999): 474–484.

Burgmer, M. et al. "Cerebral Mechanisms of Experimental Hyperalgesia in Fibromyalgia." *European Journal of Pain* 16, no. 5 (May 2012): 636–647.

Cohen, H. et al. "Prevalence of Post-Traumatic Stress Disorder in Fibromyalgia Patients: Overlapping Syndromes or Post-Traumatic Fibromyalgia Syndrome?" *Seminars in Arthritis & Rheumatism* 32, no. 1 (August 2002): 38–50.

Colloca, L., and F. Benedetti. "Nocebo Hyperalgesia: How Anxiety Is Turned into Pain." *Current Opinion in Anaesthesiology* 20, no. 5 (October 2007): 435–439.

Defrin, R., et al. "Quantitative Testing of Pain Perception in Subjects with PTSD: Implications for the Mechanism of the Coexistence between PTSD and Chronic Pain." *Pain* 138, no. 2 (2008): 450–459.

Del Casale, A., et al. "Pain Perception and Hypnosis: Findings from Recent Functional Neuroimaging Studies." *International Journal of Clinical and Experimental Hypnosis* 63, no. 2 (2015): 144–70.

Harvard Medical School. Harvard Health Publishing. "Depression and Pain." March 21, 2017. www.health.harvard.edu/mind-and-mood/depression-and-pain

Epel, E.S., et al. "Wandering Minds and Aging Cells." *Clinical Psychological Science* 1, Issue 1 (January 1, 2013): 75–83.

Grachev, I.D., B.E. Frederickson, and A.V. Apkarian. "Brain Chemistry Reflects Dual States of Pain and Anxiety in Chronic Low Back Pain." *Journal of Neural Transmission* 109 (2002): 1,309–1,334.

Grachev, I.D., B.E. Fredrickson, and A.V. Apkarian. "Dissociating

Anxiety from Pain: Mapping the Neuronal Marker N-acetyl Aspartate to Perception Distinguishes Closely Interrelated Characteristics of Chronic Pain." *Molecular Psychiatry* 6 (2001): 256–260.

Hasset, A.L., and D.J. Clauw. "The Role of Stress in Rheumatic Diseases." *Arthritis Research & Therapy* 12 (June 7, 2010): 123.

Juhan, D. *Job's Body: A Handbook for Bodywork*, 3rd ed. Barrytown, NY: Barrytown/Station Hill Press, Inc. (2003).

Keefe, F.J., et al. "Pain and Emotion: New Research Directions." *Journal of Clinical Psychology* 5, no. 4 (April 2001): 587–607.

Keltner, J.R., et al. "Isolating the Modulatory Effect of Expectation on Pain Transmission: A Functional Magnetic Resonance Imaging Study." *Journal of Neuroscience* 26, no. 16 (April 19, 2006): 4,437–4,443.

Kling, M.A., V.H. Coleman, and J. Schulkin. "Glucocorticoid Inhibition in the Treatment of Depression: Can We Think Outside the Endocrine Hypothalamus?" *Depression and Anxiety* 26, no. 7 (2009): 641–649.

Kroenke, K., et al. "Association between Anxiety, Health-Related Quality of Life and Functional Impairment in Primary Care Patients with Chronic Pain." *General Hospital Psychiatry* 35, no. 4 (2013): 359–365.

Lin, P.Y., Y.C. Huang, and C.F. Hung. "Shortened Telomere Length in Patients with Depression: A Meta-Analytic Study." *Journal of Psychiatric Research* 76 (May 2016): 84–93.

McEwen, B.S. "Glucocorticoids, Depression, and Mood Disorders: Structural Remodeling in the Brain. *Metabolism* 54, no. 5, Suppl 1 (May 2005): 20–23.

McEwen, B.S. "Stress and Hippocampal Plasticity." *Annual Review of Neuroscience* 22 (1999): 105–122.

McIntyre, C.K., and B. Roozendaal. "Adrenal Stress Hormones and Enhanced Memory for Emotionally Arousing Experiences." In

Neural Plasticity and Memory: From Genes to Brain Imaging, edited by F. Bermudez-Rattoni. Boca Raton, FL: CRC Press, 2007.

Mengshoel, A.M., and K. Heggen. "Recovery from Fibromyalgia— Previous Patients' Own Experiences." *Disability and Rehabilitation* 26, no. 1 (January 7, 2004): 46–53.

Murphy, B.E.P. "Steroids and Depression." *Journal of Steroid Biochemistry and Molecular Biology* 38, no. 5 (May 1991): 537–559.

Otis, J.D., T.M. Keane, and R.D. Kerns. "An Examination of the Relationship between Chronic Pain and Post-Traumatic Stress Disorder." *Journal of Rehabilitation Research and Development*, 40, no. 5 (2003): 397–406.

National Institute of Arthritis and Musculoskeletal and Skin Diseases. "What Is Fibromyalgia?" www.niams.nih.gov/health-topics/fibromyalgia

National Fibromyalgia Association. "Prevalence." www.fmaware.org/about-fibromyalgia/prevalence/

Roth, R.S., M.E. Geisser, and R. Bates. (July 2008). "The Relation of Post-Traumatic Stress Symptoms to Depression and Pain in Patients with Accident-Related Chronic Pain." *Journal of Pain* 9, no. 7, 588–596.

Salomons, T.V., et al. "Perceived Controllability Modulates the Neural Response to Pain." *Journal of Neuroscience* 24, no. 32 (August 11, 2004): 7,199–7,203.

Sapolsky, R.M. "Stress and Plasticity in the Limbic System." *Neurochemical Research* 28, no. 11 (November 2003): 1,735–1,742

Sapolsky, R.M. *Why Zebras Don't Get Ulcers: The Acclaimed Guide to Stress, Stress-Related Diseases, and Coping*, 3rd ed. New York, NY: Holt Paperbacks/Henry Holt and Company, LLC, 2004.

Schwarz, M.J., and M. Ackenheil. "The Role of Substance P in Depression: Therapeutic Implications." *Dialogues in Clinical Neuroscience* 4, no. 1 (March 2002): 21–29.

Sharp, T.J., and A.G. Harvey, A.G. "Chronic Pain and Posttraumatic Stress Disorder: Mutual Maintenance?" *Clinical Psychology Review* 21, no. 6 (August 2001): 857–877.

Simon, E.B., et al. "Losing Neutrality: The Neural Basis of Impaired

Emotional Control without Sleep." *Journal of Neuroscience* 35, no. 38 (2015): 13,194–13,205.

Thiagarajah, A.S., et al. "The Relationship Between Fibromyalgia, Stress and Depression: Why Does Stress Lead to Fibromyalgia in Some Patients?" *Medscape CME & Education,* October 17, 2014.

Watanabe, Y., E. Gould, and B.S. McEwen. "Stress Induces Atrophy of Apical Dendrites of Hippocampal Ca3 Pyramidal Neurons." *Brain Research* 588, no. 2 (August 21, 1992): 341–345.

Yuen, E.Y. et al. "Acute Stress Enhances Glutamatergic Transmission in Prefrontal Cortex and Facilitates Working Memory." *Proceedings of the National Academy of Sciences* 106, no. 33 (August 18, 2009): 14,075–14,079.

Chapter 4: How You Develop Muscle Memory

Adams, J.A. "Historical Review and Appraisal of Research on the Learning, Retention, and Transfer of Human Motor Skills." *Psychological Bulletin* 101, no. 1 (1987): 41–74.

Attwell, P.J.E., S.F. Cooke, and C.H. Yeo. "Cerebellar Function in Consolidation of a Motor Memory." *Neuron* 34 (2002, June 13): 1,011–1,020.

Bear, M.F., B.W. Connors, and M.A. Paradiso. *Neuroscience: Exploring the Brain,* 3rd ed. Baltimore, MD: Lippincott Williams & Wilkins. (2007).

Berlucchi, G., and H.A. Buchtel. "Neuronal Plasticity: Historical Roots and Evolution of Meaning." *Experimental Brain Research* 192, no. 3 (January 2009): 307–319.

Dekaban, A.S. "Changes in Brain Weights during the Span of Human Life: Relation of Brain Weights to Body Heights and Body Weights." *Annals of Neurology* 4, no. 4 . (1978, October): 345–356.

Doyon, J., and H. Benali. "Reorganization and Plasticity in the Adult Brain during Learning of Motor Skills." *Current Opinion in Neurobiology* 15 (2005): 161-167.

Eden, S. "Stroke of Madness." ESPN. Golf. January 22, 2013. www.espn.com/golf/story/_/id/8865487/tiger-woods-reinvents-golf-swing-third-time-career-espn-magazine.

Hill, L.B. "A Quarter Century of Delayed Recall." *Pedagogical Seminary and Journal of Genetic Psychology* 44, no. 1 (1934): 231–238.

Houk, J. "Voluntary Movement: Control, Learning and Memory." *Encyclopedia of Behavioral Neuroscience* 3(2010): 455–458.

James, W. "Habit." Chapter 4 in *The Principles of Psychology*, Volume 1. (1890). www.psychclassics.yorku.ca/James/Principles

Ma, L., et al. "Changes in Regional Activity Are Accompanied with Changes in Inter-Regional Connectivity during Four Weeks Motor Learning." *Brain Research*, 1318C (March 8, 2010): 64–76.

Newmark, T. "Cases in Visualization for Improved Athletic Performance." *Psychiatric Annals*, 42, no. 10 (October 2012): 385–387.

Packard, M.G.l., and B.J. Knowlton, B.J. "Learning and Memory Functions of the Basal Ganglia." *Annual Review of Neuroscience* 25 (2002): 563–593.

Roland, P.E., et al. "Supplementary Motor Area and Other Cortical Areas in Organization of Voluntary Movements in Man." *Journal of Neurophysiology* 43, no. 1 (January 1980): 118–136.

Santos, M.J., N. Kanekar, and A.S. Aruin. "The Role of Anticipatory Postural Adjustments in Compensatory Control of Posture: 1. Electromyographic Analysis." *Journal of Electromyography & Kinesiology* 20, no. 3 (2010, June): 388–397.

Shadmehr, R., and H.H. Holcomb. "Neural Correlates of Motor Memory Consolidation." *Science Magazine* 277 (August 8, 1997): 821–825.

Shutoh, F., et al. "Memory Trace of Motor Learning Shifts Transsynaptically from Cerebellar Cortex to Nuclei for Consolidation." *Neuroscience*, 139, no. 2 (May 12: 2006): 767–777.

Stefan, K., et al. "Formation of a Motor Memory by Action Observation." *Journal of Neuroscience* 25, no. 41 (October 12, 2005): 9,339–9,346.

Strata, P. "David Marr's Theory of Cerebellar Learning: 40 Years Later." *Journal of Physiology* 587 (December 1, 2009): 5,519–5,520.

Wolpert, D.M., Z. Ghahramani, and J.R. Flanagan." Perspectives and Problems in Motor Learning." *Trends in Cognitive Sciences* 5, no. 11 (November 2001): 487–494.

Chapter 5: Why You Lose Control, Sensation, and Awareness

Bear, M.F., B.W. Connors, and M.A. Paradiso. *Neuroscience: Exploring the Brain*, 3rd ed. Baltimore, MD: Lippincott Williams & Wilkins, 2007.

Feldenkrais, M. *Body & Mature Behavior*. Berkeley, CA: Frog Books/North Atlantic Books, 2005.

Hanna, T. *The Body of Life*. Rochester, VT: Healing Arts Press. 1993.

Hanna, T. *Somatics: Reawakening the Mind's Control of Movement, Flexibility, and Health*. Cambridge, MA: De Capo Press, 2004.

Juhan, D. *Job's Body: A Handbook for Bodywork*, 3rd ed. Barrytown, NY: Barrytown/Station Hill Press, Inc., 2003.

Melzack, R., and P.D. Wall. *The Challenge of Pain*, 2nd ed. London, England: Penguin Books, Ltd., 2008.

Webster, M.A. "Evolving Concepts of Sensory Adaptation." *F1000 Biol Reports* 4, no. 21 (2012).

Chapter 6: The Pros and Cons of Common Pain Relief Treatments

American Chiropractic Association. "Origins and History of Chiropractic Care." www.acatoday.org/About/History-of-Chiropractic

Avela, J., H. Kyrolainen, and P.V. Komi. "Altered Reflex Sensitivity after Repeated and Prolonged Passive Muscle Stretching." *Journal of Applied Physiology* 86, no. 4 (April 21, 1999): 1,283–1,291.

Bear, M.F., B.W. Connors, and M.A. Paradiso. *Neuroscience: Exploring the Brain*, 3rd ed. Baltimore, MD: Lippincott Williams & Wilkins, 2007.

Biller, J., et al. "Cervical Arterial Dissections and Association with Cervical Manipulative Therapy: A Statement for Healthcare

Professionals from the American Heart Association/American Stroke Association." *Stroke,* 45 (2014): 3,155–3,174.

Calvert, R.N. "Pages from History: Swedish Massage." *Massage Magazine,* April 24, 2014.

Cherkin, D.C, et al. "A Comparison of Physical Therapy, Chiropractic Manipulation, and Provision of an Educational Booklet for the Treatment of Patients with Low Back Pain." *New England Journal of Medicine* 339 (October 8, 1998): 1,021–1,029.

Coombes, B.K., L. Bisset, and B. Vicenzino. "Efficacy and Safety of Corticosteroid Injections and Other Injections for Management of Tendinopathy: A Systematic Review of Randomized Controlled Trials." *Lancet* 376, no. 9,754 (November 20, 2010): 1,751–1,767.

Ernst, E. "Adverse Effects of Spinal Manipulation: A Systematic Review." *Journal of the Royal Society of Medicine* 100, no. 7 (July 2007): 330–338.

Ernst, E. "Chiropractic Care: Attempting a Risk-Benefit Analysis." *American Journal of Public Health* 92, no. 10 (October 2002): 1,603–1,604.

Ernst, E. "Deaths after Chiropractic: A Review of Published Cases." *International Journal of Clinical Practice* 64, no. 8 (July 2010): 1,162–1,165.

Fritz, J.M., et al. "Physical Therapy for Acute Low Back Pain: Associations with Subsequent Healthcare Costs." *Spine* 33, no. 16 (July 15, 2008) 1,800–1,805.

Gelhorn, A.C., et al. "Management Patterns in Acute Low Back Pain: The Role of Physical Therapy." *Spine (Phila Pa 1976),* 37, no. 9 (April 20, 2012): 775–782.

Gergley, J.C. "Acute Effect of Passive Static Stretching on Lower-Body Strength in Moderately Trained Men." *Journal of Strength & Conditioning Research* 27, no. 4 (April 2013): 973–977.

Gouveia, L.O., P. Castanho, J.J. Ferreira. "Safety of Chiropractic Interventions: A Systematic Review." *Spine (Phila Pa 1976)* 34, no. 11 (May 15, 2009): E405–413.

Hernandez-Reif, M. et al. "Breast Cancer Patients Have Improved Immune and Neuroendocrine Functions following Massage Therapy." *Journal of Psychosomatic Research* 57, no. 1 (July 2004): 45–52.

Juhan, D. *Job's Body: A Handbook for Bodywork,* 3rd ed. Barrytown, NY: Barrytown/Station Hill Press, Inc., 2003.

Marks, L. "Bridging the Great Divide: Touching Our Most Basic Humanity." *Spirit of Change Magazine,* June 1, 2005. www.healingheartpower.com/article1.html.

National Center for Complimentary and Integrative Health. National Institutes of Health. "Massage Therapy for Health Purposes: What You Need to Know." www.nccih.nih.gov/health/massage/massageintroduction.htm

Radcliff, K., et al. "Epidural Steroid Injections Are Associated with Less Improvement in Patients with Lumbar Spinal Stenosis: A Subgroup Analysis of the Spine Patient Outcomes Research Trial." *Spine* 38, no. 4 (February 15, 2013): 279–291.

Rapaport, M.H., P. Schettler, and C. Bresee. "A Preliminary Study of the Effects of Repeated Massage on Hypothalamic-Pituitary-Adrenal and Immune Function in Healthy Individuals: A Study of Mechanisms of Action and Dosage." *Journal of Alternative and Complementary Medicine* 18, no. 8 (August 13, 2012).

Schleip, R. "Fascial Plasticity—A New Neurobiological Explanation: Part 1." *Journal of Bodywork and Movement Therapies* 7, no. 1 (January 2003): 11–19.

Simic, L., N. Sarabon, and G. Markovic. "Does Pre-Exercise Static Stretching Inhibit Maximal Muscular Performance? A Meta-Analytical Review." *Scandinavian Journal of Medicine & Science in Sports* 23, no. 2 (2013, March): 131–148.

Tsao, J.C.I. "Effectiveness of Massage Therapy for Chronic, Non–Malignant Pain: A Review." *Evidence-Based Complementary and Alternative Medicine* 4, no. 2 (June 2007): 165–179.

Wellens, F. "The Traditional Mechanistic Paradigm in the Teaching and Practice of Manual Therapy: Time for a Reality Check." PhysioAxis, 2010. www.physioaxis.ca/realitycheck.pdf

Zwanger, M. "Narcotic Abuse," *eMedicine Health*. www. emedicinehealth.com/narcotic_abuse/article_em.htm

Chapter 7: The Evolution of Somatic Education

Alexander, F.M. *Man's Supreme Inheritance*. New York: Dutton, 1910.

Alexander, F.M. *The Use of the Self.* Great Britain: Methuen & Co, Ltd., 1932.

Alexander, G. *Eutony: The Holistic Discovery of the Total Person*. Great Neck, NY: Felix Morrow, 1986.

Behnke, E.A. *Friends Passing: Thomas Hanna (1928–1990).* 1990. www.somatics.org/library/bea-passing.html

Feldenkrais, M. *Body & Mature Behavior*. Berkeley, CA: Frog Books/ North Atlantic Books, 2005.

Feldenkrais, M. *Practical Unarmed Combat.* London, England: Frederick Warne & Co., Ltd. 1942.

Gelb, M.J. *Body Learning: An Introduction to the Alexander Technique*, 2nd ed. New York, NY: Henry Holt and Company, LLC., 1996.

Hanna, T. *Somatics: Reawakening the Mind's Control of Movement, Flexibility, and Health*. Cambridge, MA: De Capo Press, 2004.

Hanna, T. *The Body of Life*. Rochester, VT: Healing Arts Press, 1993.

Huebner, M. "The Life and Teachings of Elsa Gindler." *Rosen Method International Journal* 3, no. 1 (2010): 17–21.

Klinkenberg, N. "The Encounter between Moshe Feldenkrais and Heinrich Jacoby." In *Feldenkrais und Jacoby—Eine Begegnung, Volume I.* 2002. www.davidzemach-bersin.com/2012/09/the-encounter-between-moshe-feldenkrais-and-heinrich-jacoby/

Melville, T. "Eutony." www.scribd.com/document/283132552/ Eutony-Gerda-Alexander

Milz, H. "A Conversation with Thomas Hanna, PhD." *Somatics: Magazine—Journal of the Bodily Arts and Sciences* VIII, no. 2 (1991): 50–56.

Mower, M. "In Memory of Thomas Hanna." *Massage,* Nov/Dec

(1990): 73.

Pinchas, R.L.B. (1986). "'The Energy Is in the Bones': Eutony's Gerda Alexander." *Yoga Journal Issue* 66 (January/February 1986): 21–24.

Weaver, J. "The Influence of Elsa Gindler—Ancestor of Sensory Awareness." *United States Association of Body Psychotherapy Journal* 3, no. 1 (2004): 22–26.

Chapter 8: Clinical Somatic Education

Hanna, T. *Somatics: Reawakening the Mind's Control of Movement, Flexibility, and Health.* Cambridge, MA: De Capo Press, 2004.

Chapter 9: Stress and Posture

Blouin, J.S., G.P. Siegmund, and J.T. Inglis. "Interaction between Acoustic Startle and Habituated Neck Postural Responses in Seated Subjects." *Journal of Applied Physiology* 102, no. 4 (April 1, 2007): 1,574–1,586.

Eaton, R.C. *Neural Mechanisms of Startle Behavior.* New York, NY: Springer, 1984.

Fowler, K., and L. Kravitz. *The Perils of Poor Posture.* www.ideafit.com/fitness-library/the-perils-of-poor-posture

Guimond, S. and W. Massrieh. "Intricate Correlation between Body Posture, Personality Trait and Incidence of Body Pain: A Cross–Referential Study Report." *PLOS ONE* 7, no. 5 (May 18, 2012): e37450.

Hanna, T. *Somatics: Reawakening the Mind's Control of Movement, Flexibility, and Health.* Cambridge, MA: De Capo Press, 2004.

Hansraj, K.K. "Assessment of Stresses in the Cervical Spine Caused by Posture and Position of the Head." Neuro and Spine Surgery, Surgical Technology International, Vol. 25 (November 2014): pp. 277-279.

Hazlett, R.L., D.R. McLeod, and R. Hoehn-Saric. "Muscle Tension in Generalized Anxiety Disorder: Elevated Muscle Tonus or Agitated Movement?" *Psychophysiology* 31, no. 2 (March 1994):

189–195.

Juhan, D. *Job's Body: A Handbook for Bodywork*, 3rd ed. Barrytown, NY: Barrytown/Station Hill Press, Inc., 2003.

Lundberg, U., et al. "Psychophysiological Stress and EMG Activity of the Trapezius Muscle." *International Journal of Behavioral Medicine* 1, no. 4 (December 1994): 354–370.

Malmo, R.B., C. Shagass, and J.F. Davis. "Electromyographic Studies of Muscular Tension in Psychiatric Patients under Stress." *Journal of Clinical & Experimental Psychopathology* 12 (1951): 45–66.

Malmo, R.B. *On Emotions, Needs, and our Archaic Brain.* Austin, TX: Holt, Rinehart and Winston, Inc., 1975.

Rideout, V.J., U.G. Foehr, and D.F. Roberts. *Generation M2: Media in the Lives of 8- to 18-Year-Olds.* Menlo Park, CA: The Henry J. Kaiser Family Foundation, January 2010.

Sainsbury, P., and J.G. Gibson. "Symptoms of Anxiety and Tension and the Accompanying Physiological Changes in the Muscular System." *Journal of Neurology, Neurosurgery, & Psychiatry* 17, no. 3 (1954, August): 216–224.

Straker, L.M., et al. "Computer Use and Habitual Spinal Posture in Australian Adolescents." *Public Health Reports* 122, no. 5 (2007): 634–643.

Chapter 10: Why You Bend to the Side

Bear, M.F., B.W. Connors, and M.A. Paradiso. *Neuroscience: Exploring the Brain*, 3rd ed. Baltimore, MD: Lippincott Williams & Wilkins, 2007.

Blouin, J.S., P. Corbeil, and N. Teasdale. "Postural Stability Is Altered by the Stimulation of Pain but Not Warm Receptors in Humans." *BMC Musculoskeletal Disorders* 4 (2003, October 17): 23.

Carter, O.D., and S.G. Haynes. "Prevalence Rates for Scoliosis in US Adults: Results from the First National Health and Nutrition Examination Survey." *International Journal of Epidemiology*, 16, no. 4 (1987): 537–544.

Erwin, W.D., et al. "Clinical Review of Patients with Broken Harrington Rods." *Journal of Bone & Joint Surgery* 62, no. 8 (December 1980): 1,302–1,307.

Ha, K.Y., J.S. Lee, and K.W. Kim. "Degeneration of Sacroiliac Joint After Instrumented Lumbar or Lumbosacral Fusion: A Prospective Cohort Study Over Five-Year Follow-Up." *Spine* 33, no. 11 (May 15, 2008): 1,192–1,198.

Hanna, T. *The Body of Life.* Rochester, VT: Healing Arts Press, 1993.

Hanna, T. *Somatics: Reawakening the Mind's Control of Movement, Flexibility, and Health.* Cambridge, MA: De Capo Press, 2004.

Horne, J.P., R. Flannery, and S. Usman. "Adolescent Idiopathic Scoliosis: Diagnosis and Management." *American Family Physician* 89, no. 3 (February 1, 2014): 193–198.

Johnston, D.W., et al. "Nature's Experiment? Handedness and Early Childhood Development." *Demography,* 46, no. 2 (May 2009): 281–301.

Kebaish, K.M., et al. "Scoliosis in Adults Aged Forty Years and Older: Prevalence and Relationship to Age, Race, and Gender." Spine (Phila PA 1976) 36, no. 9 (April 20, 2011): 731–736.

Levin, D.A., J.J. Hale, and J.A. Bendo. "Adjacent Segment Degeneration following Spinal Fusion for Degenerative Disc Disease." *Bulletin of the NYU Hospital for Joint Diseases* 65, no. 1 (2007): 29–36.

Martin, B.I., et al. "Reoperation Rates following Lumbar Spine Surgery and the Influence of Spinal Fusion Procedures." *Spine,* 32. no. 3 (February 1, 2007): 382–7.

National Scoliosis Foundation. Information and Support. www.scoliosis.org/info.php

Reamy, B.V., and J.B. Slakey. "Adolescent Idiopathic Scoliosis: Review and Current Concepts." *American Family Physician* 64, no. 1 (July 1: 2001): 111–117.

Schwab, F., et al. "Adult Scoliosis: Prevalence, SF-36, and Nutritional

Parameters in an Elderly Volunteer Population." *Spine* 30, no. 9 (May 1, 2005): 1,082–1,085.

Shah, S.A. *What Is Scoliosis?* Alfred I. duPont Hospital for Children. 2009. www.nemours.org/content/dam/nemours/wwwv2/filebox/service/medical/spinescoliosis/scoliosisguide.pdf

Trobisch, P., O. Suess, and F. Schwab. "Idiopathic Scoliosis." *Deutsches Arzteblatt International,* 107, no. 49 (December 2010): 875–884.

Uomini, N.T. "The Prehistory of Handedness: Archaeological Data and Comparative Ethology." *Journal of Human Evolution* 57, no. 4, 411–419. (October 2009).

Voos, K., O. Boachie-Adjei, and B.A. Rawlins. "Multiple Vertebral Osteotomies in the Treatment of Rigid Adult Spine Deformities." *Spine* 26 (2001): 526–533.

Weiss, H.R., and D. Goodall. "Rate of Complications in Scoliosis Surgery—A Systematic Review of the Pub Med Literature." *Scoliosis* 3, no. 9. (August 5, 2008).

Wong, G.T.C., et al. "Persistent Pain in Patients following Scoliosis Surgery." *European Spine Journal* 16, no.10 (October 2007): 1,551–1,556.

Chapter 11: Personality and Posture

Bohns, V.K., and S.S. Wiltermuth. "It Hurts When I Do This (Or You Do That): Posture and Pain Tolerance." *Journal of Experimental Social Psychology* 48, no. 1 (January 2012): 341–345.

Burgoon, J.K., L.K. Guerrero, and K. Floyd. *Nonverbal Communication.* Boston, MA: Allyn and Bacon, 2009.

Carney, D.R., A.J.C. Cuddy, and A.J. Yap. "Power Posing: Brief Nonverbal Displays Affect Neuroendocrine Levels and Risk Tolerance." *Psychological Science,* 21, no. 10 (October 2010): 1,363–1,368.

Guimond, S., and W. Massrieh. "Intricate Correlation between Body Posture, Personality Trait and Incidence of Body Pain: A Cross–Referential Study Report." *PLOS ONE* 7, no. 5 (2012, May 18): e37450.

Mehrabian, A. *Silent Messages,* 1st ed. Belmont, CA: Wadsworth, 1971.

Meurle-Hallberg, K. "Relationships between Bodily Characteristics and Mental Attitudes: Bodily Examined and Self-Assessed Ratings of Ill Health." *UMEA Psychology Supplement Reports,* Supplement No. 9 (2005). www.umu.diva-portal.org/smash/get/diva2:154411/FULLTEXT01

Chapter 12: Automatic Imitation

Bassolino, M., et al. "Training the Motor Cortex by Observing the Actions of Others during Immobilization." *Cerebral Cortex* 24, no. 12 (December 2014): 3,268–3,276.

Bavelas, J.B., et al. "Experimental Methods for Studying 'Elementary Motor Mimicry.'" *Journal of Nonverbal Behavior* 10, no. 2 (1986): 102–119.

Chartrand, T.L., and J.A. Bargh. "The Chameleon Effect: The Perception-Behavior Link and Social Interaction." *Journal of Personality and Social Psychology* 76, no. 6 (June 1999): 893–910.

Davis, J.I., et al. "The Effects of Botox Injections on Emotional Experience." *Emotion* 10, no. 3 (June 2010): 433–440.

Heyes, C. "Automatic Imitation." *Psychological Bulletin* 137, no. 3 (May 2011): 463–483.

Lakin, J.L., and T.L. Chartrand. "Using Nonconscious Behavioral Mimicry to Create Affiliation and Rapport." *Psychological Science* 14, no. 4 (July 2003): 334–339.

Mukamel, R., et al. "Single-Neuron Responses in Humans during Execution and Observation of Actions." *Current Biology* 20, no. 8 (April 27, 2010): 750–756.

Neal, D.T., and T.L. Chartrand. "Embodied Emotion Perception: Amplifying and Dampening Facial Feedback Modulates Emotion Perception Accuracy." *Social Psychological and Personality Science,* 2, no. 6 (November 2011): 673–678.

Paukner, A., et al. "Capuchin Monkeys Display Affiliation toward Humans Who Imitate Them." *Science* 325, no. 5,942 (2009): 880–883.

Rizzolatti, G., et al. "Premotor Cortex and the Recognition of Motor Actions." *Cognitive Brain Research* 3 (1996): 131–141.

Romero, T., A. Konno, and T. Hasegawa. "Familiarity Bias and Physiological Responses in Contagious Yawning by Dogs Support Link to Empathy." *PLOS ONE* 8, no. 8 (August 7, 2013): e71365.

Shaw, D.J., and K. Czekoova. "Exploring the Development of the Mirror Neuron System: Finding the Right Paradigm." *Developmental Neuropsychology* 38, no. 4 (2013): 256–271.

Stefan, K. et al. "Formation of a Motor Memory by Action Observation." *Journal of Neuroscience* 25, no. 41 (October 12, 2005): 9,339–9,346.

Tanner, R., et al. "Of Chameleons and Consumption: The Impact of Mimicry on Choice and Preferences." *Journal of Consumer Research* 34 (2008): 754–767.

Chapter 13: Athletic Training

Abernethy, L., and C. Bleakley. "Strategies to Prevent Injury in Adolescent Sport: A Systematic Review." *British Journal of Sports Medicine* 41 (2007): 627–638.

Hennessey, L., A.W. Watson. "Flexibility and Posture Assessment in Relation to Hamstring Injury." *British Journal of Sports Medicine* 27 (1993): 243–246.

Loudon, J.K., W. Jenkins, and K.L. Loudon. "The Relationship between Static Posture and ACL Injury in Female Athletes." *The Journal of Orthopaedic and Sports Physical Therapy*, 24(2) (1996). 91–97.

Safe Kids Worldwide. "Interview with an Expert." www.safekids.org/blog/interview-expert

Stop Sports Injuries. "An Injury Prevention Curriculum for Coaches." 2011. www.stopsportsinjuries.org/STOP/Downloads/Resources/CoachesCurriculumToolkit.pdf

Watson, A.W. "Ankle Sprains in Players of the Field-Games Gaelic Football and Hurling." *Journal of Sports Medicine and Physical Fitness* 39, no. 1 (1999): 66–70.

Watson, A.W. "Sports Injuries in Footballers Related to Defects of Posture and Body Mechanics." *The Journal of Sports Medicine and Physical Fitness*, 35, no. 4 (1995): 289–294.

Watson, A.W. "Sports Injuries Related to Flexibility, Posture, Acceleration, Clinical Defects, and Previous Injury, in High-Level Players of Body Contact Sports." *International Journal of Sports Medicine* 22, no. 3 (2001): 222–225.

Zullig, K.J., and R.J. White. "Physical Activity, Life Satisfaction, and Self-Rated Health of Middle School Students." *Applied Research in Quality of Life* 6, no. 3 (2011): 277–289.

Chapter 14: How Your Patterns Lead to Common Pain Conditions

Alfredson, H., and R. Lorentzon. "Chronic Tendon Pain: No Signs of Chemical Inflammation but High Concentrations of the Neurotransmitter Glutamate. Implications for Treatment?" *Current Drug Targets* 3, no. 1 (February 2002): 43–54.

Juhan, D. *Job's Body: A Handbook for Bodywork*, 3rd ed. Barrytown, NY: Barrytown/Station Hill Press, Inc., 2003.

National Headache Foundation. "Fact Sheet." www.health-exchange.net/pdfdb/headfactEng.pdf

Sainsbury, P., and J.G. Gibson. "Symptoms of Anxiety and Tension and the Accompanying Physiological Changes in the Muscular System." *Journal of Neurology, Neurosurgery & Psychiatry* 17 (1954): 216–224.

Schwellnus, M.P. "Cause of Exercise Associated Muscle Cramps (EAMC)—Altered Neuromuscular Control, Dehydration or Electrolyte Depletion?" *British Journal of Sports Medicine 43* (2009): 401–408.

Werner, R. *A Massage Therapist's Guide to Pathology*, 4th ed. Baltimore, MD: Lippincott Williams & Wilkins, (2008).

Chapter 15: How to Keep Yourself out of Pain

Atlas, L.Y., and T.D. Wager. "How Expectations Shape Pain." *Neuroscience Letters* 520, no. 2 (2012): 140–148.

Keltner, J.R., et al. "Isolating the Modulatory Effect of Expectation on Pain Transmission: A Functional Magnetic Resonance Imaging Study." *Journal of Neuroscience*, 26, no. 16 (April 19, 2006): 4,437–4,443.

Kong, J., et al. "A Functional Magnetic Resonance Imaging Study on the Neural Mechanisms of Hyperalgesic Nocebo Effect." *Journal of Neuroscience* 28, no. 49 (December 3, 2008): 13,354–13,362.

Leboeuf-Yde, C., et al. "Coping and Back Problems: Analysis of Multiple Data Sources on an Entire Cross–Sectional Cohort of Swedish Military Recruits." *BMC Musculoskeletal Disorders* 7, no. 39: (2006, May 3).

Vlessides, M. "Catastrophic Thinking Positively Related to Post–Op Pain, Study Shows." *Pain & The Brain* 11: (August 2013).

About the Author

Sarah Warren is a Certified Clinical Somatic Educator and owner of Somatic Movement Center. She has helped people with chronic muscle and joint pain and many chronic musculoskeletal conditions become pain free by practicing Thomas Hanna's method of Clinical Somatic Education. Sarah is passionate about teaching her students how to take care of themselves and helping them through their journey toward lasting health.

Connect with Sarah Warren

Sign up for Sarah's newsletter at

somaticmovementcenter.com/signup

To find out more information visit her website:

somaticmovementcenter.com

Facebook Page:

www.facebook.com/SomaticMovementCenter

Twitter:

twitter.com/MovePainFree

Pinterest

www.pinterest.com/somaticmovement

Book Discounts and Special Deals

Sign up for free to get discounts and special deals
on our bestselling books at

www.TCKpublishing.com/bookdeals

One Last Thing ...

Thank you for reading! If you found this book useful, I'd be very grateful if you'd post a short review on Amazon. I read every comment personally and am always learning how to make this book even better. Your support really does make a difference.

Search for *The Pain Relief Secret* by Sarah Warren to leave your review.

Thanks again for your support!

Made in the USA
Middletown, DE
06 July 2021